W9-CSO-163

Subalterns and Sovereigns

Subalterns and Sovereigns

An Anthropological History of Bastar,
1854–1996

Nandini Sundar

DELHI
OXFORD UNIVERSITY PRESS
CALCUTTA   CHENNAI   MUMBAI
1997

Oxford University Press, Great Clarendon Street, Oxford OX2 6DP

Oxford New York
Athens Auckland Bangkok Calcutta
Cape Town Chennai Dar es Salaam Delhi
Florence Hong Kong Istanbul Karachi
Kuala Lumpur Madrid Melbourne Mexico City
Mumbai Nairobi Paris Singapore
Taipei Tokyo Toronto
and associates in
Berlin Ibadan

© *Oxford University Press 1997*

ISBN 0 19 564116 7

Typeset by Rastrixi, New Delhi 110070
Printed in India at Syndicate Binders, New Delhi 110020
and published by Manzar Khan, Oxford University Press
YMCA Library Building, Jai Singh Road, New Delhi 110001

For Amma, Appa, Aparna and Siddharth

Acknowledgements

Like every academic project, this is a collaborative effort, but one in which I have gained unfairly. This is a mere listing of debts — adequate thanks or repayment is impossible.

Iqbal, Kala, and their children, Punee, Shabnam and Birsa have played the role of my family in Bastar, and provided long fun filled evenings drinking mand. Iqbal, a journalist, activist, guide and many other things, has illuminated, interpreted, described and discussed so much, it would be difficult to pinpoint his specific contributions. Pintoo and his parents, especially Didi (Mrs Kusum Savita) proved the best next door neighbours one could ever have had. Mr M.N. Joshi, former sarpanch of Asna, has helped in invaluable ways, as has Mr Arjun Nag, a Halba lawyer and man of deep integrity and kindness.

Lakshman Jhadi (Dada) and Trishia Didi provided another home in Pandripani. Jhadi Dada, District Secretary of the CPI, helped me identify a field village, and gave me the benefit of his deep knowledge about the area. A true organic intellectual, he and Lakshman Kashyap both kept a supervisory eye on my research. To them and to other members of the CPI, I owe my stay in Kukanar, the tour in the Kanger reserve forest and much else that it would be impossible to describe. Again, their intellectual contributions cannot be individually noted — they permeate the book. For the warmth and generosity with which they gave of themselves: Lal Salaam.

Dayaro Pujari and Iyya, Jagdish, Bertot Andil, Sonadhar, Asmati, and Bhima who shared their house with me in Bodaras, explained various aspects of Dhurwa life, and accompanied me on several explorations; Phulmati who cooked for me, Sahadev and Rathu who interpreted, all the people of Bodaras, and other hamlets in Kukanar; and the people of neighbouring Dhurwa villages — have made this book possible. I am particularly grateful to Dayaro Pujari for his interest in this research and for being so ready with his vast fund of knowledge about local history.

Ranu Guruji, Verma Guruji in Chevaras, Brother Michael, Dr Pande and Dr Sharma at Sukma, Mr and Mrs Verma, Kirit Doshi, Mr Avasthi, Mr Shiv Narayan Pande, Narmada Prasad Shrivastav, Ranger Purushottam, Mr Ramesh Dube, Mr Arun Thakur and a host of others helped in numerous ways, and along with their families, made me feel at home in Bastar.

This book originated as a doctoral thesis in the anthropology department of Columbia University, New York. My advisor, Katherine Newman, was in large part responsible for seeing it through — especially her ability to convert stream-of-consciousness material into readable chapters in record time. Her encouragement of, and warmth towards her students, as well as her own committed research has been truly invaluable. David Lelyveld taught me much of what I know about South Asian history — his close and critical reading, wide range of references, constant accessibility, and sheer human kindness make him one of my favourite academics. Joan Vincent has influenced me in ways she will not suspect, and has provided a theoretical framework which I wish I could have done more justice to. I am also grateful to Michael Taussig, Sumit Guha, Alfred and Simeran Gell, Chris Gregory, Jonathan Parry, Bill Fisher, Mahesh Rangarajan, Amita Baviskar, Savyasachi, Claire Cesareo, Steve Rubenstein, and Cathy Wanner, for reading all or parts of the original thesis and providing useful comments. Others who have helped in various ways include Nandini Gooptu, André Béteille, Walter Huber, Robert Anderson and Crispin Bates. I also thank several officials, of the Government of Madhya Pradesh, both in Bhopal and in Bastar who extended help of different kinds. I am grateful to my colleagues in the Edinburgh University JFM Project for their support.

I am grateful to The Indian Progressive Study Group, New York, for many stimulating meetings and for making me remember constantly that academics cannot be an end in itself. The memory of C.V. Subbarao, intellectual and committed human being, who died before his time, has lived with me through the writing process. This book is considerably impoverished without his comments. Rajesh, Radhika, Jagan, Sanjay, Ritu, Parag, Bela, Ishita, Reemah, Claire and others provided friendship and various kinds of assistance during the writing stage.

It is clear that both the household unit and extended kin

links are still one of the most efficient ways of organising labour. Siddharth Varadarajan, my husband, has gone through this book as many times as I have, worked on editing it for 48 hours at a stretch, while I lay blissfully sleeping, and provided references, support, and encouragement at every stage. My sister, Aparna, also edited and discussed the entire manuscript, typed up the bibliography, and provided constant moral support. How bereft are those, I often think, without sisters. My debt to my parents, Pushpa and Sundar, is too vast to even hint at in a few lines. They have both specifically contributed to the book in numerous ways — my mother, for example, provided directions for research, and calm support when field-work threatened to become overpowering. Both she and my father worked hard to make sure I got to Bastar despite their apprehensions. My uncle, S. Guhan, gave the thesis a critical and timely reading, while Ram Guha, a cousin, provided wonderfully detailed and useful comments on how to revise the thesis into a book. If this book does not come up to their expectations, it will not be for lack of their assistance. I am grateful to my grandparents, Mr and Mrs N.R. Bansod, my aunts and uncles, Asha and Sharad Upasani, the late Lovraj and Dharma Kumar, my parents-in-law, Usha Varadarajan, and M. Varadarajan — for their help and hospitality while doing research.

I thank the librarians of Columbia University, the staff in the English and Hindi Record Room in Jagdalpur; the staff at the MP State Archives at Nagpur, the National Archives of India, the South Asian Library at Cambridge and the Methodist Reports Collection at Madison, New Jersey. This research was aided by Columbia University, the American Institute of Indian Studies, MacArthur Foundation, and the Association for Women in Science Educational Foundation.

Prologue

This book traces the genealogy of the state in Bastar, central India, over a period of approximately a century and a half (1854–1996). In particular, it looks at the manner in which the state was constituted through the dialectic of administrative intervention and popular resistance. The focus is on certain critical moments when the structures set into place by the colonial state were contested. While these challenges inevitably resulted in some immediate reform, they simultaneously helped to further entrench the institutions and ideologies of the state. Yet, each act of protest remained an ember that sparked future resistance, with changing popular notions of kingship and polity acting as the matrix through which this resistance defined itself.

Prior to 1947 when it was merged with the Indian union, Bastar was one of about six hundred princely states of India.[1] Despite its large size (39,114 sq km), larger than Belgium and larger than the state of Kerala, Bastar is relatively unknown to people outside it. And those who knew or know of it have constructed it in different ways. For the first Europeans who encountered Bastar (or rather a second-hand image of it), the place did not even have a name, being merely a 'void space . . . void of the goods in general esteem among mankind, that does not tempt either their avarice, or ambition.'[2] On this under-standing, the history of peoples and regions in corners of the world far from Europe, like Bastar, was not just the history of 'others' but the history of their 'discovery' by Europeans.[3] Seventy years later, that image had changed little and Bastar was described by Glasfurd, a colonial administrator, as an

interminable forest, with the exception of a small cultivated tract around Jagdalpore, intersected by high mountain ranges, which present

---

[1] The pre-1947 portions of this book pertain to the former princely state of Bastar alone, excluding the former state of Kanker.

[2] Rennell (1976:307).

[3] *See also* Vansina (1990:xi); Pratt (1992:111–43).

serious obstacles to traffic. Its insalubrity is proverbial; the inhabitants are composed of rude, uncivilised tribes of Gonds; in some parts almost savages, who shun contacts with strangers, have but few wants which they cannot supply themselves; honest and interesting to the ethnologist perhaps, but a race who prefer the solitude of forests to the bustle of towns, and the freedom of the savage to all the allurements and comforts of civilisation.[4]

In 1938 Grigson, a former administrator of Bastar and its first major anthropologist, painted the region as:

still terra incognita to nearly all British officials and travellers . . . To the ordinary Indian of neighbouring districts . . . this remains a land of savages, seeking still for human victims to sacrifice to their fetishes, skilled in herbs and simples, and potent practitioners of magic and witchcraft.[5]

His own book was an attempt to navigate what, according to him, had been 'an almost unknown backwater of the river of Indian history.'[6] Administrators today see it in no less fetishised, if not even more instrumental terms – as an 'El Dorado of modern times – the Ruhr of the East.'[7] With its vast forest and mineral resources, 'Bastar, in its unique virginity, offers ample scope for large scale industrialization and colonization.'[8] In this vision, shared by most of the recent immigrants to Bastar who have come as state servants, traders, or shopkeepers, the main obstacle to 'development' are the people of Bastar – described variously as 'poor but carefree', 'lazy', 'backward', 'alcoholic' and 'promiscuous'.

Activists and anthropologists alike also subscribe to a romanticized view of Bastar as 'the last major frontier in India's tribal heartland.'[9] But in their perspective, Bastar needs to be protected against exploitation and degradation. In this vision, innocent tribals living in harmonious village communities in symbiosis with each other and with nature, are now in the process of being smashed and fragmented by the monolith of the repressive state.

[4] Glasfurd (1862: para 175).
[5] Grigson (1991:3).
[6] Ibid.
[7] Quoted in Anderson and Huber (1988:30).
[8] Ibid.:142.
[9] CSE (1985:86). *See also* Sharma (1994:110).

While it is true that a way of life is being forcibly transformed, one needs to paint a more layered picture. Perhaps it is the dense forests that suddenly appear enroute from the Chattisgarh plains to Bastar, as one climbs the Keskal pass to descend into the central plateau; perhaps it is the mountains in the distance that suggest the sense of enclosure; the glimpse of people walking in single file on forest tracks, the women bearing baskets on their head, and the men with a pole slung over the shoulder; or the slow moving Indravati with people washing their clothes below, that one passes over to reach Jagdalpur;[10] perhaps it is the sense of a beauty so different from that normally experienced by the stranger from a concrete city, that suggests an untouched innocence. But participation in larger political and economic processes has been a feature for much longer than either the state or those who oppose it admit, and the people of Bastar have resisted and manoeuvred their way through this history, rather than being passive victims or heroic rebels. This book, though, is not aimed at recovering a suppressed subaltern voice – what follows in this preface is in fact an account of the disastrous effects of trying to do such a thing.

My account of Bastar, like the other accounts, is situated in the specifics of my background – its personal and intellectual production, my encounters in the 'field' (one year spent in Kukanar and visits to several other villages); in the 'archives' (six months in the District Collectorate record room, where among other things, I re-arranged the files, stuck crumbling pages and observed the several romances going on in the collectorate; one month in the state archives, and four months at the national archives); and finally, encounters with my computer (watching the words on the screen take on a life of their own).

Like many before me, I too had envisioned Bastar as terribly oppressed, and in fact as a Ph.D. student, that was the reason why I had chosen to work there. After reading about the critique

---

[10] Physiographically, Bastar is constituted by a plateau in the centre, flanked by the Chattisgarh plain on the north and the Godavari lowlands on the south. It is bisected (east-west) by the river Indravati, and also drained by the rivers Kolab-Sabari, Talpeir, and Kotri-Mahanadi. There are several hilly ranges e.g. the Abujhmarh hills in the north-west, and the Bailadilla hills in the south, known for their resemblance to the hump of a bull *(bail).*

of anthropology's colonial origins, the dynamics of power employed in fieldwork and representation, and the need for 'action research,'[11] I was quite ready to put my research at the service of the struggling masses, represented by the Naxalites or some other movement. I knew that this was not a straightforward process, and there was no reason why people should trust me more than other outsiders, but one always hoped that one's good faith would miraculously shine through.

My initial aim was to study popular conceptions of the state with a view to developing an alternative, culture-specific philosophy of governance, compared to the one bequeathed by the colonial past. I keenly eyed the people I met in the hope of discovering budding peasant intellectuals who would perhaps provide me with a representation of the state, which although drawing on their own culture(s), would also be close to my own. Something like, 'by the state we mean the structures and ideologies of administration; it has a democratic mask through which we can press our own interests to some extent, but it is ultimately underpinned by capitalism, and is in fact instrumental in shaping our conception of our own interests.'

Unfortunately, or fortunately for my political conceits, I never met a single Naxalite in the approximately two years I spent in and out of Bastar, though I was sometimes taken as one by government officials and by villagers that I went to interview. Of course, this was when I wasn't being taken as a school teacher or health worker by some villagers, or an immoral woman and a drunkard by traders, local journalists and petty officials. It was still worse, however, to be recognized as an anthropologist since everyone — townspeople and villagers alike — had some previous experience of anthropologists who always seemed to have been wonderful, dedicated researchers compared to me! So much for pristine, unresearched Bastar.

As for resistance — for a long time I couldn't see any. The only resistance I found was 'everyday resistance' directed at me, by the keeper of the record room in the District Collectorate who was reluctant to give me files, and by my young assistants in my 'field village' who went dancing every night and were too sleepy or found it too boring to come translating with me in

[11] Huizer and Mannheim (1979); Gough (1968).

the morning. I found instead plenty of warmth and laughter, and even some oppression by the oppressed, casteism practiced by those who were at the bottom of the scale themselves. I was bitterly disappointed and thought of taking myself off to some other village, or even leaving Bastar altogether for more resistant pastures.

There was always the history of the major rebellions I could work on from the colonial documents, but lived memories of them seemed to be few and far between. When I went from village to village asking about Gunda Dhur, the leader of a rebellion that took place in 1910, few answers were forthcoming. Nobody seemed to know for sure who he was and what he was like except for the Tribal Welfare Department, which had manufactured him complete with bow and arrows — a tribal 'freedom fighter' — in a tableau at its stall in the government-organized Dussehra exhibition. I found irony and appropriation, but I did not find Gunda Dhur.

In more recent years, the Communist Party of India (CPI), has been active in the south of Bastar, and villagers told me stories of their former defiance against corrupt officials. The twenty-five year old *sarpanch* of Kukanar had been elected in 1989 on a communist platform, indicating a shift of power from the dominant traders who had recently settled in the village to progressive tribal youth. But by the time I reached Kukanar, the CPI's village branch was falling apart under the weight of internal squabbles and activity was at a low ebb. The traders seemed to be getting away with awful exploitation. In short, whatever resistance there had been, it always seemed just a little out of reach, in the past or in some distant place. I remembered Brecht: going 'through the wars of the classes, despairing when there was injustice only, and no rebellion.'[12]

And then it happened! The government decided to facilitate private steel plants near Jagdalpur, sparking off resistance among the potential oustees and counter-repression by the state and the local petty bourgeoise. There was also a move to carve out alternative land in Kukanar for those who would be displaced. The local *patwari* had apparently shot his mouth off about the availability of land there. Led by the CPI, the Kukanar villagers

[12] Brecht (1976:320).

too protested, saying that if any spare land was found it should be given to the local landless. Since the government could not credit the villagers with any agency of their own, I was held partially responsible. In fact, this was a completely unwarranted compliment since I was seen as a transient newcomer in the village and no one took me very seriously. The sarpanch was upset: 'Don't they think we can see for ourselves and have a mind of our own without needing to wait for outsiders?'

My own opposition to the government was very unheroic. By this time I was well into collecting oral histories of the village. But I was equally keen to observe the demonstrations against the steel plants which were happening in Jagdalpur or Maolibhata. As a result, I spent most of my time on rickety state transport buses, focussing on neither and getting spondylitis in the bargain. I also agonized endlessly about writing an article about the repression for the papers, fearing that it would limit my access to the archives. I finally wrote it but it didn't get published, and the archives were closed to me anyway. Eventually, however, due to the vicissitudes of national politics, the collector of Bastar was transferred, and I got to look at some files after all.

To conclude, I found that it is one thing to read about the travails of other people's ethnographic encounters[13] and quite another to go through it oneself. I had of course read about such things as informants who told you different things on each visit, the fact that people's perception of you colours what they tell you, that large-scale resistance is not the only sort of resistance etc. But the 'field' and the enterprise of fieldwork has its own logic. Why else would I cycle five miles at noon in the blazing heat, falling over ruts in the track and getting bogged down in rivers, only to find the person who had promised to meet me was not there, and do it not once, but several times — if not for some version of the 'truth'?

But the truth I discovered was not perhaps the one that I set out to find. I did not find Gunda Dhur as a specific historical individual. But I did find him as a metaphor for resistance, and one that cropped up again and again under different names in different times and at different places. I learnt once again that

---

[13] *See* Clifford and Marcus (1986); Marcus and Fischer (1986).

resistance cannot be produced on demand to be participated in or written about, but that it is always there as actuality and potential in the everyday structures of life, even in its most seemingly disheartened and depoliticized moments. People come together at certain critical conjunctures, which in turn re-define the future. This book attempts to probe those conjunctures, in order to comprehend the relationship between subalterns and sovereigns in the past, and how it might change in the future.

Contents

List of Maps

List of Tables

List of Photographs *(between pp. 152 and 153)*

List of Illustrations

Map 1: *Bastar in India*
Source: GOMP (1984)

Map 2: *Bastar Today*
Source: PUCL (1989)

Abbreviations

AAR	Annual Administration Report, Bastar
ADM	Additional District Magistrate
ARFA	Annual Report on Forest Administration
BS	Bastar State
CC	Chief Commissioner
CFO	Chief Forest Officer
CFS	Chattisgarh Feudatory States
Commr.	Commissioner
CP	Central Provinces
CPI	Communist Party of India
CPI(M-L)	Communist Party of India (Marxist-Leninist)
CrPC	Criminal Procedure Code
CRR	Crown Representative Records
CSE	Centre for Science and Environment
DM	District Magistrate
DS	*Dandakaranya Samachar*
DSP	District Superintendent of Police
ESA	Eastern States Agency
F.C.	Foreign Consultation
For. Int.	Foreign Internal
For. Pol.	Foreign Political
For. Sec.	Foreign Secret
GOI	Government of India
GOMP	Government of Madhya Pradesh
IOL	India Office Library, London
IPC	Indian Penal Code
JRR	Jagdalpur Record Room, District Collectorate, Bastar
MFP	Minor Forest Produce
MLA	Member of Legislative Assembly
MP	Madhya Pradesh (or, depending on context, Member of Parliament)
MPRR	Madhya Pradesh Record Room, Nagpur
MRC	Methodist Reports Collection, Madison, New Jersey

NAI	National Archives of India, New Delhi
NTFP	Non-timber forest produce
Pers. Com.	Personal Communication
Pol. Agent	Political Agent
Pro. No.	Proceedings No.
PUCL	People's Union for Civil Liberties
PWD	Public Works Department
PWG	People's War Group
SDO	Sub-divisional Officer
Sec.	Secretary
SP	Superintendent of Police
Suptd.	Superintendent
TOI	Times of India
WP	Working Plan

Introduction

The Muria Durbar: 1992

At the right hand corner in front of the Rajwada, a sprawling white-washed building in the centre of Jagdalpur, stands an unimpressive looking shed with a tiled roof, grandly known as the *sirasar*. Throughout the year it is neglected, faintly exuding the smell of urine. Crowded jeep-taxis for Bajawand and Baka-wand take off from there every day, packed with people and produce, and even an occasional disgruntled goat. A group of women and men, mostly adivasis, from Jagdalpur or the nearby villages, sit in front selling vegetables. Skulking nearby are the abandoned wooden carcasses of former Dussehra chariots, sport-ing posters of the latest Hindi film to hit Jagdalpur, or advertising some consumer item. In short, there is nothing to mark the sirasar as a place of any importance. Yet every year in October-November, history is written and re-written within its walls. An annual feature of Dussehra since 1906, the 'Muria Durbar' was started with the intention of training the king in administration and what we would today call 'communication skills' (addressing the complaints of his subjects without really solving them). It is an occasion when the adivasis of Bastar are told of the noble intentions of the state, exhorted to conserve forests and engage in improved agricultural practices, and if they behave well and co-operate, are promised the fruits of development, symbolized, inter alia, by the graduation from loin cloths to 'full pants'. It is a moment for the profession and rewarding of loyalty, and *even* for the voicing of those minor notes of dissent that are permissible within the structures of official patronage.

In October 1992, the 'Muria Durbar' started quite promptly at 4.30 pm in the sirasar, duly spruced up for the event. It was presided over by Baliram Kashyap, Bharatiya Janata Party (BJP) MLA and minister in the then BJP government, who sat cross-legged on the stage which had been covered with white cushions.

He was flanked on either side by MLAs, the commissioner, collector, tribal welfare secretary, and the last descendant of the royal family that ruled Bastar from 1323 till 1947, Bharat Chandra Bhanj Deo. Bharat was garlanded last and somewhat belatedly, but there were many cheers on this. In front of the dais on the ground sat all the *majhis* (traditional headmen), resplendent in the red and pink turbans which they had received for the occasion; to the left and right were chairs for senior journalists and other important townspeople.

After Sampat Singh Bhandari, an MLA who was also president of the Dussehra Samiti that year, had welcomed everybody, various majhis got up to speak. They spoke in Halbi. The majhi of Barsur *pargana* complained that the sarpanches made only one school or one road and then claimed that all the money sanctioned had been spent. Bedagaon Mahasing of Bade Dongar said they had been asking for a primary school for three years and had still not got one; another majhi cited an instance of a school whose doors no teacher had ever darkened. He was much applauded for raising what was evidently a very common problem. Two boys from Maolibhata tried to get up and say something about a steel plant, but were repeatedly shoved down and finally taken out of the room. Baliram Kashyap held court, smiling silkily throughout, encouraging one majhi, cutting another one short, telling one his problems would be listened to and having troublemakers taken out. Others like Congress M.P. Arvind Netam also spoke, reiterating the virtues of the Dussehra Durbar as a means of communication. After all difficult issues had been skilfully dealt with, tea was served, and the function was over by six.

Transcripts of the Dussehra Durbar are significant for what they leave out as much as for what they reveal. The Dussehra of 1992 was a particularly contested one, yet the 'Muria Durbar' reflected these concerns only elliptically. Barely a few days earlier, Chief Minister Sundarlal Patwa had come to Bastar to lay the foundation stone of a steel plant (one of two proposed) at Maolibhata, some 30 km from Jagdalpur. Although there had been rumours and mysterious surveys in the villages doomed to be displaced, in typical fashion no one had bothered to inform the villagers. It was only on the day of the foundation stone ceremony, said the sarpanch of Maolibhata, that he was

invited to share a platform with the Chief Minister. His understanding was merely that it was a gathering of some sort, not
that this was to inaugurate the replacement of the village and
its people by steel. When the chariot procession that takes place
every evening during Dussehra was delayed that day, several
people told me that the chariot pullers (who coincidentally come
from Maolibhata and neighbouring villages) had gone on strike
after hearing about the steel plant. As it turned out, they had
merely been delayed due to lengthy speech-making at the foundation site of the steel plant, where they had been roped in to
provide an 'audience'.

Shortly afterwards, however, the villagers began to protest
under the aegis of the Bharat Jan Andolan, run by Dr B.D.
Sharma, a former administrator of Bastar and, *inter alia*, former
Commissioner, Scheduled Castes and Scheduled Tribes, who has
now retired and turned activist. The movement demanded the
right for villagers to be consulted in this and all such future
projects, and a share in the profits. Reactions by the state and
townspeople – the class of officials and petty bourgeois traders
who would benefit from the increased jobs and business generated by the project – were equally sharp and immediate. On
28 October 1992, the sixty-five year old Dr Sharma was pulled
off the pillion of a scooter by activists of the BJP, stripped, and
paraded through the streets of Jagdalpur with a garland of shoes
around his neck. The incident attracted much national outrage
but predictably, no action was taken against the culprits.

Outlining the Argument

First, there was the English Government. After that there was
Congress Government like its child. Then Congress Government
grew up and became old. Now there is only half-anna jungle
left.

(Budhu Majhi, Dussehra 1992)

Budhu Majhi's genealogy of the post-colonial state goes to the
heart of the matter – drawing the connection between the loss
of jungle and the process of government that began with the
British. As in several other parts of the world, the question of

access to the means of production and reproduction, mainly land and forest, especially in the face of displacement by large industries and 'development' projects, has come to be a major one for local people.[1] In Bastar, as in other cases, the roots of this conflict can be traced to the colonial period. At the same time, it is clear that the local contexts, attitudes towards the state and modes of organizing are quite different from the colonial to the post-colonial period.[2]

There are at least three key reasons for identifying the colonial period as a significant watershed. First, the colonial situation meant that the primary impulse for the extension of administrative institutions did not come from the changing exigencies of local society but from the colonial authorities' perception of the structures necessary to govern. The structures of indirect rule, for example, which formed such an important part of the experience of colonial rule in Bastar, need to be seen as part of the movement of ideas across empire.[3]

Secondly, contrary to popular perception, 'frontier areas' like Bastar were not isolated from the rest of the larger economy in the pre-colonial period. Colonialism's distinctive contribution was not in integrating these regions into some wider system, but in changing the terms of this integration. Within anthropology, this realization is a relatively recent one, formed under the impact of modes of production and world systems theories, and the turn to history.[4] However, for many, particularly those

---

[1] Burger (1987); Hecht and Cockburn (1990).

[2] It is not immediately obvious that a kingdom represented the same sort of entity as the post-colonial state in India, and that they can both be classified together under the category 'state', unless one adheres to a broadly Marxist tradition of seeing the state as arising out of class divisions in society. Here, while I use the term state in a specific sense to refer to the structures of administration and the rule(s) they regulate in the colonial and post-colonial period, it is understood that these structures are not neutral, but a product of the balance of class forces in society. There are of course several debates about the extent to which the state is relatively autonomous, whether it is part of the 'superstructure', or enters into the organization of the economic base itself, and the precise mechanisms through which ruling class interests are articulated with state policies. For a slightly dated and by no means comprehensive, but still useful collection of essays, *see* Giddens and Held (1983).

[3] Roberts (1990), *see also* Fisher (1991:432–77).

[4] *See* Roseberry (1989); Wolf (1982); Cooper et al. (1993).

involved in implementing 'development,' the idea has not struck home yet.[5] Bastar clearly was never as commercialized as other parts of India,[6] nor were there a whole range of intermediaries between the cultivator and the state as represented by the king.[7] It was one of several hilly and forested spaces on the outskirts of more intensive plains agricultural settlements, or as some would have it, 'peripheral' from early times. In Wolf's words: 'separate agricultural regions generated separate polities'.[8] But this does not mean that they were not connected. The present adivasi or 'indigenous' populations migrated to Bastar over different periods from surrounding areas, albeit at some very early time. The various kingdoms in the area competed with others, and Banjaras, Gossains and Bairagis served as agents of trade and the cross-fertilization of information and ideas. Moreover, the people of Bastar were not necessarily subordinate to the plains dwellers and in the eighteenth century and perhaps earlier, they exercised some degree of domination through their raids on the latter.[9] This is not to deny that there was mutual prejudice between the plains and hill people, or that the latter were looked down upon by the former as savages.[10] Rather, it is to make the point that the independent political power exercised by the hill people was sufficient to ensure that negative descriptions of them by outsiders did not have the material force they were to achieve in colonial times.

Colonial transformation of local economies and polities was achieved primarily through administrative and legal means. The history of forest reservation in India is not dissimilar to that of enclosures or of struggles over the commons in Britain in the eighteenth century, relying on similar oppositions of local interest to 'general public utility.'[11] According to Thompson, unlike England where 'capitalist notions of property rights arose out of the long material processes of agrarian change,' in

---

[5] *See* James Ferguson's (1990) analysis of the assumptions on which the World Bank's study of Lesotho is based.
[6] Bayly (1983); Subrahmaniam (1990).
[7] Perlin (1985).
[8] Wolf (1982:27).
[9] For an account of the raids, *see* Blunt (1924:91–173).
[10] Thapar (1978).
[11] Arthurs (1985:22); Thompson (1975); Gadgil and Guha (1992).

England's colonies it was law (transported from England) 'which became the instrument of reorganizing (or disorganizing) alien agrarian modes of production and, on occasion, for revolutionizing the material base.'[12] However, Thompson's inversion of the European base-superstructure (material base-law) dialectic for the colonies needs to be nuanced to account for what actually happened. The enactment of laws in the colonies was both analogous and yet different, based on varied readings of local custom and imperial right. Many ideologies, practices, and modes of control, which we have hitherto assumed to have been developed in a metropolitan setting and then transported to the colonies, actually developed in the context of colonial domination and were then adopted at the centre.[13] Moreover, the role of law was not always that of straightforwardly assisting the transition to capitalism. In some instances it operated to preserve (at least partially) what were thought to be 'traditional' structures, which in fact impeded the development of private property, alienability and capitalist relations of production.[14]

Despite Bastar's insertion into a capitalist framework, the relations of production in the state or district itself were not transformed into capitalist ones. Even today, the main form of livelihood is small-scale agriculture, primarily for self-consumption. This sector comprises approximately 88 per cent of the population.[15] The farming season usually lasts from June to January and is followed by a period from February to May in which one of the main activities is collection of non timber forest produce (NTFP) for sale to either traders or state purchasing agencies. Also important is wage work for government departments or contractors, constructing or repairing roads and buildings, felling timber, demarcating fire lines etc. Despite the overall subsistence character of the economy, the existence of a capitalist framework is very evident in the purchase of NTFPs. In the colonial period, the prices of myrobalan and wages paid

[12] Thompson (1993:164).

[13] *See* Grove (1993) on the ideology of forest conservation; Mitchell (1988) for the development of the panoptical gaze as a disciplinary mechanism in the colonies; Stoler (1989).

[14] Dirks (1992:175–208); Washbrook (1981:649–721); Chanock (1991:61–84).

[15] Calculated from Census of India 1991, Primary Census Abstract — General Population, Part II, B(i), vol. I, pp. 894–901.

for its collection were linked to prices in the London market. Currently, the state-monopolized purchase of tendu leaves (used for making *beedis)* and sal seeds (used domestically and exported for making soaps and chocolates) structures local relations with capital. Although nationalization ostensibly occurred to reduce exploitation by private traders, in effect it has meant that the state acts as a monopsonist, keeping its purchasing prices low, so that it may sell at lower prices to the industrialists. Many of the localized struggles in recent years, led by the CPI, Naxalites and others, have been over attempts to get the government to raise the prices of these NTFPs.[16]

Bastar is still the most forested district in Madhya Pradesh, with a forest cover officially estimated as 55.4 per cent.[17] The Bastar forests are of the tropical moist deciduous variety, with sal shading into teak as the most important commercial species, as one goes from north-east to south-west, drawing a diagonal line from Narainpur to Tongpal. Both sal and teak have several associates, including bamboo, which today forms 20 per cent of the forest cover.[18] One explanation for its name Bastar, comes from it being known as the valley of bamboos – *banstari.*[19] One of the more common sights in Bastar today is log-laden trucks on their way out of the district, yet little profit seems to have found its way back into the hands of the adivasis. On the other hand, a group of Jagdalpur residents, organized under the banner of the Bastar Society for the Conservation of Nature (BASCON) have been successful in stalling development projects that would destroy valuable forests. A World Bank-funded industrial forestry project (1976–83) which aimed at converting 20,000 hectares of natural sal forest into pine plantations to provide pulpwood for paper, had to be abandoned, as was another Bank-funded proposal, the Bodhghat

---

[16] PUCL (1989); CSE (1985:86, 91).

[17] GOMP (1991).

[18] Sal associates include bija, saja, haldu, dhaora, mahua, char, tendu, which together constitute nearly 85 per cent of the standing crop volume per hectare today. Teak associates in the north-west and south-west comprise many of the same species as well as shisham, aonla, semur, hurra and bamboos. Palms are common – sulphi, and towards the south, chind and tar. For Latin equivalents, *see* glossary.

[19] CSE (1985:86).

hydroelectric project. The latter would have displaced about thirty-four villages as well as 5676 hectares of forest.[20] There is always a possibility however, that this project might be revived, as considerable infrastructure has already been created at Barsur in Dantewada sub-district.

Table I: *Bastar in Comparative Perspective, 1991*

Indicator	Bastar	Madhya Pradesh	India
Area (sq km)	39,114	443,446	3,287,263
Population	2,271,314	66,181,170	838,583,988
Population Density (per sq km)	58.6	149	257
Females per 1000 Males	1002	932	928
Rural Population (%)	92.9	76.8	74.3
Urban Population (%)	7.1	23.2	25.7
Scheduled Tribe Population (%)	67.35	23.3	8.08
Scheduled Caste Population (%)	5.85	14.5	16.48
Forest Area (%)*	55.4	35	23
Per Capita Forest Area (hectares)*	9.5	0.30	0.11
Literacy Rate (%)	24.89	44.20	52.19

Sources: Figures calculated on the basis of the *Census of India, 1991* Series I (Paper 1 of 1992), Final Population Totals, New Delhi, Ministry of Home Affairs, 1992.
  * Forestry figures are taken from *Madhya Pradesh Environmental Status Report*, MP Government, Bhopal, 1991.

Bastar's mineral wealth includes 10 per cent of the country's iron ore reserves, as well as rich reserves of tin, limestone, dolomite and bauxite, manganese and sulphur. The setting up of the Bailadilla iron ore mines in south central Bastar, has created a certain enclave economy. It is one of the country's

[20] Ibid.:88

Table II: *Bastar – Social Indicators*

Number of inhabited villages*	3670
Percentage of villages with an educational facility (1981)	60.80
Percentage of villages with medical facilities (1981)	3.65
Percentage of villages with problem-free drinking water*	10.1
Percentage of villages with post and telegraph facilities (1981)	11.71
Percentage of villages with markets	7.67
Percentage of villages with paved approach road	10.36
Roads per sq km*	7.10
Percentage of villages with power supply*	53.49
Est. percentage of households with power supply* (1992)	26.7
Irrigated area* (1993–4)	2.9
Percentage of villages where the following facilities are more than 10 km away	
Education	5.96
Medical facilities	43.71
Post and telegraph	18.67
Rate of growth of employment under different groups (1981–91)	
Agriculture and Allied Activity	3.9%
Mining and Quarrying	27.4%
Trade	46.8%
Marginal Workers	56.2%

Source: *Census of India, 1981* (Series II – Madhya Pradesh, Bastar District Census Handbook) (New Delhi/Bhopal: 1984).
    *   *Madhya Pradesh Human Development Report*, 1995, Bhopal.

largest foreign exchange earners, but provides no employment to local adivasis. Mining effluent has turned the rivers Sankhini and Dankhini red, and destroyed the water supply of fifty-one villages downstream. In the meantime, residents of the mining town of Kirandul are supplied with piped filtered water.[21] There are 8336 small-scale and four large-scale or medium-scale industries in Bastar.[22] The total effect, however, is one of the absence of industrialization. Neither this, nor the temporary moratorium on major changes in the forestscape, should be taken to imply a lack of integration into a larger capitalist process. As Roseberry notes, the development of both capitalist modes of production in some regions and non-capitalist modes in others were part of 'the same historical movement'.[23] In the colonial period, as in the present, the precise path taken was often dictated by political considerations such as the need for the preservation of the colonial regime. It is important therefore to look not just at economic imperatives but also at the 'epistemological procedures and institutional interests' that underlay the colonial state.[24]

Thirdly and finally then, we come to what several writers have argued was one of the most fundamental aspects of the exercise of colonial power: the creation of sociological and epistemological categories through law, and other state-organized activities, such as the production of census records, gazetteers, official or semi-official ethnographies, grammars, linguistic surveys, and land tenure records.[25] These outlived particular colonial regimes and determined the questions asked by future generations of researchers as well as the self-perception of those being researched. Perhaps nowhere is this more evident than in the category of 'tribes' or the 'tribal' and in the Indian context, the question of tribes versus castes. The characterization of the tribal in India was similar to that in Africa, drawing on evolutionary classifications based on race and anthropometry, the denigration of any indigenous kingship in favour of an acephalous, kinship-bound society, and the perceived primitiveness of modes of production. But the Indian 'tribe' was further understood to be differentiated by religion and culture from the Indian 'caste'.[26]

[21] Ibid.:86–7.

[22] GOMP (1995:171).

[23] Roseberry (1989:222, 144).

[24] Prakash (1990b:383–408).

[25] *See* for example, Cohn (1990); Lelyveld (1993); Dirks (1989:59–76).

[26] For some early debates about the differences between tribes and castes, *see* Bailey (1961); Dumont (1962); Mandelbaum (1984). There were of course dissenters from the conventional view, e.g. Béteille (1974).

Much recent work has been directed against these early con-
structions.²⁷ There has also been a resurgence of interest in
understanding how the categories 'tribal', 'primitive', 'savage' or
'wild' were imbricated in domination and anxiety, providing
both the justification for colonial rule, and the means towards
it in the stipulation of necessary techniques of administration,
including the gratuity of colonial violence.²⁸

Yet these processes were never completely hegemonic, and
colonial rule was often a contradictory, internally contested
process with several unintended outcomes. Missionaries and
anthropologists, among others, espoused different visions of
rule.²⁹ And despite the Foucault-inspired emphasis on seeing
subjectivities as constituted through particular discursive mechanisms, it is not clear how 'efficient' the disciplining and making
over of indigenous groups has been. In particular, how do we
make sense of all the resistance that has historically occurred,
and that continues to take place, and which cannot be reduced
to localized reactions within an increasingly hegemonic system?³⁰
In Bastar, apart from the major rebellions that have taken place
in the past, in recent years (1980-90s) demands for land, wages,
health and education have been articulated by the Marxist-
Leninist 'People's War Group'.

To sum up thus far, colonialism transformed local societies,
polities and economies in three crucial ways: through the imposition of alien structures of government, through unequal
integration into larger capitalist processes, and through epistemological means. But ideologies and modes of control trans-
posed across empire are only one aspect. Local histories and
popular responses, including large-scale rebellions, quotidian
resistance and selective collaboration were critical to the way
structures of rule expressed themselves and were reconstituted.

²⁷ *See* Stocking (1983, 1984); Clifford (1988:189-214). In the Indian context,
regarding tribes and castes, *see* Cohn's (1990) essays on colonial sociology;
Sengupta (1986, 1988); Bates (1995); Corbridge (1988); Jones (1978), and Saha
(1986, 1988).

²⁸ Spurr (1993); Taussig (1987).

²⁹ For anthropologists, *see* Asad (1973); Stocking (1991); for missionaries
see Comaroff and Comaroff (1992); Padel (1995:185-241).

³⁰ *See* Kahn (1985); Roseberry (1988:161-85); Nash (1981:393-423), for
overviews of studies on resistance to capitalism.

In the process, the modes of resistance and the resisting agents themselves changed. There is perhaps rather less in this book on everyday life than one would have liked, all those intervening days between birth and death, and between insurrections. The focus on certain insurgent moments is justified, however, along the lines advanced by Karen Fields in her study of the watchtower movement in central Africa: 'Since millennial revival exposes the lines along which order could break down, its analysis yields unusual evidence about the processes by which order was sustained.'[31] The same could be said of the rebellions studied here.

People and Places

Both ecologically and culturally, Bastar is part of the Dandakaranya forest belt which was broken up by the different administrative provinces delineated by the British.[32] The reorganization of the states in the 1950s followed similar lines, maintaining the division of the central Indian forest belt into the states of Madhya Pradesh, Andhra Pradesh, Orissa and Maharashtra. Demands for separate Gond and Bhil states have been periodically taken up but have failed.[33] In any case, the principle would have to be different from that of linguistic reorganization which formed the basis for the creation of states in India. In Kukanar alone, people with at least three different languages co-exist and take part in collective village events. In the Dandakaranya region as a whole, there are seventy-two identified dialects and several languages.[34] Telugu influences dominate across the southern tract, Marathi is mixed with Gondi in the west, and Bhatri has a large admixture of Oriya. However, Halbi has served as the *lingua franca* of Bastar since at least the seventeenth century, when the Halbas of Bade Dongar (Kondagaon tahsil) entered the Bastar king's service as soldiers and were posted to different parts of the country.[35]

Officially the Bastar tribes are distinguished by the following

---

[31] K. Fields (1985:22).
[32] PUCL (1989:4).
[33] Cinemart Foundation (1984:113–17).
[34] PUCL (1989:4).
[35] Grigson (1991:5–6).

names: Halbas, Bhatras, Dhurwas (formerly Parjas),[36] Dorlas, Abujhmaria (Hill Maria), Ghotul Muria, Jhoria Muria, Damdami (Bison-horn) Maria and Raja Muria. There are also small pockets of Mundas, Saoras and Gadabas, tribes which are found in large numbers towards the east, in Bengal, Bihar and Orissa. Finally, there are a range of groups which fall under the official category of 'castes' (as opposed to 'tribes'), since they are relatively more 'Hinduized', and generally speak Halbi or some version of Hindi. These castes include Maharas, Pankas, Gandas (all weavers), Kallars and Sundis (both distillers), Rauts (cowherds), Kumhars (potters), Telis (oil pressers), Kewat (fishermen), Dhakads, Panaras, Marars, and Ghasias (brass workers, musicians). It is obvious that the concept of the 'indigene' and the 'tribal' is an impossibly problematic one. But when one talks of a 'Bastar culture', it is the composite one created by these groups that comes to mind.

Secondly, there are groups that have come in under the aegis of the state at different historical periods, such as the Orissa Brahmans, of whom the first contingent of sixty families was brought in by Purushottam Dev in the fifteenth century to spread settled agriculture and provide brahminical legitimacy. They were followed in the time of Rajpal Deo (1649–1721) by three hundred Brahman families from Paplahandi (Orissa), who according to their published caste history were fleeing from the oppression of the king of Paplahandi and were given sanctuary and land by the Bastar Raja.[37] The descendants of these Orissa Brahmans are today mostly found in Jagdalpur tahsil (central Bastar) and have become large landlords. Other early migrants included the Maithili Brahman Rajguru family who functioned as advisors to the king from the sixteenth century; Rohillas who came as mercenaries in the service of local zamindars and later settled in South Bastar as traders; and a few Kayasths and

---

[36] The Bastar Parjas apparently tired of being called Parjas as the name was used derogatorily by government servants and outsiders. In 1941 a group of them from Chitapur, Tirathgarh and Kachorapati parganas petitioned the government to have their name officially recorded as Dhurwa in the census. Dhurwa was the title used for a headman or someone who organized events. Compilation no. VII-I, Parts 21 and 23, Correspondence regarding 1941 census, JRR.

[37] Pande and Joshi (n.d.).

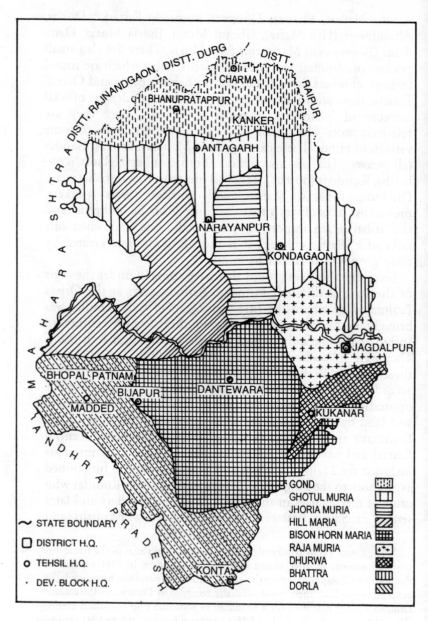

Map 3: *Ethnic Distribution in Bastar*
Source: GOMP (1984)

Marathi Brahmans who functioned as officials and scribes in the eighteenth and nineteenth century. Finally, there are the very recent immigrants from UP and Marwar, other parts of Madhya Pradesh, Bihar, Kerala and Tamil Nadu. Most of them either directly fill the bureaucracy or co-exist with it in domination over the tribals and low castes — as merchants, moneylenders, mining project staff, forest officials, bus conductors, teachers, clerks, bankers, etc. Consequently, there has been a massive boom in urbanization. The population of Jagdalpur grew by 72 per cent from 1971–81, following the Bailadilla iron ore project, and by 33 per cent from 1981–91. In 1991, it was estimated as having a total population of 84,578.[38]

The incredible mosaic of people in Bastar shows how this 'isolated tribal area' can compete with any metropolis in terms of linguistic and cultural hybridity. Among the adivasi and 'low caste' populations, economic differentiation, migration and ecological adaptation have all played a role in creating a patchwork of different groups. Grigson argues that the so-called scheduled castes were 'in reality members of primitive tribes speaking their languages and only differentiated from them by occupation.'[39] In the case of the Lohars this seems true — they are simply Gond families which took to making iron implements and became differentiated and looked down upon as Lohars.[40] Migration has been an even more prominent cause of differentiation. For instance, in Bastar and neighbouring areas, all the Gonds refer to themselves as *koitor* or *koi* (meaning people or human in Gondi), differentiating themselves by the prefix highland or lowland. The Dorlas occupying the Godavari plains in the south adapted their name to the Teluguized Dorla (meaning chief/ head) from Dor (lowland) Koitor, by which they were distinguished from the highland (Metta) Koitor or the Bison Horn Marias who occupy the villages of the Dantewara plateau. The latter in turn descended from the Abujhmarh hills and for a while continued intermarriage with the Hill Maria or Abujhmaria.[41] None of these groups

---

[38] *Census of India, 1991*, vol. 1, Final Population Totals, Paper 3 (New Delhi, 1992).

[39] Grigson (1991:37).

[40] Elwin (1991a:13).

[41] Grigson (1991:198). For Muria migrations *see* Elwin (1991:20); Grigson (1991:48–9).

are confined to Bastar, but stretch across the borders to Orissa, Maharashtra and Andhra Pradesh. In short, while the offical history of states and regions follows administrative boundaries created under different regimes (both colonial and pre colonial), a more demographically accurate history would follow a different chronology mapped onto a different cartography.

A note on nomenclature seems necessary here. In general, I try to use the words 'people', 'locals', 'peasants' or 'villagers' instead of tribals with the knowledge, however, that these are all equally unsatisfactory since they suggest a lack of differentiation. Still, it may in fact be the best option in a situation where the majority of Bastar's population calls itself Koitor (people). 'Adivasi' has become popular only in the post-colonial period, and hence seems inapt for much of the period under study. Where I use the term 'tribal,' it is a convenient shorthand for those categorized by the state as 'scheduled tribes' (Maria, Muria, Dhurwa, etc.), and is intended more to call attention to administrative perceptions than to any particular mode of existence. On occasion, I use the term 'tribes' and 'castes' interchangeably, to indicate the impossibility of a clear separation on most grounds.

Structure and History in this Book

This book is divided into three parts: the first deals with the pre-colonial economy and polity. Society and nature in the past are constructed through Dhurwa oral histories while the polity is portrayed through the rituals of Dussehra, the annual state festival. This is a history which is embedded in rituals and relationships which re-enact the past at the same time as they refigure it through the concerns of the present. Both in this section and the next, unmediated access to the 'pre-capitalist' or 'pre-colonial' past is rendered problematic by the location of my sources for this period in anthropological fieldwork today, and in colonial documents written in service of particular administrative measures once the process of change was already underway. For instance, communal ownership of land was described in the process of determining what sort of land tenure systems to legislate. My interest in introducing this section has been to write against the dominant history which sees Bastar and places like it as untouched and isolated prior to colonialism, or even up to the present. I try to show the degree of social and political fluidity in the pre-colonial period, as well as the manner in which people acted to construct the pre-colonial polity. Relations between lineages and ritual events within a village were reflected in the polity at large. Colonial perceptions and policies gradually transformed this picture into one of a static society composed of isolated tribes and castes, and a princely state that was simultaneously despotic and weak.

The second section contains accounts of both 'major' and 'minor' resistance to the colonizing process, constructed from standard sources — colonial official records, newspapers, some secondary sources — which I have then attempted to flesh out with oral histories. Whereas in the first section, there is an attempt to be sensitive to non-linear or local modes of history telling, in this section it is the archives that provide the narrative structure. The rebellions were very differently understood by subalterns and sovereigns, by the actors involved and those commenting on it both at the time and later. Each situation comes to us through multiple histories, a polyphony of voices narrating pasts out of different presents. Not all these histories are strictly compatible, yet both the points of intersection and divergence are equally revealing. The different historical imaginations that actors bring with them are central both to their construction of and actions within a situation and to our understanding of it. While each rebellion acquires significance from its own context, each succeeding one also drew on the others, providing, in a sense, a continuum of rebellious pasts. The rebellion of 1876 (chapter 3) encapsulates several issues with which this book is concerned — the relationship between raja and *praja* or the state and the public in Bastar, from about 1854 to 1996; the transformations in kingship wrought under indirect colonial rule; the multiple histories that undergirded different understandings of and interactions within this relationship; and the manner in which past events constitute future ones. At different stages in the history of Bastar, popular allegiance to, or rebellion against the king served as the metaphor for negotiations with a changing order, an order which went far beyond the immediate relations between people and king. Taking issue with the dominant theories of divine kingship, I argue that ideologies of legitimate rule are selectively invoked at times of rebellion, and do not constitute the glue of the polity in the manner that they are claimed to.

Chapters four and six deal with the colonizing process. In chapter four, one can see clearly how the laws and regulations introduced marked a significant watershed. In chapter six, the specific historical period, 1927–50, and the specific place, Bastar, are shown as important to the telling of a larger story — how a certain discourse about tribes was created, and how it was challenged. Chapters five and seven are again about rebellions. Although the *bhumkal* or rebellion of 1910 was suppressed by force, it had enduring effects, both intended and unintended. One of these was the use of similar imagery in the resistance of the 1960s. Both after 1910 and after 1966, people found ways to read defeat as victory — if so many of their own friends and relatives died, they claimed to have succeeded in killing as many of the enemy (the soldiers or police) in return. Popular resistance or the threat of it was one of the critical factors in determining the initial choice of indirect rule and was responsible for its continuation throughout. It also limited the degree of economic exploitation of resources.

In the final section, 'Uncertain Futures', I bring this history up to date. At each period, whether in 1876, 1910, 1966 or 1996, there is no unitary insurgent consciousness that we can capture, rooted in 'culture.' In the process of individuals making collective choices of whom to support, what culture to adopt, when to rebel and when not to rebel — whether to organize under a 'traditional' system, whether to support a king or the communists, whether to represent themselves as indigenous people or as an exploited class or both, culture is redefined, sometimes in old and sometimes in new terms. These are not entirely free or conscious choices, but they are choices nonetheless.

Recreated Pasts

In order to make modern life intelligible I have made a construct which is called the Middle Ages. What may have been the actual conditions of that era is a matter of complete indifference to me, and it is ridiculous to claim to refute my theories with objections drawn from historical essays.

Werner Sombart

What histories, rulers, heroes, perhaps transcending all others,
What laws, customs, wealth, arts, traditions,
What sort of marriage, what costumes, what physiology and
    phrenology,
What of liberty and slavery among them, what they thought of
    death and the soul,
Who were witty and wise, who beautiful and poetic, who brutish
    and undevelop'd
Not a mark, not a record remains — and yet all remains.

Walt Whitman

Recreated Pasts

1

Village Histories in South Bastar

In the old days of which the aged tell, the songs sing and the imagination brings alive as one walks in the dusk through the forest and chances upon an isolated house: People lived in small groups, sometimes even one or two houses to a village, scattered in the clearings of the forest. And then a group of men, with no fixed abode, would come hunting and see the lone and distant fire burning in the night and ask for fire. Daughters would go in marriage and the newcomers would be shown where they too could harness land. And so the villages grew. On the slopes of hills, men and women cut down the trees and cleared the land and sowed seeds that had been consecrated by the Perma. Sometimes the harvest was like gold; sometimes they came one morning to find the crop ruined by wild beasts presumably because the spirits of the forest had not been appeased. Too good or too bad a harvest, sickness and death, a pot falling unexpectedly — were signs of the Earth mother's unwillingness to give them a place, signs that it was time to move on. And the forests would regenerate (Field Notes, 1992).

This chapter looks at how people narrate their own history, as against the official accounts of it, and the contrast between the administrative concept of 'backwardness' and the people's more ambivalent attitude towards their own past. Even when they refer to a civilizing process, it is one where they are actors rather than objects. I collected these narratives in the form of stories and songs, from Dhurwa villages in south-east Bastar. Although some of the names that recur in the stories are specific to Dhurwas, the underlying pattern is common to most groups in Bastar.

The aim here is twofold: first, to set the stage for the next section on colonial rule by highlighting the fluidity and freedom it was contrasted against; secondly, to check the concept of tribal people as always either victims or conversely as heroic agents resisting the state. These stories are essentially about the concerns of village politics, while at the same time they connect to a larger history — indicating the basis on which claims to land were founded before land records and the possession of a written title deed became necessary; the importance of marriage alliances as a way of harnessing fresh labour and organizing production in a situation of plentiful land but scarce labour, as well as the resultant flexibility of social relations.

The accounts presented here, even those pertaining to the settlement of villages, are not about any one period in particular. Indeed some of the migrations described here occurred as late as the end of the nineteenth century (based on approximations from known genealogies). Moreover, the names of founding members of lineages are used for their descendants too and thus events which may have taken place at very different moments in time, appear to have taken place simultaneously due to the use of the same actors. The narratives also share certain similarities of names and structure, with those that are told as stories. However, these accounts were specifically described to me as origin histories, the word *katav* (history) being used rather than *dugga* (story). What further distinguishes them as history is the fact that they bring in specific details of names and places touched upon during migration, and are embedded in the current relations between lineages. They are especially relevant in weddings and in certain ritual requirements which require the presence of founding families at collective village ceremonies. Thus, these narratives provide a different sort of history, one that is spatially or socially mapped. As these relations change, it is possible that the histories of origin change too.[1]

Histories through Oral History

The framework used here draws partially on that of Vansina, one of the foremost scholars of oral history. Vansina starts from 'words and things' found in the present to go backwards into time, through the combination of historical linguistics,

---

[1] The gender of the local expert(s) on these histories varied between hamlets and villages. The English translations from Dhurwa are fairly literal, with some modifications for readability. I was helped in the translation by Sahadev Nag and others in Bodaras.

ethnographic and archaeological data, and literary sources, to
arrive at a picture that is claimed to have some correspondence
to what actually happened. In other words, oral histories, if
properly treated, are thought to yield the same sort of narrative
as a history constructed from more traditional sources.[2] But
often, as Gyan Prakash has argued, oral histories and written
records have a more complex relation, being quite 'different
modes of historical reconstruction.'[3] In some cases, oral histories
are informed by written records. This happens, especially, as
memories become more feeble and the written word acquires
greater authenticity, or when subordinate groups internalise the
characterization by others of their past. In other cases, as in
the Dhurwa histories described here, the story of their 'civilization' is conveyed through tropes that are quite different from
the standard categories, and which make them and the relations
they enter into the agents of their own history. However, it is
not just a question of comparing a Dhurwa historiographical
tradition to a 'Western' one, or of two different sources for
telling the past — the written chronological and the oral. Apart
from the fact that there are several schools of history writing,
every mode of telling the past involves a process of representation.[4] There could be several Dhurwa constructions. Different aspects of the past get emphasized, depending on the
aims of the present.[5] And depending on the context and the
audience, the same narrative may perform different functions:
describe a historical process, contest, or reinforce existing
relations of power at the household, village or state level.[6]

Located 70 km south of Jagdalpur in the Godavari-Sabari
lowlands, Kukanar is one of the largest villages in Bastar, with
a population of approximately 7000 people (1981 census)
distributed between twelve hamlets. The hamlets are placed 2
to 5 km away from the main road, stretching towards the hills
all around. The path to Bodaras, where I lived, curves through
one and a half km of government 'waste' land, to finally end
in a large ground which serves as a meeting place and dancing

[2] Vansina (1990:3–33); (1985).
[3] Prakash (1990a).
[4] White (1978).
[5] Daniel (1989).
[6] Appadurai (1991); Blackburn (1989); Blackburn and Ramanujan (1986).

space. The houses, neatly arranged in rows on either side, are
brown mud structures set in their own compounds under leafy
tamarind trees, or hedged by prickly date palms. Kukanar is
a heterogeneous village with Dhurwas being predominant and
recognized as the founders, though subsequently large numbers
of Gonds have settled there. There are also concentrations of
Kumhars and Rauts, and some Dhakads, Kallars, Sundis, Lohars
and Pankas. In Kukanar *khas*, the hamlet on the main road,
there are about forty families of UP Thakurs.

Within each hamlet, kinship and relations of subordination
of certain lineages to others continue to be the idiom in which
local politics is conducted. Although this is now overlaid with
the power derived from economic standing, party affiliations
and government positions, the history of how the hamlet was
founded is generally agreed upon by all. But between the ten
hamlets, there are almost as many variants of the same story.
The men of each hamlet claim an importance in the founding
of the village, which the other hamlets deny. The women are
less involved in this aspect since they move between lineages
and villages. When I first started collecting oral histories, the
discrepancies I encountered in my search for a neat narrative
built up to a stage where I was confused and fed up with the
different accounts and complained bitterly about it to people.
The villagers blamed it on their loss of memory and on the
death of elders who might have known, as well as to rivalries
and jostling for influence within the village. In the best traditions
of colonial codification, I then thought of holding a panchayat
or assembly so that people could thrash it out among themselves,
instead of giving me any old story, or as sometimes happened,
using me as a conduit to challenge someone else's version. The
panchayat never took place and fortunately, I soon realized that
even if there was no one consistent account of the village's
history that would suit the purposes of all rival groups, I was
being provided a 'history' sufficient for *my* purposes: to understand the changes wrought by colonialism.

In summary then, the intention here is not to focus on or
unravel the differences in accounts and relate them to people's
current politics within the village and their relations to each
other, which is the subject of another paper. Rather, I use the
stories in my own construction of their past. Villagers may

disagree on who came first and from where, but they broadly
agree on the normative principles of how villages were created
and what constituted the basis for political authority in the
'traditional system'. The fact that they can disagree about particulars indicates that there is a shared discourse, a framework
within which the past can be re-created and contrasted to the
present.[7] Ethnographic observations in the present are used
merely to *evoke* the past, and do not amount to a claim to have
documented it.[8]

Deities and Deifiers

Talking about forest and pastoral deities in Maharashtra, Sontheimer notes that the coming of a group to a village is often
told as the coming of their gods to the village.[9] Broadly speaking
there are three main categories of deities in Bastar which must
be propitiated: the Earth, the Mother Goddess and the deity of
each lineage or clan. Among Dhurwas, the earth is generally
referred to as *jaga*, or sometimes simply old man *(murtak)*, or
old woman *(murtal)*. Elsewhere, the earth is also called *bhum* or
mati. The earth includes the spirits of the forest and rivers who
must be separately appeased, or else they are said to appear as
tigers and cobras and bite humans. All the major agricultural
festivals (e.g. the seed sowing ceremony or the new-mango eating
festival) are celebrated at the shrine of the earth.[10]

The village mother goddesses *(Matas* or *Devis)* on the other
hand, have names and distinct personalities. For instance, Jalni
Mata, the Mother Goddess for all 12 hamlets of Kukanar, who
has a big temple in the market square in Kukanar unlike the
mud shrines of the other Matas, is said by some to be the
daughter or daughter-in-law of Gangna Dei *(Murtal)*. In yet
another version narrated by Bhaisaku, priest of Bodaras, she is
held to be the youngest sister of the Bodaras Devi:

There were 3 sister devis – the eldest one, Dular Dei, stopped in

[7] Sabean (1984:29).
[8] Price (1990:281).
[9] Sontheimer (1989).
[10] For some details on festivals, *see* Elwin (1991:29, 31-2); Grigson (1991: 208-21).

Pratapgarh. The second one stopped under a mango tree at the present site of the Devi shrine in Bodaras and the third one went on to the present Jalni shrine in Kukanar proper. The youngest sister had no name, but decided to adopt the name of her elder sister. *The two elder sisters because they lived in the mountain and the forest, became less famous,* while the youngest sister made a fuss and insisted that she would handle all of Kukanar on her own. (emphasis mine)

The reference to the unknown nature of the Devis who lived in mountain and forest might be read as a metaphor for the people themselves, who are treated as inferior by the plains dwellers, and their gods relegated to obscurity, while those of the later comers, the groups associated with the state, are given prominence in big temples. The original object of worship is generally only a stone or a tree, but when taken visiting elsewhere, the Matas are represented by a flag and umbrella. Matas perform the function of warding off sickness and calamities, and accordingly *jatras* and *mandais*, which are festivals intended for these purposes, are celebrated in the Mata shrines of the hamlet/village and pargana respectively.

Every lineage also has its own ancestor spirits represented by an empty pot, which is usually kept in the back of the house or in a special room. Only actual or potential daughters-in-law, or pre-pubertal girls can go near this. Jaga is generally stationary and does not go anywhere. If all the people of the village migrate, they establish a new shrine in the name of the old Devi, but often come back to their old sites to propitiate the earth or clan Gods. The Devis on the other hand travel, sometimes migrating with a lineage. Sometimes, every lineage in a village will have its own Devi, all of them becoming subordinate to and helpers of the original Devi. The relation between humans and their Gods is an intimate one, as this extract from Bhaisaku Pujari's prayer to mark the end of the threshing season reveals. He addresses himself to all the gods concerned:

> I have cleaned my teeth and bathed, I have prostrated.
> On cattle, goats, fruits, flower and grain
> Kali Mai Phiranta roams with Rahat Kali
> Causing the eruption of poxes inside and outside
> Peacefully take it away, take the road, take it away
> When you are used to roam so much, don't sit here
>   any longer. . . .

Rice and incense are living, a chicken too is alive
Bananas are alive — you will get all these definitely
Sukhrau, Munnarau (spirits of the forest) — they will be given
separately, from now on don't cause bad dreams at night . . .

Here the Devi is being asked to take away the illness she has
brought, being promised the blood of live things in return, and
assured that she will have enough for herself. The pujari continues, invoking all the Gods of field and forest, swamp and
river (Singhraj and Kamini), earth (Jaga) and mountain. He
names the mountains (Banal) and the rivers (Malangeir and
Talpeir), and calls the ancestors (Boda Dhur, Koklu Dhur, Sargi
Dhur and Dangdi Dhur):

Turn one house into two houses, one seed into two seeds
One basket into two baskets
Even after this (offering), if you don't do this
Man's soul will be angry
Don't prevaricate, there is rice for you
here is the witness (reads the rice omens)

The sacrificial chicken refuses to eat the rice, which would
indicate that the Devi has not accepted the offering or answered
whatever request the pujari put. He gets angry:

After all this, you stall my words and prevaricate
After all this, you don't listen, but caw like a crow
roar like a tiger.
Why do you do this? Be happy with this much . . .

In the old days, villagers say, the world was dangerous and
difficult, but their ancestors too had power and could look
their gods in the eye and speak. The Mata was powerful and
capricious, yet she could be reasoned with. Colonial rule
brought new gods — revenue officials and forest rangers, the
police and soldiers — in front of whom the villagers lost their
ability to speak. This reinforced the colonial perception of
them as inarticulate 'children'.[11]

---

[11] *See also* Elwin (1954). Of course, this infantilizing was not confined to
tribals alone but was an idiom intrinsic to colonization, what has been called
the 'Peter Pan theory of India: the East is unchanging and the Orientals are
like children'. J.A. Spender, quoted by Iyer (1960:24).

Founding Villages

In the 'traditional' order, it is the earth which gave humans and their other deities permission to settle and determined the boundaries of the village, in contrast to the present system, where the government decides this. The founding lineage thus had special powers of intermediation with the earth, and one of its male members, known as *perma* in the south, generally functioned as its priest. His task was to perform all the rituals connected with agriculture to propitiate the earth. The power of the lineage lasted insofar as its members continued to be successful in mediating with the earth; any disaster, natural or otherwise was seen as a sign of the deity's displeasure, indicating that it was time for the villagers to leave.[12] In some cases, the earth showed its favour to someone else, whose lineage then became the perma lineage. The choice of perma was tested by the villagers by going out hunting in his name. If they were successful, the new perma was seen as having the approval of the earth. This also makes sense in a society where hunting and gathering were important elements. Thus the power to propitiate the Gods and gain their favour was the currency in which ritual offices were exchanged. The following story from Hamirgarh in south-east Bastar supports this. There once lived a Dhurwa headman there by the name of Gogria Majhi (colloquially Gogir Dora). One day, in the words of Chendru Murtak of Nandrasa, a village in Hamirgarh pargana, whom I interviewed in 1993:

A cheetah started terrorising the 12 villages of the pargana. Everyday it would take off with one child. People didn't know what this scourge was — they had never seen it. A Bairagi came from Champakar in Orissa and built his hut on Hamirgarh hill, where Danteswari Devi lived. Gogir Dora went and asked him: 'How is it that you can live here alone? A kind of *bhumkal* (anger displayed by the earth) has broken out in our pargana — a cheetah is chasing us The mendicant muttered: 'Hah, the Devi recognises a foreigner.' He bound his enclosure with spells so that the Devi in her guise as cheetah could not enter. Everyday the mendicant would see the cheetah going into its hole in a big bamboo pole. It would emerge in the evening and creep back in at about four am.

Gogir Dora and the villagers tried propitiating the Devi, but

---

[12] *See also* Grigson (1991:197).

nothing worked. They went on a hunt in her name, but got nothing. Many days passed and the terror continued. Finally, the villagers went and asked the mendicant where he was from, and said they would try hunting in his name. He acquiesced, saying modestly that he was only a foreigner. This time, as soon as they went into the forest, they succeeded in killing a twelve-antlered stag. They brought it back to the village and showed it to the mendicant. Then the mendicant took a tendu branch and closed up the cheetah's bamboo hole. He told the villagers to watch out for unusual signs or a big commotion. But nothing happened. The next day he asked them if the cheetah had appeared, and told them to go on a hunt again to test his power. Again they killed a stag.

Then the villagers said: 'We are successful in your name. We will entrust you with the work of Danteswari priest.' The mendicant demurred but the people insisted. They said: 'Cattle or wealth will not give you a lasting name, but the position of priest will. On dying, you can eat the articles left in the grave; while living, you can live off the sacrifices offered at rituals and panchayat fines.' Thus they also made him majhi. Then the villagers gathered wood and burnt the bamboo log and all lived happily after.

The office of perma and majhi, religious and secular headman respectively, were generally combined in some initial stage.[13] According to Grigson, there was a separation in the colonial period under the pressure of demands for corvée and supplies by state officials. The tendency then became to 'put forward a dummy as the headman for secular matters, the real leadership of the village remaining with the religious headman . . . the dummy being able to bear the brunt of official wrath, though powerless to effect anything without the consent of the village elders'.[14] But from many accounts, the office of perma and/or majhi changed hands for more mundane reasons, such as dwindling numbers in the original lineage. There appears to be no consistent pattern — sometimes, the position of priest was given away and sometimes the position of headman.

Apart from the perma and majhi there are other ritual functionaries. Dhurwa lineages are sometimes known by the

---

[13] The term 'majhi' is usually reserved for the headman of a pargana, an administrative division comprising several villages, but may also be used for headmen of large villages like Kukanar. Some local names for village headmen are *pedda, dhurwal, mukaddam, patel.*

[14] Grigson (1991:285).

name of a founding or famous member[15] and sometimes by the functions they perform in village rituals, especially those connected with agriculture.[16] In Kukanar which is a multi-caste village, only Dhurwas perform the rites at the main earth shrine, indicating their prior connection to the earth. But in the *mandai*, which takes place in the Jalni shrine at Kukanar, all the castes and not just Dhurwas have roles to play. The pujaris for Jalni and Kankalin are from a Dhurwa family of Punguda hamlet but the work of cleaning the place and bringing water is done by a Raut. Maharas are necessary to play the pipe and drums; Kallars have to make the alcohol from mahua flowers required for all rites, and Kumhars make pots. Mandais involve weeks of planning, sending out invitations to neighbouring villages, collecting grain and money from every household to feed and house the visiting Gods and humans. Thus village festivals serve as miniature models for the Bastar-wide Dussehra ceremony.

Occasionally in Dhurwa villages, when Dhurwas themselves were lacking for ritual work connected to the earth shrine, other castes were adopted. For instance, in Kandanar in the Kanger forest, the ancestor of the current perma lineage used to be a Lohar (blacksmith caste), who got shot with an arrow by mistake. His wife happened to be pregnant, and when she gave birth to a son, the village decided to make him the perma in compensation. So they upgraded the family to Dhurwa caste. It was not only what are now considered lower castes who changed their affiliation. The Rauts are the village cowherds and consider themselves higher to Dhurwas and will not accept food from them. But when the Durras Rauts were orphaned at some stage, they came to live with the Dhurwa headman's family in Durras, and gradually, they too became Dhurwas. As mentioned in the previous chapter, it was not just individual families, but whole groups which changed castes, due to migration and adaptation.

---

[15] e.g. in Chitapur, the Kandki (searcher) lineage got their name from an ancestor who was an aubergine-thief and came to search for refuge in Chitapur; Chevaras hamlet in Kukanar is more commonly known as Majhirasa, since the majhi lives there.

[16] For instance, the *bodka* lineage cooks food and cleans the hearth in the Murtak shrine; the *pat bodka* does the same work in the Murtal shrine; the *kicek* lights fire by rubbing bamboo; the *bhandarin* distributes food etc. *See also* Thusu (1965:66).

Kinship as a Mode of Organizing Labour

In every village and hamlet in Kukanar, there are several lineages. Apart from the founding lineages, the rest came as sons-in-law or servants, or immigrated for a variety of reasons and were given land, cows and marriage partners by the dominant lineage. For instance, the Dangdi lineage is claimed to be the founding lineage of Kukanar as a whole, because not only did they bring the Gods, but they also gave daughters and land to the founding lineages of several hamlets. Given below is one representative story from the hamlet of Bhandarras, recounted by a group of old men there:

They took birth in Barsur. Seven brothers, twelve brothers and their younger sister went from there to Warangal. Their younger sister gave birth to a child in the jungle. There was no water to bathe it or to feed it. So the brothers cut a *siadi* creeper and water began to flow and was changed into milk. With that they bathed the child. They stayed there for some days and then taking 12 caskets of snakes and 12 caskets of tigers with them, they came to Kokawada and other villages. Because of the tigers and the snakes, no one gave them a place to stay so they finally came to Nagerkonta (a mountain).

Then they were in need of fire. They saw the smoke of Dangdi Dhur's cigar which was a foot long — so big that the trees shook from the smoke, and they went in that direction. Two daughters were pounding grain. All the brothers asked for fire in turn, but the girls kept silent. Finally, the last brother said: '*Andil*, give me fire,' whereupon they gave him some. Then the father asked where they were from and what they had brought. The boy said, 'We have brought 12 caskets of snakes and 12 caskets of tigers.' The father said: 'No wonder no one is giving you a place. Do what I say. Leave the snakes among the other snakes on the mountain and the tigers among the tigers and people will give you a place to stay.' The youngest brother took the fire and went to his elder brothers. The brothers asked 'How come they gave you fire?' so he related the whole story. They took the father's advice and married the girls and settled there for some time.

The motif of a group carrying tigers and snakes and not being given a place or alternatively a hunting party coming upon a house in the middle of the forest and requesting fire is a common one. In the case of the tigers and snakes, it could indicate that they lived with wild animals in the forest till they were domesticated through the setting up of marriage links and learning the art of cultivation. The travellers invariably get no response till they use the term '*mama*' (mother's brother) or as in this case, *andil* (elder sister-in-law). Among Dhurwas, as among other Dravidian groups, cross-cousin marriage is the preferred norm. The 'mama' or the mother's brother is also the father-in-law, and all parents-in-law are referred to by the terms for mother's brother and his wife, *anya*. Anya is also father's sister. Fire plays a significant role here, through what Savyasachi describes as the 'cult of cross-cousin marriage: the movement of women who carry fire from one household to kindle the hearth of another'.[17]

Through the custom of bride price, marriage alliances were a way of appropriating resources and labour for the dominant lineage which generally gave daughters to begin with. Land in itself could not be the basis of power since it was plentiful; instead, power depended on the size of one's own family and the corresponding labour available, as well as the prestige of the lineage and the labour it could consequently command from others for purposes of agriculture, weddings, and other rituals.[18] Unlike settled agriculture where land assumes importance, in shifting cultivation it is labour which is at a premium. Labour was organized on the basis of lineages, and sometimes on the basis of *bethia* — a system whereby all the people of the village turned out to work for one household for one day in exchange for a feast of meat and rice beer or alcohol. Bethia still persists in some villages, but it has been predominantly replaced by wage labour.

The need to establish marriage links was so important that it often over-rode considerations of clan exogamy or rather the division of lineages into clans often adapted itself to the requirements of marriage links.[19] Inder Baghel of Bokadabadr, another hamlet of Kukanar, related the following story which supports this:

While the Elbaks were coming from Elubnad, they saw Koklu Dhur's lineage coming from Marjum Mountain. Each looked at the other

---

[17] Savyasachi (1992:153).

[18] For more detailed debates on kinship as a way of organizing production, *see* Wolf (1982:88–100); Roseberry (1989:134); Cooper (1993:99).

[19] *See also* Gell (1992:42).

for some time wondering what the other's clan was. When the Koklu Dhurs broke the stand off by saying they were of the cobra clan, the Elbaks (who were also actually of the cobra clan) immediately said they were from the tiger clan, so that they could live compatibly in Durras, exchanging daughters and sisters.

Today, the system of clan exogamy would appear to have weakened — there are several Nag-Nag marriages in Kukanar for instance, and Thusu too found several in neighbouring Marenga during his fieldwork in the late 1950s. It would seem, however, from these early stories of migration that it may never have been a rigid textbook system of clan exogamy in the first place, and the requirements of production and reproduction ensured cultural innovation as and when necessary.[20]

The 'Civilizing Process'

The founding lineage not only gave the others land, but also taught them how to live and cultivate. We see this process at work in the following story about the lineage that settled Pedaras, another hamlet of Kukanar, narrated by Dayaro Pujari of Bodaras and later corroborated by Chainu of the Peda lineage. The story begins in the same way as that of the Bhandarins, with a party of twelve brothers coming to the Dangdi house and asking for fire. The Dangdi told the brothers to settle near Gurbe, and gave them a daughter. They also sent a Devi, articles of worship, pots, vessels and clothes. Then, the youngest brother had a boy.

For seven days the boy didn't drink milk and kept crying. So the father of the boy came to Dangdi's house to ask his advice. His father-in-law told him to mark out a boundary of trees, rivers, stones, jungles and mountains — to do one round of the whole (and thus establish the village of Pedaras). The boy then began to drink milk. The son-in-law came again to invite the Dangdi house for the naming

---

[20] Names change, castes change, clans change — yet through all these changes, knowledge of the village of origin or clan is still preserved. At the same time as these stories demonstrate fluidity, one could argue that they indicate an underlying rigidity. The original categories, even if changed for expediency several generations ago, are preserved in memory. The interesting question then becomes whether these identities are being read backwards, and if not, what identity or belonging to a particular group meant for people then.

ceremony. The father-in-law told him to go on a Monday, taught him how to make landa, and told him to keep a goat ready. But while waiting the brothers thought that if the Dangdi came, he would eat up the whole goat and there would be nothing left for them. So before the father-in-law reached, they started eating the goat alive, biting its ear, and dipping the whole gourd in the landa and licking it. When the Dangdi saw this he was horrified. He taught them how to kill and cook the goat and how to make a ladle of the gourd. Then the boy was named Pandra Peda (after whom Pedaras got its name). The boy's father was embarrassed and said: 'From now on I will not eat goat,' and from that day the Peda household in Pedaras does not eat goat. As brideprice which they did not give initially, every year this family brings twelve big pots of landa to the Lundel festival.

New families were thus settled, assigned lands and taught the ways of life. These initial encounters continue to be replicated and acknowledged ritually even today, at the same time as there is much innovation. In Bodaras hamlet, all the other lineages describe themselves as porters to the Boda family. The Murwaks claim they came out of a bamboo clump, in response to a call by the Boda lineage for help to carry their game home. The Kondan Baghels who are much later migrants from Kondanpal to Bodaras, have a similar story of being discovered in the course of a hunting expedition by the Perma lineage of Kondanpal:

Our ancestors lived in a cave. When the hunters came by, the ancestors ran into the cave, as they were absolutely naked. Thinking they were animals, the hunters shut the cave up, thrusting only one long stick in. Whereupon the Kondaks said: We are men, but naked. So the perma lineage gave them twelve hands of cloth, and only that many people came out of the cave as there was cloth for. The rest remained inside.

What these stories illustrate is the manner in which the other lineages express their obligations to the founding lineages of their hamlet. As Mahadev Dhurwal said: 'They showed us the land, they could even now tell us to leave and go.' It is invariably this lineage which gives them land, shows them the arts of civilization (represented here by cloth or a drinking ladle) and because of their superior authority to mediate with the gods of that particular land, exercises temporal authority as well. Perhaps all tribal areas, because of being constituted by others as 'wild', also have stories to explain how they became civilized. But in these stories, unlike in colonial or upper caste narratives, it is local people who are the civilizing agents.

While the perma lineage is primary among the founding lineages in terms of exercising sacred and political power, all the original lineages are known as *matidars* or *dorel*, and have superior rights in land to that of later immigrants, e.g. they can perform certain agricultural rituals such as the pre-harvest sacrifice on their own land, without the aid of the perma. Later immigrants require the perma to do this for them.[21] The original founders of a village are commonly (but not always or necessarily) from one clan, and are known as *toler vaub* (brothers), while the lineages of the other clan are known as *saga* (affines). The (men of) founding families of the hamlets largely continue to exercise dominance in matters social, political and economic, on the basis both of their origins and the good use to which they put their earlier power, and built up an economic base.

The dominance of certain lineages does not imply that there was no overt conflict. Villages were not static over time. People fought with each other, left and came back. Old men in Bodaras said that in the time of their grandfathers (mid- to late-nineteenth century), there were only two houses in Kandkipara, a sub-hamlet of Bodaras, and three in Bodaras proper. The Tewal and Diral lineages of Kandkipara, were at war with the Boda lineage over sulphi trees located in Bodaras proper. Boda wouldn't give them any sulphi (juice), so they used to steal it and were correspondingly beaten if and when caught.[22] Finally, the Diral lineage went to Badanpal, but when their numbers there dwindled, they decided to return home.

Village of Memories: Field and Forest

A village is not just a collection of different lineages, it is a place marked by memories and particular spirits inhabiting particular spots. Specific stones and bends in the river, specific trees and paths — all have their stories. A stranger might go by and never realize that she was walking through history. But

---

[21] *See also* Thusu (1965:64-7) for a discussion of *matidars* among Dhurwas.

[22] Elwin (1942) noted that in the last twenty years there had been several cases of murder in Bastar over the right to collect juice from sulphi trees in common lands, or over thefts of sulphi juice from privately owned trees.

travellers who know, whose ancestors have built the human landscape which appears to others as so much 'wild nature', make offerings at certain spots, just a sprinkle of alcohol on the earth, a handful of rice – whatever they are carrying – or the spirits remind them by causing misfortune. Even the rivers Malangeir and Talpeir came into being due to the actions of the ancestors – as thirsty and tired on their way from Warangal to Bastar, they cut open bamboo stalks to let loose a stream of water. History in this account is mapped spatially across the landscape.[23] In the following story told by Sonadhar Sarpanch to a group of people waiting for the seed-sowing hunt to begin, individual features of the Kukanar landscape are explained thus:

In the days when the Jimmedar Murtak was still alive, all of Kukanar used to gather at Dangdi hill where Dangdi Dhur lived. Each hamlet had only a couple of houses. They would gather at Dangdi hill to perform the *kuraal* dance and the dust they raised would settle on the river bank fields of Tongpal, Hamirgarh, and Littiras (villages about 13 km north of Kukanar), ruining their tobacco crops and choking their children. So the villages of Hamirgarh pargana sat the medium and divined the cause and came to kill Jimmedar Murtak, who was resting on a rock behind Bodaras. He already knew of their coming and pretended to be sleeping with a bamboo stick under his head, having smeared *beeja* seed on his backside which made it red. When the attackers came, his old woman said: 'Look, he's such an old man, and is suffering from blood in his shit, how could he have raised such a dust?' But the attackers wouldn't listen and continued to advance towards him. So the old man took up his stick and chased them to beyond the Gutteir river, where he planted the staff to mark the boundary of Kukanar. Since then it has grown into a whole clump of bamboo.

Every seven or twelve years, the Hamirgarh villagers offer a white goat there to placate him. Recently, say the Bodaras villagers, a wedding party from Hamirgarh on their way past the rock where the Murtak sat failed to make an offering there. Consequently, their pot of landa unaccountably broke.

When it comes to dense forests, it is even more difficult for the outsider to perceive the marks of human action, rather than seeing it as areas where humans have *not yet* penetrated. Yet in

[23] *See also* Vitebsky (1993:75); Carter (1987); Lan (1985).

the cycle of shifting cultivation as practiced in areas with large tracts of land and little population, forests regenerated to obliterate the immediate evidence of human action. And in many cases, humans actually manoeuvred towards particular types of forests. For instance, Agarwal reports villagers' claims that outlying patches of sal in south central Bastar near Bailadilla were really 200 year old plantations. Possibly oil (from sal seed) was the main output expected, given the paucity of sources of oil in those days.[24] G.C. Homans, in his wonderful discussion of English landscapes as 'enduring memorials' to human activity, emphasizes the effects of different types of cultivation and systems of property in shaping different landscapes.[25] The same perspective needs to be extended to see forests as landscaped too, in opposition to and in symbiosis with fields.

The forests have been critical in defining life for people in Bastar, providing among other things: roots, tubers and fruits which are essential for monsoon months; medicines for different illnesses; wood for agricultural and domestic implements; leaves for plates and cups; bamboos for fencing, baskets, umbrellas and arrows; *siadi* creepers for ropes and cot weaves; oil from *mahua* seeds and *kirich*; alcohol, and cash income from the sale of sal seeds, mahua flowers and other NTFPs. Among several little known uses is the thorny bark of the *semur* tree which acts as a natural grater. It is clear that the forests contain wealth far beyond our urban imaginings.

Forests have not always been perceived by local villagers in purely beneficial ways however. The forest which both men and women roam so freely by day and through which they can chart their way with the help of trees and rocks, is also seen as full of wandering spirits, dissatisfied ghosts and, in the old days, wild beasts. Hunting was a dangerous business earlier, by all accounts. Men went out in large bands for a fortnight or so *(parads)* and battled with bears and wild buffaloes, and the

[24] Agarwal (1979:76-7). Normally, sal is not conducive to plantations. But, Sumit Guha (forthcoming) makes the same point for teak in Western India. He argues that grazing, shifting cultivation and firing of undergrowth, practices commonly seen as detrimental to forest cover, in fact led to teak expanding into new areas would not normally have been found in. Royal protection to teak, strengthened its dominance.

[25] Homans (1942:12-28).

women waited for them at home, guarding the house and going in groups to the forest to collect forest produce. Those were the days when the horns echoed to each other from hill to hill, and the men coming home would have their feet washed in welcome, like visitors, and the women would dance with the catch and everyone would have bunches of white flowers behind their ears because they were so happy.[26] Today people are lucky if they can catch a rabbit, provided of course they themselves are not caught by the forest guards.

Shifting Cultivation *(Penda)*

In the 'old days', even more than today, forests were inextricably connected to the agricultural cycle of the people. Villages would expand, as new settlers carved out fields for themselves in the midst of forests. This was no easy task as they had to fell the trees and level the land, and keep a constant watch for the depredations of wild beasts. The *kuraal* preserves the memory of this time. It is a multigenre ritual performance (dance, song, drama) held on winter nights from September to January in Dhurwa villages, three years in a row, with a gap of three years. The sequence bears the outward form of a story of the girl's life — her engagement, her marriage and finally, the death of her child. The kuraal dance comes from the Devi (i.e. is sacred), but is also a means of training the young in the ways of life, and simultaneously enjoyment, satire, history, and current commentary. In the '*chirmul tapiyan*' (wild buffalo or gaur shooting) episode a boy sings to his andil.

> We'll cut the penda, lets cut the penda, andil
> We'll gather the wood, lets gather the wood, andil
> We'll cut the small shrubs, lets cut the shrubs, andil
> We'll burn the field, lets burn the field, andil
> We'll turn over the field, raking it lengthwise and crosswise,
>   turning it the other way
> We'll finish the penda, I finished the penda, andil
> We'll sow the aikul, I've finished the aikul, andil
> We'll sow the rathel; I've finished the rathel, andil

He goes, all excited, to see how the *aikul* and *rathel* (millets) are

---

[26] Field Notes, 1992-3.

doing, whether they have sprouted; and sees happily that the ears are filling with milk and they are ripening. And then one day he sees that the chirmul have attacked it. The boy moans:

My aikul, the cunning chirmul has started on
A fence was made, he didn't heed it
A ditch was made, he ignored it
My rathel, the wicked chirmul is eating it
My aikul, the stupid chirmul is drinking it
He drank, and drank every drop
He ate and ate every ear
He ate it clean, from top to bottom.

He wanders in search of an experienced hunter and eventually finds one. The hunter kills the chirmul, and the boy sings gleefully and vengefully of plans to roast it, cut it in pieces, cook it and drink the gravy. Unfortunately, even once inside him, the wicked chirmul doesn't give up. The boy gets a stomach ache from overeating and they have to go in search of a doctor *(wadde)*. But all ends well. The wadde bites out the animal flesh, the patient recovers, and the curer is rewarded with grain. When I saw the dance performed, a bamboo frame covered with cloth was made to resemble a buffalo and two boys inside rushed around madly, scaring the crowd; the hunters came swathed in straw stomping away like abominable yetis, and the shamans got suitably possessed for the cure. In 1909, DeBrett noted that wild buffalos and bisons (gaur) were by then 'comparatively rare' in Bastar.[27] Hence, in depicting a situation where they posed a common threat, the kuraal goes back at least over a hundred years. Moreover, the aikul grain is now very rare. Only the older people could remember what it was.

There were different forms of shifting cultivation, depending on the quality and position of land. Dhurwas distinguish them as *kont penda* (hill cultivation), *bat penda* (flat cultivation) and *dukkil* (old fallows cultivation). In kont penda, or simply penda as it is referred to, cultivation is done by felling and firing patches of forests on hill slopes. The seeds are broadcast in the ashes after the first monsoon rains, (May–June). The crop ripens by October–November and is harvested. This is followed by

[27] DeBrett (1988:32).

threshing in December–January. Plots are cultivated for a couple of years and then left fallow for the forest to regenerate for anything between 12 to 18 years.[28] Bat penda (*marhan* in Halbi), is level land on which the same process of felling forests, burning wood etc. is applied. In the third system, called *dahya* in Halbi – old fallow plots are used, with the wood for firing being brought from elsewhere. In the other two systems, unlike in hill penda, the ashes are spread evenly over the ground, and hoed or ploughed in after the rains.[29] While intercropping of pulses and millets on marhan and penda is common, providing the advantage of different harvest times, there is little seasonal double cropping.[30] In addition, every household has always had an enclosure around their house where they grow maize, tobacco, mustard, turmeric, beans, gourds etc. Vegetables were and are grown on the fertile banks of rivers.

In the common perception of most people, rice was relatively rare in Bastar much less than a hundred years ago, and the majority of people lived by shifting cultivation, growing cereals, millets and, sometimes, early ripening paddy.[31] Today, rice has become the dominant crop in Bastar. Permanent rice cultivation involves different methods, follows a different cycle and leads to changes in social, including gender, relations.[32] Apart from the good rice land – flat, low lying with moisture retention – other fields cannot be cultivated every year, and are therefore left fallow for a period.[33] At the same time, wet rice cultivation sets up a permanent opposition between field and forest, and leads to the loss of the latter.[34] Rice requires standing water, fields must be embanked and there must be no shade. Millets, on the other hand, coexist with trees, the thick layers of fallen leaves providing nutrient, and a breeding ground for edible mushrooms.

Coarse grains like *kutki, kodon* and *mandia* have other advantages as well, such as having a higher nutritional content than rice or wheat, maintaining soil fertility and being drought

---

[28] Grigson (1991:127–8); Savyasachi (1993).
[29] *See also* Elwin (1991:24–5).
[30] Thusu (1965:142).
[31] Corroborated by Sly's settlement note, 1899, LI–13–1, JRR.
[32] Savyasachi (1993:65).
[33] DeBrett (1988:54); Grigson (1991:149–50).
[34] Savyasachi (1993:65).

and pest resistant.[35] Sadly, their virtues are being discovered by
scientists at a time when the villagers are themselves beginning
to abandon them under the pressure of being thought 'backward'
by upper castes and government extension workers. But it is
important not to see the move away from shifting cultivation
and millets in the past to permanent cultivation and rice in the
present in evolutionary terms. Rather, they are two different
systems of cultivation occupying different ecological niches and
representing different types of human investment. It was and is
possible for them to coexist and for people to move from
predominantly practicing rice cultivation to shifting cultivation
if they lost access to draught cattle, taxes on rice fields became
too heavy, or if they were displaced from their land by large
development projects.[36]

Further, the choice of methods in agriculture and the crops
sown have always varied between different areas of Bastar, and
between different groups. Some of these differences, e.g. that
between the Abujhmarias who rely largely on millets grown in
penda plots and the Halbas and Bhatras of the plains who grow
more rice, appear to be of long standing. Sugarcane has been
grown around Jagdalpur at least since the middle of the nineteenth century.[37] In other areas, differentiation is somewhat more
recent. For instance in Kukanar, the Gonds continue to carve
out penda plots on the hills unlike most Dhurwas, but as is
evident from the kuraal account of penda and other oral
histories, Dhurwas also practiced shifting cultivation. Gond
women still plough but in other groups they have ceased to do
so, partly out of 'Hinduization'.[38] It is true that different agricultural styles meant that British restrictions on shifting cultivation
affected groups in different ways, engendering different responses. However, what appears to have provoked uniform resentment in Bastar, at least as far as the 1910 rebellion went, was
the wholescale reservation of forests, and the expulsion of
villages from sites of long occupation.

Regarding the degree of individual ownership and

[35] Shiva (1988:124). *See also* Tyler (1978).
[36] *See* Grigson (1991:144-5). *See also* Dove (1993).
[37] Glasfurd (1962: para 137).
[38] Field Notes, 1992-3. *See also* Grigson (1991:125-50); Agarwal (1979:139-
42) for variations in agricultural practices.

egalitarianism too, there were differences among the various groups in Bastar from quite early on. Among the Hill Maria, shifting cultivation plots were (and still are) annually apportioned between families according to need and capabilities, but during a cultivation cycle the field belonged to the family which cultivated it. Among Dhurwas and Bison Horn Marias, freshly carved penda fields belonged to whichever household initiated them. Permanent rice fields were however always individually owned, even among the Hill Maria.[39] Possibly this was because rice cultivation involves long term care in the form of constructing embankments, making irrigation channels, and levelling the land. Nowadays, property ownership among all groups is becoming increasingly standardized as lineage land is being divided among different households in the lineage, each with its own title deed. Forests, village waste-lands (pasture and grazing lands, dancing squares, burial grounds) and natural ponds, rivers etc. were (and continue to be) held in common by the people of the village, though occasionally certain trees on these common lands (e.g. mahua, tamarind and sulphi) were privately owned.

Women occupy a different position in this structure.[40] Their rights to land vary: widows for instance have usufructory rights (but not ownership) in their husband's land for the period of their lives. If they leave the village or marry out of their former husband's lineage, they forfeit these rights. But unlike the upper castes, any asset, land or property that has been purchased out of a woman's own earnings from sale of forest produce or outside wage labour, belongs to her. And the involvement in all aspects of labour has also meant that women in Bastar are far more assertive than women in mainstream Indian society. But because rights to land are not transmitted across generations to women, and because women move between villages, they do not exercise power over other women or groups in any systemic way; and although their status often derives from, it cannot be simply equated with that of men from the lineage (natal or marital). In their marital villages, they are often simply called by the names of their natal villages – e.g. Pungudin (for a woman from Punguda), and their own names may be totally forgotten

<hr/>

[39] Grigson (1991:125–6); Savyasachi (1992); field notes, 1992–3.
[40] *See also* Kelkar and Nathan (1991:88–109); Agarwal (1994).

or unknown to others. In other words, the dominance exercised by the founding lineage is often a specifically gendered one, with men exercising power over the women of their own lineage; as well as over other lineages. Gathering together on dark kuraal nights, women sing of their lives:

> In the absolutely moonless night
> Dying, dying they are pounding
> With new grain, they are pounding . . .
> Having sat the child who sits
> having sat it, they are pounding
> Having walked the child who walks
> having walked it, they are pounding.

Markets and Trade

Along with the earth and the Mother Goddess, there are various ancestor spirits known as *sein* or *dangda/dangdi* which could be roughly translated as friends and young boys and girls respectively. Once upon a time they used to live and dance with humans. Now they live on Gurbe mountain (south-west of Kukanar) and have to be propitiated during the ceremonial hunt that takes place around the seed sowing festival.

Previously, says Dayaro Pujari, there wasn't sufficient cloth for weddings and mandais. So people would go to the mountain and ask for cloth from the dangda/dangdi and the sein. The village people would wear the cloth, wash it and return it the next day. Once, a child shat on a cloth that was being used to line its cradle, and by oversight it was returned unwashed. Since then, however much they asked and pleaded, the seven dangda and seven dangdi refused to give them cloth.

At Ropil, a festival which takes place once a year in August during the three years that the kuraal is not performed, women give bread at the Murtak shrine in the name of the dangdi and sein, in return for the cloth. The reference to cloth here and elsewhere (the giving of cloth to groups found in caves and bamboo clumps and thus civilizing them and making them a part of the village community) provokes some thought. There is no evidence of the Dhurwas or any other tribal group in Bastar ever having manufactured cloth by themselves. Gandas and Maharas are the traditional weavers. But cloth was also procured through Banjaras, who went with their pack bullocks up and down the sub-continent.[41] They left their traces in Bastar in the form of Banjarin Mata, a goddess whose shrine is often found at hill passes on major routes, and the costumes worn by mediums at festivals, which are typical Banjara skirts and blouses. Perhaps it was thought that these traders had some greater power of intercession with the Gods. Salt and cloth appear to have been the most important commodity the Bastar cultivators purchased from the Banjaras, in return for lac, resin, wax, galls, horn, dyes, teak, silk cocoons etc.[42] Bastar was also a 'great source of supply of elephants in medieval times'.[43]

Another group which seems to have travelled the country extensively bearing news and produce, and who appear frequently in Dhurwa stories (trying to make off with Dhurwa girls), are Gossains and Bairagis, Shaivite and Vaishnavite mendicants. Blunt describes an encounter with a Gossain from Benaras who had procured lac from the mountain people of Corair (Central Provinces) in exchange for a little salt and cloth.[44] Russell and Hiralal also remark upon their missionary work: 'In former times the Gosains travelled over the wildest tracts of country, proselytizing the primitive non-Aryan tribes, for whose conversion to Hinduism they are largely responsible.'[45] Conversely, the Gossains were also responsible for the adoption of pastoral or forest deities by settled castes, through the Bhairava cult, which assimilated them to a form of Shiva.[46]

Conclusion

The stories given above highlight the degree of migration that was prevalent in the past. Families routinely uprooted themselves

[41] We know from Blunt's account written in 1795 that one common Banjara route was through Bastar — from Dongar to Jagdalpur to Kotpad to Jeypore and from there to Vizianagram (Blunt, 1924). In 1862 the annual volume of traffic from Raipur to Hyderabad passing through Bastar was as high as '10,000 laden bullocks'. Glasfurd (1862: para 32).

[42] Glasfurd (1862: paras 45 & 46). *See also* Gell (1986:120–21) on the imported nature of Muria 'traditional' clothing and jewelry.

[43] Sherwani (1973:15).

[44] Blunt (1924).

[45] Russell and Hiralal (1969:159).

[46] Sontheimer (1989:95).

and moved on due to a variety of causes. This was partly to do with low population levels and the absence of a strong central authority that could enforce revenue demands that might have tied people down to particular fields, as well as the nature of the production system — hunting-gathering and shifting cultivation. In the cultural logic through which people depict their past, the right to cultivate, and the demarcation of village boundaries rested not on written title deeds but upon 'permission from the Earth', of course as interpreted by the founding lineage and the mediums. Claims to political authority were derived from religious authority, which in turn depended on one's powers of intermediation with the earth. Yet, authority was not rigidly fixed in one lineage and could be transferred, and was subject to a variety of checks. Social relations were also fluid, as might be expected in a situation of plentiful land and scarce labour. It was possible for people to change their clan and even their caste, in order to cement marriage alliances, or ensure that the necessary rituals were performed. Marriage assumed a special importance as a way of organizing labour. Over time, these relations hardened, as villages expanded and began to cultivate permanent fields. Minor disputes, for instance over sulphi, could cause significant heartburn — yet this did not disrupt the underlying sense of political and social cohesiveness.

Feelings towards the past are ambivalent — on the one hand, they may have more to eat under permanent rice cultivation, mills do remove some of the pressure of pounding by hand, and there are fewer deaths from wild animals. But the colonial restrictions on forests set in motion a process of alienation from which people have found it difficult to extricate themselves. A life without forests is difficult to imagine, yet they can see the rapid deforestation happening before their eyes and are aware of their own contribution to this process.

Emerging work on forest polities from the 17th to the 19th century shows that tribals were involved in a variety of networks with the contesting states in their vicinity. Sumit Guha points out that they too had assets to trade for power and wealth, most notably their intimate knowledge of the area.[47] Some were converted into settled agricultural labourers, some joined contending

---

[47] Guha (1996:153).

armies leading to monetization and stratification of their economies, while others retreated into the remaining hills and forests, continuing with hunting–gathering and shifting cultivation, as well as periodic raids on the villages of the plainspeople below.[48] As the stories in this chapter also make clear, at no point did pre-colonial 'tribal' groups in Bastar live in complete isolation, either from each other or from the so-called Hindu castes or traders, and there was mutual symbiosis between the two. An 'isolated and backward tribal society' had yet to fully take shape.

[48] Bayly (1988:31).

2

The Dialectics of Dussehra:
Raja and *Praja* in the Bastar Polity

The year 1912, the year in which Teso district was crystallized
within a colonial territory still in the making, represents no
more than an instant when the movements of countless peoples
over five hundred years were peremptorily halted, to be embedded in colonial history. . . . Over time as 'peoples' were
created and the district given shape, an imbricated social map
became a political reality. To derive the landscape and people
of Teso district from all else that it might have been, one is led
initially to a much larger arena. That the arena shrinks is what
politics is all about.

Joan Vincent, Teso in Transformation

The political history of pre-colonial Bastar reveals that far
from being 'void of the goods in general esteem among
mankind'[1] the region was, in Grigson's words, 'a country worth
invading in quite early times,'[2] and, one might add, advanced
enough to compete in the various power struggles of the region.
The eleventh to the fourteenth centuries saw the rise of Naga
kings who established themselves by conquering previous kingdoms in the area.[3] The ruins of Shiva temples with several images
of Sanskritic Gods and Goddesses can still be found at their
capital in Barsur. There are also various stone inscriptions
regarding administrative issues and land grants which mention
the presence of a variety of castes 'from various countries'
including traders and priests, as well as decisions taken by heads
of assemblies.[4] Both the ruins and the inscriptions indicate the
presence of high Hinduism and a supra-local organization.

---

[1] Rennell (1976:307).
[2] Grigson (1991:4).
[3] Shukla (1988); Yazdani (1982:579); Hira Lal, 'Inscription no. 4' (1910:26).
[4] Hira Lal, 'Inscription no. 23' (1908:311–16); Hira Lal (1916).

Today outsiders find it difficult to reconcile this with their image of 'primitive', 'tribal' and 'isolated' Bastar.

The Naga kings were supplanted by the Kakatiyas of Warangal who ruled Bastar from 1323 till 1947, when the last king of the dynasty, Pravir Chandra Bhanj Deo acceded to the Indian union. The founder of the Bastar dynasty, Annam Deo, fled northwards after the defeat of his brother, Pratap Rudra the king of Warangal, by Ulugh Khan (later Muhammad bin Tughluq) on his second Telengana expedition.[5] Although the Kakatiyas may have had nominal suzerainty over the area even prior to this, their rule in Bastar had to be established by defeating both the Naga kings and several minor chiefs.[6] According to Kedarnath Thakur, a local historian writing in 1908, these chiefs were found at a distance of 8–10 *kos* (ten to twenty miles) — at Bhairamgarh, Pratapgarh, Chindgarh, Hamirgarh, Killepal, Keshlur etc.[7] In many of these places, traces of old forts and oral histories attest to the existence of these minor chiefdoms. For instance, in south-east Bastar, Dhurwa villagers tell the stories of Gogria Majhi and a Hamirshahi king in Hamirgarh, Ruda Majhi of Chindgarh who fought with the Malkangiri king, Sargi Perma and Dangdi Dhur of Dangdi Koppe in Kukanar, and Boda Dhur of Pratapgarh. Indeed, this picture is characteristic of the whole central Indian belt, including Orissa. While the more powerful dynasties contended for power, local authority remained in the hands of local chieftains or headmen.[8]

The Dhurwas of Bodaras hamlet in Kukanar claim that their ancestors fled to the current area they occupy, from Barsur via Antagarh, Partabpur, and then Pratapgarh, after the defeat of the Nagvanshi kingdom. This was the only time anyone claimed to have emigrated from Barsur. The place of origin most commonly cited by all groups in Bastar is Warangal. This may have been true for some groups, while for others it may have

[5] Venkataramanayya and Sarma (1982:642–57). There appears to be some controversy over the date of Annam Deo's arrival in Bastar. *See* Hira Lal (1908:165–6). Grigson (1991:3) and the DeBrett (1988:37), erroneously date this event a century too late at approximately AD 1425, in the period of Ahmad Shah Bahmani.

[6] Thakur (1982:132); Grigson (1991:4).

[7] Ibid.

[8] Mahapatra (1987:11).

been caused by a desire to establish some connection with the ruling dynasty of Kakatiyas who are known to have come from there. Possibly Dayaro Pujari, who narrated the flight from Barsur, learnt of the fall of the Nagvanshi kingdom from someone in one of those back and forth borrowings between recorded history and oral traditions. But that there was some connection between the Nagvanshi kingdom in Barsur and the earlier Dhurwa settlement in Pratapgarh is indicated by the presence of old stone statues of Nandi the bull and other Sanskritic Gods and Goddesses in a clearing in the forest. The Dhurwas of Bodaras refer to them as their old Gods and Goddesses whom they had to leave behind. For many years they would go back and perform the annual rituals but eventually the distance and rains, which caused the stream to be in flood, made it impossible for them to do so, and they entrusted the Gods to the Halbas who had migrated there.[9]

Possibly the Parjas, a derivation from praja meaning people, were the original citizens of the Nagvanshis and other local kingdoms, or so Lakshman Jhadi, native of Bastar and CPI district secretary argues, based on what he has pieced together over the course of many years and many travels in Bastar. According to him, the Parjas lived in the old centers of the Nag kingdom — Barsur, Bhairamgarh, Chitrakote, Chote and Bade Dongar. When the Kakatiyas came, they retained existing centres of power but substituted their own chiefs. There were major battles — in besieged Bhairamgarh, an army had to be sent from Barsur. Those who surrendered to the Kakatiyas were killed, while others managed to escape by different routes. The group which came to Kukanar came from Barsur via Pratapgarh. Different groups of Parjas took different routes — but they mostly all settled in the hills and forests on the eastern side. Whether the Parjas constituted a 'tribe' is doubtful. In fact Grigson argues that the obvious derivation of the term Parja from praja indicates that the current 'tribe' is probably a mixture of the remnants of several tribes or confederations of tribes, all speaking different languages.[10] The oral histories I collected also support this — with some Dhurwa villages saying they came

[9] Field Notes, 1991-3.
[10] Grigson (1991:36).

from Warangal and others like Mundagarh close to the Orissa border claiming they came from Kotwapadar in Orissa.

Throughout Kakatiya rule, the kingdom was subject to attacks from both inside and outside. The zamindaris in the south and west of Bastar, some of which were given by the king to retainers and others which pre-dated the Kakatiyas[11] continue to have been fractious well into the nineteenth century. In 1856 we find the Bastar raja complaining to the British government at Nagpur about raids into his territories by the zamindars of Cherla, Loongoor and Albaka, which were formerly part of Bastar state.[12] This warfare also affected the local population. Hajra writes that in the mid-19th century the depredations of the Bheji rulers caused the depopulation of much of the country up to the Rampa region of Andhra, and that they maintained bands of Rohillas as mercenaries.[13] The Kakatiyas changed their capital several times before settling at Jagdalpur — e.g. Mudhota, Rajpur, Bade Dongar, Bastar — indicating the unsettled political situation.[14]

There were also periodic incursions from larger powers.[15] In 1563, there is evidence of the Bastar kings paying the Haihaibanshi kings of Ratanpur (north of Bastar) an annual tribute of Rs 5,015,[16] while from 1612 to 1672, they came under the suzerainty of the Qutb-Shahis of the Deccan to their south.[17] In 1780, Bastar became a tributary of the Bhosala (Marathas) at Nagpur, paying Rs 4000 p.a. in return for aid in an internal family quarrel.[18] The collection of tribute under Maratha paramountcy was often fraught with tension on both sides, with the Marathas

[11] e.g. the Sukma zamindari and its branches of Chintalnar and Bheji. The Sukma zamindar is still referred to as king in all his villages. There was intermarriage between the families of the Bastar king and the Sukma zamindars (who claim to be Rajputs). *See also* Hajra (1970:13–15).

[12] C. Elliot, Dy. Commr. Chattisgarh to G.A.C. Plowden, Commr. Seetabuldi, 11 December 1856, Chattisgarh Divisional Records, Nagpur, MPRR.

[13] Hajra (1970:14); *see also* Glasfurd (1862). He mentions several raids by zamindars on each other's territories, on their own villages and on travelling Banjaras.

[14] Thakur (1982:136).

[15] Shukla (1988:160–4).

[16] Wills (1919:238).

[17] Sherwani (1973:460); the year 1672 as a closing date is provided by Shukla (1988:179).

[18] Grigson (1991:6).

ordering the sack of Bastar villages and the raja and zamindars retaliating with raids.[19] Throughout its history, Bastar occupied a place in both northern and southern politics. It was only as late as the eighteenth century with Maratha suzerainty, that there was a real move towards integration into Chattisgarh and the north. This was strengthened during British rule by its positioning within the Central Provinces, when the rest of the Upper Godavari district was transferred to Madras, but was fully realized only in the post-1947 period.

On the eve of colonial rule then, the picture in central India was one of numerous kingdoms locked into a fairly stable routine of contention and co-existence. Some of them, like Bastar, were subordinated to one or the other overarching political formation (e.g. the Mughals, Marathas, or the Bahmani kingdom), on the basis of tribute payments. But largely due to the inaccessible nature of the terrain which was hilly and forested, they retained 'their identity, their cults and their own form of political organization', at the same time as they adopted some of the administrative practices and royal rituals of the Mughal and Maratha states, including the patronage of temples and Brahmans.[20] In short, both in terms of the political engagements of its rulers and in terms of the affiliations of its peoples, Bastar was not outside the 'mainstream' of Indian history but part of the composite development of events, the mosaic of states and polities that interacted sometimes hierarchically and sometimes horizontally.

State Formation and Legitimation in the Pre-Colonial Period: Existing Interpretations

Bayly has argued that 'power and authority in India had always been more like a complicated hierarchy than a scheme of "administration" or "government"'. Little kings and warrior farmers who exercised control at the village level also participated in the 'mystique of kingship' and were, in fact, the real government at the local level.[21] What exactly did this 'mystique of

[19] Blunt (1924).
[20] Bayly (1988:25-6).
[21] Ibid.:13-14.

kingship' consist of? Why and how did different indigenous groupings come to accept the Kakatiyas as rulers? Initially of course, there might have been the brute force of conquest. But beyond that, how was legitimacy, or rather royal hegemony, created and sustained? And to what extent?

One early explanation can be found in C.U. Wills' argument, based on a study of the administrative units of medieval Chattisgarh kingdoms, that they were successful in maintaining legitimacy because they retained local tribal organization and local chieftaincies. He deduced that the system of *garhs* (political and administrative divisions centred around a fort) derived from the earlier tribal clan territories, which Rajput rulers standardized.[22] The result was 'a system of feudalism superimposed on an earlier tribal organization'.[23] Sinha and others have argued the new rulers need not have been Rajputs in every case, but could have been tribal chiefs,[24] or tribal chiefs claiming Rajput status.[25] The latter invented exalted genealogies and styles of ruling for themselves, thereby distancing themselves from kinspeople.[26] At the same time, the role of the original tribe had to be acknowledged through their leading role in investiture ceremonies and state festivals like Dussehra.[27]

Bastar presents a more complicated case because the history of state formation goes so far back. Besides, the vast size of Bastar allowing for the co-existence of different types of polities in the pre-colonial period, and the different kinds of regional powers, both northern and southern under whose influence it came, also make it difficult to talk with specificity of a standard

[22] Wills (1919:199).

[23] Ibid. (1919:235, 255).

[24] e.g. the Gond states of Garha-Katangi (later Garha-Mandla), Kherla, Devgarh and Chandrapur. Garha-Mandla for instance lasted from the fourteenth till the eighteenth century when it was finally taken over by the Marathas. It was considerably prosperous, based on expanding agrarian settlement and the immigration of different groups like Brahmans, Kurmis, Lodhis and Rajputs from surrounding areas. Baker (1993:16–20).

[25] In states such as Bonai, Kalahandi, and possibly Mayurbhanj among others in Orissa, while the rulers claimed to be Rajputs, they were probably from indigenous groups. Sinha (1962, 1987).

[26] Even among Rajputs, however, state formation followed a similar route with an abrogation of kinship links in favor of tribute extraction. Fox (1969).

[27] Mahapatra (1987:25).

type of administration or standard terminology in the pre-colonial period. Thus today we find place-names ending with *nad* and *ur*, which are characteristic southern terms referring to micro-regions and villages respectively, along with terms like garhs and parganas which were categories of the medieval Chattisgarh and Mughal administrations respectively. In short, an attempt to explain state legitimation by purely structural features alone — the retention of some original tribal structure within an overarching feudal formation — is inadequate.

A second type of explanation for Kakatiya legitimacy comes from Anderson and Huber. They divide the process of legitimation into several stages. For the first stage, they essentially follow Wills' argument that 'faced with the problem of incorporating tribal societies under centralized hierarchic authority, the Kakatiyas adopted . . . the solution of weak central authority structurally congruent with tribal polity'.[28] In the next stage, the Kakatiyas adopted more classical models of kingship, by importing Brahmans and other service castes. In the last stage, caste headmen were created for the khalsa parts, i.e. the areas under direct management. The result was that the kingdom, comprising both the khalsa and zamindari areas, was implicitly bifurcated into two parts: 'a Hindu center and an outer, tribal part. Thus, one part took on an increasingly Hindu character with close connections to the state, while the other remained distinctly tribal, and in political and economic terms, experienced comparatively little intervention in customary practices.'[29]

The state was integrated, however, on a ritual plane. The king's relation to his tutelary deity and chief goddess Danteswari was both homologous to and encompassed the clans' relation to Tallur Mutte, the earth Goddess at the village level. In return for their minor tribute payments, the people got the 'highly valued benedictions of protection and prosperity from their God-Kings'.[30] Anderson and Huber appear to be following the model of the 'segmentary state' postulated by Southall in the African context and later adopted by Burton Stein for South India.[31] In Southall's latest definition, the segmentary state is

---

[28] Anderson and Huber (1988:33).
[29] Ibid.:33–4.
[30] Ibid.:34.
[31] Southall (1956); Stein (1980).

'one in which the spheres of ritual suzerainty and political sovereignty do not coincide. The former extends widely towards a flexible, changing periphery. The latter is confined to the central, core domain'.[32]

Some critics have argued that the segmentary model is flawed on the grounds of an illegitimate separation of social structure and 'cultural meaning'.[33] Others have pointed to the dangers inherent in identifying particular cosmologies as the basis of state legitimacy, and in assuming that these are unproblematically shared throughout the culture, especially in the absence of more mundane links.[34] But there is yet another reason why Anderson and Huber's model is inadequate, as is Wills'. Both treat 'Hindu' and 'tribal' as two distinct entities brought into relations with each other, instead of seeing how they are historically meshed in the service of royal hegemony. This issue is addressed later in the section on Danteswari.

The best parallel to state formation in Bastar is found in Kulke's work on the neighbouring states of Orissa, particularly the analytical distinction between vertical and horizontal legitimation. Vertical legitimation was achieved through an appropriation of indigenous deities into royal cults, while horizontal legitimation, whose stakes were prestige and acceptance within other kingdoms, involved bringing in Brahmans and building temples. The two processes were not separable as successive stages, but co-existed.[35] While the focus here is on the processes of vertical legitimation, in practice, of course, the distinction is not always clear. The importing of Brahmans was not for religious reasons alone or even for the purpose of competing with other kingdoms. Kulke argues that they were intended to provide 'administrative and ideological specialists' to counter centrifugal feudal forces.[36] Mahapatra gives two other significant reasons for this practice. On the one hand, the kings were dependent on tribal support, but on the other, they saw the dominant tribes as 'politically like a double-edged sword' in that they could lay claim to a countervailing authority and make

[32] Southall (1988:53).
[33] Dirks (1993:401–4).
[34] Gailey (1985:85).
[35] Kulke (1986).
[36] Ibid.:135.

demands on the king. Secondly, kings needed resources to
support the royal family as well as to meet the costs of defence
and administration. Settled agriculturalists were needed to generate a larger surplus; they could also be taxed more (except for
Brahmans and other retainers given revenue-free lands), unlike
the older groups who had traditionally negotiated fixed tri-
butes.[37] It is notable that the chariot processions and the celebration of Dussehra in Bastar coincided with the introduction of
Brahmans, as two aspects of the process of achieving greater
legitimacy among other kingdoms. But simultaneously, Dussehra and the mobilization of groups in a joint effort at making
the chariots are crucial to maintaining legitimacy within Bastar.

In the absence of adequate inscriptional or written material,
the representation of the pre-colonial state here is heavily dependent on ethnographic enquiries today. Contemporary descriptions of popular relations with the king revolve primarily
around the issues of corvée and the Dussehra festival. Hegemony,
it seems, was primarily achieved through two mechanisms – the
ritualization of corvée as both a right and an obligation and
the materiality of ritual within Dussehra – the integration
through labour of different groups within the kingdom, and
the integration of their Gods. Through the various rituals of
Dussehra, the political history of the kingdom was expressed –
the defeat of the various zamindaris and other territorial groups,
as well as the fragility of Kakatiya rule and the king's dependence
on the people.

Corvée

Corvée was the prime mechanism that sustained the state, both
in its ritual (Dussehra) and mundane (defence, building of public
works etc.) aspects, and the success of the Kakatiya state lay in
equating the two types of corvée such that service to the king
and the kingdom was seen as both an obligation and a right.
Corvée in Bastar was generally known as *begar* or *beth-begar*, both
terms common across North India.[38] In the hallowed light that

[37] Mahapatra (1987:23–7).
[38] Fukazawa (1991:132) notes that these terms came from the Persian *begar*
and the Sanskrit *visti* leading to *veth*.

all things connected with the kingship have currently acquired, people refer to their work for the king as *seva-bethia*. Bethia refers to a practice of reciprocal help within villages, while seva means service. Turning out to work for the king is thus portrayed in familiar, communal terms.[39]

The mechanisms of mobilization for everyday corvée and Dussehra were essentially the same — through village institutions and in the case of Dussehra, upwards through the pargana majhi. Revenue, cesses and corvée were collected from household heads by the village headman on the basis of the land owned (measured by the number of ploughs owned) by each household. Throughout the state every village maintained a *thanagudi* (rest house), an *atpaharia* and *raut* to serve the needs of visiting officials. The atpaharia brought firewood, cleaned up the place, and acted as general factotum and messenger while the raut cooked.[40] The other villagers contributed grain to them annually, in essence paying to have the service performed by one of them as part of a collective service they performed for the king, zamindar or any state official.

While the king's power over outlying areas had to be constantly reinforced by military means,[41] in Bastar there was a close overlap between areas of ritual and of political-economic integration. For the Kakatiya king, both were concentrated around Jagdalpur tahsil; and labour was drawn more from Jagdalpur tahsil for both mundane work and Dussehra, than from any other area. Villagers around Jagdalpur performed a variety of tasks: carrying firewood, grass and bamboos to the palace and temples, making fences, cleaning the palace, carrying loads for visiting officials etc. Nine persons from the three parganas of Chitapur, Tirathgarh and Nethanar were employed in rotation throughout the year as atpaharias in the palace alone, doing domestic work. They were given free rations during the period

[39] Field notes, 1991–3.

[40] Atpahria literally means someone who is available for the entire eight (*ath*) periods (*pahar*) into which a 24 hour cycle is divided. Rauts are cowherds and considered 'cleaner' than other low caste or tribal groups, and hence qualified to cook for 'superior' visitors.

[41] Hence the presence of Halbas — agriculturists conscripted as soldiers — in all the old centres of the Nag kingdom and minor chieftaincies like Bhairamgarh, Pratapgarh and Chindgarh.

of their stay and some cloth, provisions and cotton blankets when they returned.[42] Villages around Jagdalpur which performed specified tasks for the kings were exempt from other sorts of corvée; sometimes when the load of begar increased, it was ameliorated by a concession in the assessment of land revenue.[43] Villages in the Sukma zamindari performed similar corvée in the private lands and house of the zamindar, and correspondingly looked upon him as king. Visits to Jagdalpur for Dussehra were comparatively rare owing to distances. Under the colonial expansion of administration and the increase in number of touring officials, the incidence and extent of *kavad begar* (porterage duties) increased drastically, as did probably the visits of the king to outlying areas.[44] Thus colonial rule paradoxically increased both ritual and administrative integration. Under colonialism, a change in cultural meaning and the financial exigencies of 'rule on the cheap' led to an essentialization of corvée as a return for rights of access to land and forest, which were seen as owned by the state (see chapter four). As we saw in chapter one, this was not the popular perception for the basis of land ownership. Common lands were owned by particular clans or lineages organized in villages and the king's rights were limited to revenue and corvée.[45]

Encapsulating Hegemony Historically: Dussehra over Time

The fifteen-day long annual Dussehra festival which takes place in Jagdalpur in September–October, is critical to the understanding of the Bastar polity. It illustrates the establishment of royal hegemony, its transformation under indirect colonial rule, and the manner in which both have been accepted and contested. At the same time as Dussehra illuminates the standard political chronology of Bastar, it also provides an alternative history — one that is not laid out in linear time, but as several co-existing

[42] Compilation no. xxii (Forced Labour), JRR.
[43] DeBrett (1988:62).
[44] Field Notes, 1991–3.
[45] *See also* Kamath (1941:72–2). He argues that historically there was no connection between begar and nistar, the tenants only tilling that portion of the lands of village lessees or zamindars as was necessary to meet collective village expenses, or feed travellers and state servants on tour.

and contestatory stories; one that subsumes in a single event the dialectically produced and historically sedimented relations between subalterns and sovereigns in Bastar.

First, Dussehra encapsulates the process of state formation under the Kakatiyas — both spatially and historically. Spatially, Dussehra incorporated all the areas within the kingdom — conversely, as different garhs and zamindaris were alienated from Bastar, their people continued to attend the Bastar Dussehra for a while and then gradually drifted away. Each ritual of the festival provides a glimpse of the textured construction of hegemony though time, e.g. the manner in which the organized and orderly routines and imagery of imperial durbars was based on and refashioned 'old regime' assemblies; how 'sports days' and agricultural exhibitions co-existed with the wild dance of the devis in possession; and finally, how the Collector and the Commissioner, the MLA and the MP have succeeded to the mantle of the king in this disenchanted but not de-hegemonised world.

Secondly, Dussehra has always been and remains a performative act of legitimation, a process whereby, to paraphrase Corrigan and Sayer, the state states — it defines individual and collective identity.[46] Within the agricultural mode of production, Dussehra was an extension of the village jatra — local festivals necessary to preserve fertility and avoid sickness. The king was seen as necessary to the performance of this function for the kingdom as a whole. In turn, by the incorporation of different groups as participants and contributors to the ceremonies, the Kakatiyas simultaneously ensured their contribution in terms of corvée and revenue to the more mundane and regulated aspects of state construction and sustenance. The latter was the real service the people performed for the state, but its ritual overlay — Dussehra — came to be seen as equally central to the continued existence of the polity.

While Dussehra was a moment for the expression of public loyalty, it was simultaneously contingent on the king's proper behaviour and acknowledgement of the role of his subjects. Moreover their loyalty could fracture, as happened in 1876 and even earlier in 1774, when the Halbas of Dongar rebelled against

---

[46] Corrigan and Sayer (1985:3).

the king, Daryaodev, led by his half-brother, Ajmer Singh.[47] The establishment of hegemony is not a one-time accomplishment, but something which is ceaselessly contested, and constantly re-established.

Dussehra as Royal Ritual

Elsewhere in India, Dussehra is also celebrated as Durga-Puja, or Navratri (nine nights), held as it is on the first nine days/nights of the lunar month Asvina (September–October). The tenth day was known as Vijay Dasami or victory day, of which the common mythological referents are a commemoration of the victory of Ram over Ravan, the protagonists of the epic, *Ramayana*, or the Goddess Durga over Mahishasura, the buffalo-demon. However, in Bastar, as elsewhere, the central place of Durga was taken by Danteswari, the tutelary Goddess of the royal family, and Dussehra was celebrated as the state festival *par excellence*. Following the worship of professional tools, especially arms, throughout the festival, and their processional honouring on the ninth day, the tenth day traditionally marked the beginning of military campaigns (which also made sense in the context of the ending of the monsoons). The other ubiquitous features of Dussehra are the sacrifice of animals, especially buffaloes; the entrusting of the well-being and safety of the kingdom, usually in the shape of a sceptre or sword, to the Goddess (or an ascetic) for the period of the festival; and the ceremonial of processions and assemblies *(durbars)* which required the attendance of all notables and invited the spectatorship of all commoners.[48] The central theme of the Dussehra festival, taken generically, is said to be the worship of the Goddess by the king on behalf of the kingdom, in order to ensure its well being. However, the various rituals of Dussehra in Bastar are multi-layered accretions of different meanings going back to different historical periods and events, and drawing upon different ensembles of tradition — some pan-Indian and high-Hindu, and some specific to Bastar.

---

[47] *See* Shukla (1992:13–24) for further details of the Halba uprising.
[48] Dubey and Mohril (1961:105); Fuller (1992:106–28); Dirks (1993:39).

Village Rituals and State Performances

Jatras are village festivals held to appease the local Mother Goddess through sacrifice such that she feeds off the animals and not human lives (by causing death through sickness and drought); and to invoke her aid in the well-being of the village. The majhis and pujaris whom I interviewed in 1992, had similar explanations for Dussehra – with the benefits being intended for the area as a whole rather than a single village. This suggests that in the popular imagination, the direction of cosmological understanding goes from the rootedness of village life and everyday experiences upward to the state, rather than the other way around, as Fuller claims. In his view, village rituals were minor replicas of royal rituals, with a village headman assuming the king's function.[49]

Dussehra is also similar to a mandai (the pargana level equivalent of a village jatra) in that it is a meeting place for Gods and humans, albeit on a much larger scale. In 1992, eighty-eight village mother goddesses were invited to attend Dussehra in Jagdalpur.[50] The ritual division of labour between different groups for Dussehra parallels that of different lineages in the propitiation of village Gods. However, it is essential to remember that groups living closer to the capital are naturally far more involved through the assignment of specific tasks than those further away. Although people came to attend Dussehra from all over the state, often walking several days and several hundred miles, it is not the central festival in people's lives, as is often claimed, but a royal or political ritual – one that binds people to the state. For instance, from 1930-6, due to the Queen's illness or absence from Jagdalpur, Dussehra was not held. It would have been inconceivable for any important village ritual to go uncelebrated that long. The leading headmen who were consulted by the Administrator on due procedure replied that although they were anxious to celebrate the event, its main significance for them was the opportunity to see the Queen, and they would rather not celebrate the festival in her absence. The Queen, too, seemed piqued to think it could be held without her.[51] After Pravir's

---

[49] Fuller (1992:140-2).
[50] Tahsil Office List, 1992.
[51] XLVI 28/2, Note from Admin., 21 March 1932, JRR.

death and the internecine quarreling among the remnants of the ex-royal family, the royal place on the chariot was taken by the umbrella of Danteswari held by her senior priest. This turned what was centrally a royal ritual into a religious festival, and elevated Danteswari to cardinal importance.

Danteswari

The history of Danteswari embodies the history of the region and in understanding how she came to power, it is possible to understand how the Kakatiya dynasty came to power. In the received wisdom, Danteswari was seen as the chief Goddess of the land, and the king merely owed his power to his role as her chief priest.[52] According to popular legend, Danteswari came with the Kakatiyas from Warangal. She asked Annam Deo to proceed in front. As long as he could hear the sound of her anklets, she is said to have told him, he was not to look back. All the land that he could cover in this fashion was to be his. At Dantewara, however, the sands of the Sankini and Dankini rivers muffled the sound of the anklets. When the tinkle ceased, the king turned around, whereupon the Goddess stopped still in her tracks and refused to go further. Hence a temple was built on the spot (Dantewara) and another shrine established in the palace at Jagdalpur, for the king's convenience.

However, a closer look at both the rituals of Dussehra and the actual distribution of Danteswari shrines across the state suggests that her position as Chief Goddess is tenuous, and had to be constantly re-inforced during Dussehra, as a part of the process whereby the king re-inforced his own power over subordinate forces. Danteswari's position has to be seen through a hall of mirrors. Like Mother Goddesses elsewhere who were appropriated from indigenous cults[53] and adopted as tutelary Goddesses by royal families, she represented what Kulke calls the integration rather than displacement of tribal elements in the development of 'nuclear areas of sub-regional power'. Ultimately, it was this fusion which helped legitimize rule in these areas.[54] The site of the Danteswari temple, according to the inscription

---

[52] Anderson and Huber (1988); Grant (1984:37-8).
[53] *See* Sontheimer (1989); Eschmann (1986); Kosambi (1983); Nandi (1973).
[54] Kulke (1986:127-9).

in front of it, represents the spot where one of Parvati or Sakti's teeth *(dant)* fell, as her dead body was being carried by her husband Siva across the land, and is thus one of the *sakta-pithas* (sakti cult centres) of India. But the sakta-pithas themselves result from a process whereby the original object of worship, an animal or tree spirit and then a local Mother Goddess, is first worshipped through different, more pan-Indian rituals (flowers and incense as against animal sacrifice and medium possession) and then associated with one of the Goddesses of the Hindu pantheon, generally Durga/Kali/Sakti in order to form regional cults. The phenomenon has been well described by Nandi for the Deccan and by Eschmann for similar deities in Orissa.[55]

However, local manifestations of Danteswari all over Bastar are refractions of the royal deity and not the other way around. Simeran Gell notes of Muria cults in the north that while both Tallur Muttay (Earth Goddess) and Yayal Muttay (Danteswari's local name), are part of a unified cosmology, 'the Muria cults of *pen* and Tallur Muttay are transactional cults between men and other worldly beings in which the effort is to achieve a sort of balance between demands on both sides; hierarchy is however intrinsic to the cult of Yayal Muttay.'[56] In south and south-east Bastar, Danteswari is just one of the many Devis, but she is superior to the other Goddesses in the area, and at mandais where all the Devis and their mediums are assembled, they go to greet her rather than vice versa. In other words, Danteswari is worshipped locally only because the king was able to establish and maintain his political power, and gradually assimilate Dussehra and the worship of Danteswari to local festivals like mandais.

Thus, when I say that Danteswari's position has to be seen through a hall of mirrors I mean that the rulers adopt 'tribal' gods and change them, and the tribals in turn adopt these changed gods and change them . . . and so it goes on in endless mimesis. What is 'tribal' here, and what is 'Hindu'? Contra Ghurye, who used the phrase 'backward Hindus' for aboriginals,[57] we might equally see the Hindus as overdetermined aboriginals. For the same reason, the concepts of 'Sanskritization', 'Kshatriyzation'

[55] Nandi (1973:114-23); Eschmann (1986:79-97).
[56] Gell (1992:72-3).
[57] Ghurye (1963).

and the newer variant, 'Hinduization', popularized within the South Asian literature to refer to scheduled caste or tribal imitation of Brahmanical, dominant caste or Hindu customs, are not adequate to capture the nature of mutual appropriation and the resultant contradictions that co-exist in popular religion. Paraphrasing Sontheimer, one might instead use the term 'religious (re)configuration'.[58]

Yet another complication in Bastar is the long history of state formation. By the time of the Kakatiyas, the search for the *adi vasi* or original inhabitant becomes highly problematic with the influences of Sanskritic Gods and multi-caste territorial assemblies preceding animistic worship and tribal clan divisions on occasion. Even if the Nagvanshi kingdom was just an enclave of agriculturists surrounded by hunting-gathering groups, there must have been a mutual exchange. In understanding the relation between the Kakatiyas and the defeated Nagvanshi kingdom, the relation between Danteswari and Manikeswari (locally known as Mawli), whose temple is across the road from the palace in Jagdalpur, is of particular interest. Manikeswari appears to have been a Nagvanshi goddess, though the existing literature on this as well as local knowledge is most confusing.[59] It appears to me that Mawli who is deemed older to Danteswari by local tradition, and whose unanthropomorphized shrines are found all over the state, became the Nagvanshi Manikeswari through the process of appropriation described above.[60] However she also stayed in her

---

[58] Sontheimer (1989:vii).

[59] *See* Elliot (1856: para 11). A Barsur inscription speaks of the Nagas as worshippers of Manikyadevi or Manikeswari, who was an incarnation of Durga or Mahisasuramardini. Hira Lal argues that the Kakatiyas merely adopted the same Goddess and renamed her Danteswari (1908:164; 1910:25, 27). Local priests are no better at providing clarity. According to Lallu Pujari, the Danteswari priest, Manikeswari was the Goddess of the Nagvanshi kings, and Danteswari that of the Kakatiyas. The Queen continued the worship of Manikeswari and the king worshipped Danteswari. The Manikeswari (Mawli) Pujari on the other hand says that both Mawli and Danteswari came with the king from Hastinapur to Warangal, and Danteswari stopped at Dantewada, while Mawli went on to Jagdalpur.

[60] Naga inscriptions refer to several Gods, including Manikeswari, Narayana, and Vindhyavasini. This Vindhyavasini, writes Thapar (1978:168) was worshipped by the Sabaras, Barbaras and Pulindas, which were generic names for 'barbarian tribes'.

form as Mawli, meaning simply Mother.[61] With the conquest of the Nagvanshis, their Goddess Manikeswari became subordinate to the Goddess of the Kakatiyas – Danteswari. Yet, as part of the process of achieving hegemony, the defeated had to be accommodated, albeit in a subordinate position: thus while the festival is seen as dedicated to Danteswari, Manikeswari or Mawli is acknowledged in every ritual of Dussehra.

In all the events of Dussehra, the procession must follow a route from Danteswari to Mawli, which suggests that the latter is somehow senior. According to the Mawli Pujari, when there was a ruler, all the major rituals that now take place in the Danteswari temple used to take place in the Mawli temple. The chariot's path is further determined by the position of the Mawli and Jagannath temples – around which it must circumambulate. The Mawli Parghav event in which Danteswari is welcomed from Dantewada, and which is one of the bigger events of the festival, is also suggestive of the importance of Mawli's role – except once again there is no consensus on the precise meaning of it.

As part of the same process of hegemonic reconfiguration, the priests of all the temples in Jagdalpur (e.g. Malkarnath, Kalkanath, Karnakotin, Sitala, Kankalin, Telangin and Mawli) who used to be aboriginal or low caste, have been replaced by Brahmans within the living memory of people. The Mawli priest (a Dhakad, aged approximately 60) remembers that a Dhurwa priest used to look after the Danteswari temple, but died with the Raja in 1966. Lallu Pujari's Oriya Brahman family then took over.[62] In short, the history of the rise to power of any group can be read through the history and relative position of their Gods, and vice versa. Similarly, the recent adoption of Ram and Hanuman in Bastar is an index of the power of their devotees, the migrant traders and officials, over the lower classes.

Dussehra: Integration Through Labour

Every single group in the kingdom, however small in number, has some role in the festival – ranging from the small groups

---

[61] As Sontheimer (1989:205) notes, the original notions about a deity co-exist with newer ones. There can be several layers of meaning and references within a religious configuration.

[62] This is corroborated in DS, 2nd Oct. 1966; 28 November 1971.

of Mundas in and around Potenar, the Saonras in Bade Umargaon and its environs, to the more populous Murias and Marias. Certain functions are carried out on a caste basis and certain others on a regional basis — for instance, there may be several castes in a particular village which is assigned to bring wood. Upto the mid-twentieth century, the villages in a pargana would pool resources and send rice, goats and other presents to the king through the majhi. Certain parganas contributed supplies, while others contributed labour. For instance, in Kachorapati pargana, two kg rice and eight annas per household were collected, of which approximately forty to sixty kg and one goat were marked for Dussehra contributions. The rest was kept for pargana events.[63] A Dussehra tax was levied at the rate of three paise per rupee of rent in Jagdalpur tahsil, and anywhere from eight annas to three rupees per village elsewhere.[64] This cess was similarly collected through the majhis. The supplies thus collected would be used to feed people who had specific functions to perform at Dussehra.[65] Today, ironically, when there are no cesses or special taxes levied, the mass feeding is not seen as an act of largesse (as it was considered during the days of the king) but the fulfillment of a duty on the government's part. In 1938 the state contributed Rs 5600 annually for the festival, which was managed by the Palace Superintendent.[66] By 1992, the budget had risen more than forty-fold, albeit in nominal terms, to Rs 2,13,500. Except for a brief period in the 1960s when the festivities were managed by the king and his supporters on their own, all arrangements have been co-ordinated by the tahsildar's office in Jagdalpur. Currently there is also a Dussehra committee comprising of majhis and former supporters of the king — men and women known as members and membrins respectively — to formally oversee the arrangements. While expenditure has increased, people complain of skimpy portions, nostalgically looking back to the liberality of the king when, they claimed, an extra sack of rice would be thrown in now and then. There

[63] Interviews with majhis, Dussehra 1992.
[64] DeBrett (1988:64).
[65] XLVI 28/2, Palace Superintendent to Administrator, BS, 15 May 1939, JRR.
[66] XLVI 28/2 (Dussehra Programme for 1938), JRR.

are also accusations of corrupt government officers and MLAs; whether true or not, in view of inflation and the fiscal oversight exercised by the Dussehra committee, these accusations are symptomatic of the present day status of the state.[67] In short, although people still come voluntarily and suffer the income loss of fifteen days or more away from home and work, and say they would 'jump on the *sarkar*' if it was not celebrated, the most striking feature about Dussehra as it is celebrated today is the extent to which it is regarded as a government responsibility *(Sarkari Dussehra)*, rather than a people's event.

In 1992, the Dussehra festivities started on 26 September and continued till 10 October. Preparations, however, began at least two months earlier — in August, with the construction of the chariot. According to popular legend, the chariots date back to the period of Purushottam Deo (AD 1407–1439) who made a pilgrimage to the temple of Jagannath at Puri. He prostrated himself along the entire route, and so pleased the Lord Jagannath that he gave him a twelve-wheeled chariot for the return journey. However, since the original chariot was too big to be easily pulled, it was divided up into two smaller chariots, a four wheeled one and a bigger eight-wheeled one. Purushottam Deo started Dussehra in his then capital at Dongar, where even today a minor version of the event is held.

Every year, one of the chariots is made afresh. The entire process of construction is carried out through the co-operation of different villages. In 1957, an effort was apparently made to give out a contract for chariot making but the lessee had to withdraw in the face of popular resentment.[68] Each stage in the construction of the chariot is marked by certain offerings and sacrifices, e.g. the *pata* jatra which inaugurates the work, when people from village Billori bring logs of sal to Jagdalpur for the construction of the pata (wheels).[69] Different parts of the chariots are given different names and made of different woods — for instance, the base is known as *magar muhi* and is made of sal

[67] According to the tahsil accounts, the sum allotted barely covers expenditure, which includes feeding all the people who take part as well as providing for the cleaning of the temples, lights, fireworks, musical bands etc.

[68] Verma (1958).

[69] Amanullah (1988).

wood brought by the villages of Pandripani, Bade Marenga, Bade Morathpal, Lendra and Rajur; the roof is made of dhaman wood brought by Tondapal, Badebadam, Chilkuhuti and Dongriguda. These villages are given special forest passes for the purpose. The coal for smelting the iron to be used for the joints of the chariot is brought by another set of villages, as are the siadi creepers to make the ropes to pull the chariot. In all, some seventy two villages appear to be involved in bringing construction materials for the chariots alone.[70]   •

The entire carpentry and construction, which takes about fifteen days, is supervised by the Saonra Naiks of Jhar Umargaon and Beda Umargaon, who have been traditionally designated for the task. In 1992, there were sixty-five men of different castes from Beda Umargaon, and forty-three from Jhar Umargaon at work. Muria ironsmiths make the nails and the dragging ropes are plaited by Dhurwas. In the days when the king took part, Gadbas carried the king's palanquin to the *kalas-sthapan* ceremony (installation of sacred water) at various temples. Halbas, as the militia of old, carried swords alongside the chariot, while Bhatras bore bows and arrows.[71] The four-wheeled chariot is pulled by fifty or sixty men from each of the forty assigned villages near Jagdalpur and belong to different groups – Bhatra, Dhurwa, Muria, Halba, Dhakad, Mahara, Sundi. The eight wheeled chariot is pulled solely by Marias from the villages of Killepal pargana. The division of labor is so specific as to detail every possible function – even the people who put up the ladders to ascend and descend the chariot are from a specific village.

Dussehra Rituals

Despite variations and accretions over time, as modes of representing authority changed and Durbars and sports shows were added on, the Dussehra programme has remained more or less the same over the past century.[72] In the following account, I try

[70] *Dashera Parv 1992 Ke Liye Rath Nirman Hetu Lakdi Pradai Karne Hetu Free Pass Pradai Karne Hetu Vitaran Suchi* (List of different villages and the specific logs brought prepared by the Jagdalpur Tahsil office, 1992, for the purpose of free forest passes).

[71] Menon (1938).

[72] XLVI, 28 (Meetings of leading majhis and gaitas assembled at the time

and bring out some of the distinctive features of the traditional Bastar Dussehra like the *Kachan Gadi* ritual, *Jogi Bithai*, *Mawli Parghav* and the *Kumdakote* kidnapping. The other features are more standard, though also part of an ensemble of beliefs developed from Mother Goddess cults.[73]

Table III: *Dussehra Programme (1992)*

Days	Time	Events
1.	Evening	Kachan Gadi ritual
2.	Morning	Kalas-Sthapan
	Evening	Jogi Bithai
3–9.	Morning	Navratri Puja
	Evening	small chariot procession
10.	Morning	Durga Ashtami/Mahaashtami
	Evening	Nisha Jatra
11.	Morning	Kunvari Puja
	Evening	Jogi Utthayi
	Night	Mawli Parghav
12.	Morning	Bheeter Raini Puja
	Evening	Big chariot procession
13.	Morning	Bahar Raini Puja (Kumdakote)
	Evening	Chariot returns to palace
14.	Morning	Kachan Jatra/(Ran Jatra)
	Evening	'Muria' Durbar
15.	Morning	Gangamunda (Kutumb) Jatra
	Afternoon	Ohadi: Farewell to village deities
16.	Morning	Farewell to Danteswari

Source: Official Dussehra Programme, 1992, Tahsildar's Office, Jagdalpur.
NB: Exhibition runs throughout the festival

---

of Dashera), JRR. This file contains programmes and state speeches at the time of Dussehra for several years from 1906 onwards. Apart from my own observations of Dussehra in 1992, I have also consulted the following descriptions which were written at different periods: Menon (1938). Majumdar (1939), Verma (1958); Dubey and Mohril (1961).

[73] *See* Fuller (1992); Nandi (1973); Kulke (1986) for Mother Goddess rituals in Dussehra.

The Kachan Gadi takes place in the evening, on the last day of the waning moon in the month of Kunwar (September–October), which elsewhere is observed as *Pitramoksha Amavasya*, when people make offerings to their departed ancestors. In Bastar, it marks the start of the Dussehra, with permission to hold it being taken from Kachan Devi. In the ritual, a pre-pubertal Mrigan girl[74] becomes possessed by Kachan Devi in the course of circumambulating a swing made of thorns seven times, accompanied by a group of singing women. Once possessed, she engages in a mock fight with a man from the Khati caste.[75] After defeating him, the girl (in her role as Devi) is laid down to swing on the thorns, apparently without ill effects. The king (and since the death of the last king, Lallu Pujari holding the umbrella representing Danteswari) puts his request through the priests of the temple, which is granted when the Devi takes off her garland and gives it to them. According to the Mawli priest, the significance of this is the symbolic exchange of the king's weapons and the safe-keeping of the kingdom in return for the garland during the period of the festival. In royal times apparently, a durbar was held at night, whereby the king 'abdicated' — exchanging his clothes and ornaments for the simple clothes of an ascetic. In this guise, he could perform ceremonies in the temples of Danteswari, Mawli and Kankalin.

There are several meanings attached to the Kachan Gadi rite. Dube and Mohril claim that it is a fertility ritual, which they surmise from the fact of Kachan being an earth Goddess associated with fertility and reproduction, and the song sung by the women. The version they heard mentions 'an old Mother Goddess peeping out from a grove'. The mock fight represents an evil spirit trying to disrupt Dussehra. In the version narrated to me by the Mrigan priests' family, a Mrigan shaman helped a childless queen to conceive. In return, she was asked to pray to Kachan Devi, who they say is a goddess worshipped for

[74] The Mrigans are thought to be a sub-caste of the Maharas. They are also weavers. In 1992, the medium, Radha, was twelve years old, and studied in the 7th grade. She had fasted all day for the event.

[75] This mock warrior is not a Teli man as other versions claim. There is a Teli, however, who is referred to as the 'malik' (owner/master) and seems to supervise the whole affair.

children and general prosperity. Kachan is not their tutelary deity, but the queen's 'menstrual goddesss'. The Mrigans are her priests. One could also speculate on the connection between the history of Jagdalpur as a former Mahara settlement, and the permission taken from their deity in this rite. Possibly, Kachan was some variant of an earth Goddess for the area.[76] But it is equally possible, as Sumit Guha has pointed out, that because of the association of Mrigans or Maharas with impurity and tantrik rites, their prior permission is taken to ward off danger.[77] Scattered speculations aside, the Kachan Gadi ritual represents one moment of inversion in the entire year, when the Maharas/ Mrigans are given some recognition in the polity. This suggests, in turn, a situation of power that while normally subordinated or held in check, still needs to be acknowledged.

In the ritual known as Jogi Bithai (seating of the ascetic), a 'jogi' is incarcerated sitting cross legged in a pit dug in the sirasar for nine days, during which time he can neither eat nor move. The public comes and sees him and makes money offerings. The logic behind the ritual is that the jogi is a substitute ascetic for the king, who would otherwise have had to perform similar penances during Dussehra. This is strongly suggested by the fact that the king and the jogi never see each other. However there are other less serious philosophies behind the mutual abstinence, which indicate that there is often a wide gap between the high philosophy behind ritual and its popular reception. One such allegation is that a jogi once soiled his seat, and the raja who went to pick him up got soiled in the process, and thereafter refused to have anything to do with him.

The four-wheeled chariot begins to circulate from the evening of the third day and this is kept up for six days. It now creaks its way around the central market winding up again in front of the palace, preceded by the Munda and Panka musicians,

---

[76] According to popular legend, King Dalpat Deo (18th century) was hunting on the banks of the Indrawati and found his hunting dog being chased by a hare on the opposite bank. Convinced that there was some special power there, he asked permission from the local headman, Jagtu Mahara, to build his capital there. This is a very common story, invoked in other kingdoms too. *See* Sontheimer (1989:157).

[77] Pers. Comm.

a group of women waving incense before it and shouting *jai*, and as is inevitable in this modern day and age, a brass band! For night processions they have fire torches and tube lights held by rows of men and trailed by a generator on a push cart. Getting the chariots, especially the eight wheeled one, around street corners is an unwieldy task and the rope pullers have to invest much energy. There is great shouting and excitement. As the chariots turn, people also run around trying to escape being run over. If the chariot breaks down, the circuit is completed by jeep, replacing the elephant of former times. The streets as well as the rooftops of shops and houses are lined with crowds, especially on the last two days that the big chariot emerges.

People say that formerly (presumably in the late nineteenth, early twentieth century), there used to be a massive sacrifice of hundred and eight goats on the eighth and ninth day. Nowadays, only about forty goats in total are sacrificed at Dussehra. The buffalo sacrifices stopped about twenty five years ago. The Mawli Parghav, referring to the welcome of Danteswari, which takes place on the eleventh day, is the first major crowd puller of Dussehra. The events preceding this are mostly attended only by townspeople or neighbouring villagers. In royal times, the king (now replaced by the Raj Guru), went some distance bare foot to receive the palanquin of Danteswari which had been carried on foot all the way from Dantewara, 57 miles south. He would then carry it back to the palace. Following internal family quarrels after Pravir Chandra's death, the palanquin was kept in the Danteswari temple. In 1992, this event was followed by fireworks and performances. There was a dance by a group of Marias — the male drummers with their distinctive horned headware, and the women all in red sarees, as well as other non-local popular entertainment like acrobatics. The big day-time events are invariably accompanied by hawkers selling ribbons and rope, tobacco and knives, combs and earrings to local youth. At the beginning of the twentieth century, when local traders were fewer, merchants would come from as far as Calcutta and camp in Jagdalpur for the festival.

The big chariot emerges on what is elsewhere celebrated as Vijay Dasami. As long as there was a king, the Mawli

(Manikeswari) image − a golden, eight armed Durga, said
to be a very old statue − was brought to the durbar hall
and placed on the throne. The king ascended the chariot
from this hall and came back to it, where he was re-enthroned
after his nine days of asceticism, followed by a durbar.[78]
On the twelfth day of Dussehra as it was celebrated in royal
times, the king (and chariot) was 'kidnapped' to a place
called Kumdakote, to the east of Jagdalpur, where his subjects
presented him with gifts such as cash, game, fruit, brooms,
mats, and hawks. The practice was known as *Joharni*, johar
being a term of greeting in Halbi. It is also a time when
the king partook of new grains *(Nayakhani)*. In the context
of the quick ripening millet and coarse paddy grains of the
shifting cultivation cycle that was prevalent all over Bastar,
Dussehra made sense as a harvest festival. The Mawli Pujari
claimed that the offering of forest produce represented an
assurance to the king that the people and hence he too,
would not starve even during drought; while Menon writes
that the ceremony resulted from the tribals feeling aggrieved
that they, the majority of the King's subjects, could not
take part in the essentially Hindu celebrations. They wanted
their own Dussehra, 'which, they said, could only be held
in their own home, the jungle.' So they kidnapped the king
when asleep and took him and his chariot to Kumdakote,
which was a dense jungle then. The king came to some
understanding with them, and rode the chariot back in
triumph. As various observers have noted, there was often
a mutual feeling of possessiveness and loyalty between monarch
and subjects bred by the paternalist relation.[79] In yet another
interpretation, I read the offering of grains and first fruits
as a symbolic assertion of the people's rights to the forest
in the first place.

The Kumdakote nayakhani makes it possible to read Dussehra
as an act of negotiation between people and king. The king
legitimized his own position as essential to the well being of
the land through the ritual eating of the first grains and fruit,
sacrifices, and other rituals. The subjects, in turn, subordinated

[78] Dubey and Mohril (1961).
[79] Menon (1938); Mahapatra (1987:25).

the kingship to their own ends of preserving fertility and avoiding sickness — treating Dussehra as a state extension of village mandais and jatras. They also asserted through this, their rights to the land and its produce, and the king's dependence on them for his own livelihood.

The 'Muria Durbar': 'Representing Authority' in Colonial and Post-Colonial Bastar

Under colonial rule, there were accretions to the festival which reflected British modes of legitimation. This reworked Dussehra proved the ideal form for the ritual display of indirect rule. Cohn describes how British attempts to work through Mughal and other indigenous idioms of rule, such as the giving of gifts by nobles, led to continuing tensions over titles, forms of address, questions of precedence and even dress. While grappling with these forms, colonialism inevitably changed their meanings to more contractual relations. Eventually, the British substituted their own forms of legitimation — the laying of foundation stones, coronations, jubilees, the ranking of princely states by gun salutes, not to forget cricket matches and agricultural exhibitions.[80]

Yet the language of custom remained. Describing the celebrations for the silver jubilee of King George V and Queen Mary in Bastar, which included 'processions, illuminations, fireworks displays, and aboriginal dances with distribution of goods to the poor and sweets to the school children', Hyde claimed that there was considerable enthusiasm: 'Indians know all about Rajas and Emperors and greatly enjoy "tamashas" associated with them.'[81] Thus empire was translated into local rituals, and indigenous rituals now added to the greater glory and diversity of empire.[82]

The 'Muria Durbar' was first begun in 1906 as part of the Dussehra programme as a means of communication between the administration and the public. Since then, it has served as the real microcosm of the polity. The scale was evidently never

---

[80] Cohn (1990:632–82); Haynes (1990:459–92); Roberts (1990:225).
[81] E.S. Hyde, Autobiographical Memoir, Box 10, Hyde Papers.
[82] Vincent (1988).

large, and a specification in the 1947 programme gives us a glimpse: 'Uniform, darbar dress or clean clothes will be worn so far as those attending the darbar may be in possession of such.' All officials, zamindars and majhis were required to attend, and the majhis were given red turbans to signify their authority. In later years, this symbol too became a site of contestation as Pravir Chandra appointed his own majhis and gave them blue turbans as against the red-turbanned majhis who were supports of the state. Since approximately 1923 onwards, the Durbar speech was given by the Administrator rather than the Sovereign. Although the state still formally functioned in the royal name, this was as close to a ceremonial public acknowledgement of a de facto transfer of power as one might get.

The various issues raised by the administrators, though couched in a language of administrative largesse, provide a glimpse of the concerns of the people. From 1906 to 1947, complaints and queries regarding the reservation of the forests, grazing and commutation dues, begar and purchases of supplies by officials at less than the market rates *(bisaha)* were routine. At the same time, the colonial state presented its own version of the truth to its subjects. Just after the rebellion of 1910, the raja castigated his subjects for not co-operating with the administration and maintaining a 'universal conspiracy of silence' with respect to the rebellion.[83] In a situation where several villages had been burnt, hundreds of villagers flogged, large fines extracted and people were still fleeing to neighbouring provinces, it would seem odd to us if they had done anything else. In these Dussehra speeches, colonialism emerges as an essentially patriarchal phenomenon – the wise and stern, all-knowing priest or father giving advice to wayward folk on the need to extend cultivation, look after the forest, accept innoculation, attend schools, stop drinking, and desist from running off with marriage partners. Year after year, exhorted to virtue or castigated for their vices, the assembled adivasis either kept silent, or concurred heartily, sometimes perhaps a shade too heartily.[84]

[83] Speech made by Raja Rudra Pratap Deo, Feudatory Chief at the Dashera Meeting Darbar, 1911, xlvi, Raj Family, JRR.

[84] xlvi, 28, 38/3, Durbar Speeches from 1906–47, JRR.

Exhibiting the State

The Government exhibition, started in 1938/39, along with a sports day that concluded the events, represented the colonial administration's 'improvement' drive to supplement the indigenous rituals of Dussehra. The exhibition was designed to encourage local manufactures such as carpentry by aboriginal youth. The games included archery, elephant rides and lotteries. A livestock exhibition was also held. As Burton Benedict argues, exhibition displays were not about the actual products on exhibit at all: 'Systems of classification revealed differences in national views of the ideally constructed world.'[85] Thus 'British exhibits tended to show colonial products and the use of native labor to obtain these products', i.e. natives in the service of empire and commerce. The French, on the other hand, concentrated on showing natives as natives, while the American exhibits showed natives as having been transformed into good, civilized Americans.[86]

Like everything else, the exhibition was continued over into the post-colonial state. The main government exhibition runs parallel to the evening events almost throughout the festival and is perhaps the best barometer of the state of the state in its most reformist mode. Each department (Health, Tribal Welfare, Education, Fisheries, Forest, Sericulture, Irrigation, Electricity, Municipality, and Archaeology) has its own stall, paid for out of its own budget. These provide information and advertise their achievements. There are also dances and other items performed by different schools. Similar exhibitions are held in the larger mandais — such as in Narainpur. The Anthropological Survey of India, which has its offices next to the exhibition grounds in Jagdalpur, has its own exhibition of 'tribal' artifacts, which are really made by non-tribal artisanal 'castes'. As Alfred Gell points out, these items are increasingly being seen by outsiders as symptomatic of the authentic tribal, while the tribals themselves have been taking to consumer items produced elsewhere, in a process that has gone on much longer than is commonly

---

[85] Benedict (1983:29).
[86] Ibid.:51.

thought.[87] To paraphrase Clifford, the pure products have been going crazy for a while, and therein lies the predicament of culture.[88] Therein lies also the predicament of the anthropologist trying to recover a pre-colonial polity in order to contrast it with the present.

[87] Gell (1986:137).
[88] Clifford (1988:5).

Rebellious Pasts

I pondered all these things, and how men fight and lose the battle, and the thing that they fought for comes about in spite of their defeat, and when it comes turns out not to be what they meant, and other men have to fight for what they meant under another name.

William Morris

The class struggle ... is a fight for the crude and material things without which no refined and spiritual things could exist. Nevertheless, it is not in the form of spoils which fall to the victor that the latter make their presence felt in the class struggle. They manifest themselves in this struggle as courage, humour, cunning and fortitude. They have retroactive force and will constantly call in question every victory, past and present, of the rulers ...

Walter Benjamin

Map 4: *Bastar and Neighbouring States in the Colonial Period*

Source: Adapted from Verrier Elwin (1991: 4) and Grigson (1991:29).

3

'We Are Yours, but the Land is Ours': Kingship Contested*

The King who rules cherishing his people
Has the world at his feet.

Where a King is unjust
Rains are withheld.

Tiruvalluvar, *Tirrukural*

On 29 February 1876, the raja of Bastar set out from his capital at Jagdalpur to meet the Prince of Wales. He had refused at least one such previous summons, but now felt compelled to attend. But barely a day later and a mere 13 km south of Jagdalpur at Bade Marenga, his porters threw down their burden and refused to go further. 'Why are you going?', they asked, 'the English will not let you return. The Munshis loot our money, why don't you send them in your place instead?' The men then attempted to leave. The raja, or according to some, his diwan, Gopinath Kapurdar, reacted quickly. Eighteen men were picked out, taken to nearby Burungpal, flogged and then sent back to be incarcerated in the Jagdalpur jail. But on the way there, the prisoners were rescued by a party of peasants who snatched the warrant and chased away the accompanying guards.[1] On hearing about the skirmish, the raja decided to return to Jagdalpur. At Arapur, he was met by a deputation of approximately 1500 men.[2] They complained bitterly about the

* The phrase is taken from Blum (1961:469).
[1] XLVI–30–II, Statement by Lal Kalandar Singh, recorded 26 August 1908, JRR. The description of the rebellion is taken from this statement as well as For. Pol. A August 1876, Pro. nos. 163–72, NAI; For. Pol. A, April 1876, Pro. nos. 331–6, NAI.
[2] There is no mention of women being present, which normally need not mean that they were not present. But given the fact that men had assembled for a seige here, I assume they were not.

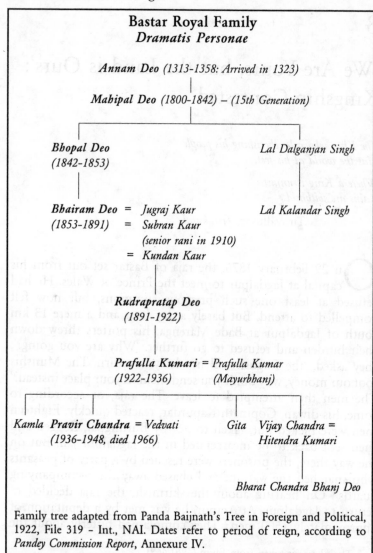

Bastar Royal Family
Dramatis Personae

Annam Deo (1313-1358: Arrived in 1323)

Mahipal Deo (1800-1842) – (15th Generation)

Bhopal Deo
(1842-1853)

Lal Dalganjan Singh

Bhairam Deo = *Jugraj Kaur*
(1853-1891) = *Subran Kaur*
           (senior rani in 1910)
        = *Kundan Kaur*

Lal Kalandar Singh

Rudrapratap Deo
(1891-1922)

Prafulla Kumari = *Prafulla Kumar*
(1922-1936)   *(Mayurbhanj)*

Kamla **Pravir Chandra** = *Vedvati*   *Gita* *Vijay Chandra* =
(1936-1948, died 1966)   *Hitendra Kumari*

Bharat Chandra Bhanj Deo

Family tree adapted from Panda Baijnath's Tree in Foreign and Political, 1922, File 319 – Int., NAI. Dates refer to period of reign, according to *Pandey Commission Report*, Annexure IV.

diwan, and Adit Prashad, the munshi in charge of the criminal courts, and said that despite being

ryots of the Raja who paid him revenue, worked as begars for him, and who venerated his person (they were) subjected to so many years of oppression, in which their rice, goats, and other goods and chattels were generally taken for nothing, and sometimes for a nominal sum, they thought it hard after enduring all this for years to be at last flogged for no fault and then committed to jail for an indefinite period and feeling they could endure this no longer they asked him in justice to remove these men.[3]

The peasants insisted that if they did not get justice, they would be forced to migrate elsewhere and the kingdom would be ruined. They crowded behind the raja's palanquin trying to make their petition. In their version of subsequent events, Gopinath ordered the guards to fire upon them. The raja on the other hand said that there was a sudden flurry of clods of earth, stones and cow bones, one of which hit him, and frightened him into ordering the firing. The peasants fled, with two dead and six badly injured by both gun shot and sword cuts. By the evening of 3 March, the king was back in Jagdalpur, with the four entrances of the fort fortified with canons.

Mango boughs were then sent around villages as a call to assemble and within a few days, peasants, primarily from the seven parganas of Jagdalpur tahsil, gathered in their thousands for a siege of the fort.[4] Led by Kesari Majhi of Raikera pargana, Ranga Majhi of Agarwara pargana, Kunhaiyya Majhi and others, they refused to give passage for grazing to the king's elephant or horses or allow mail to go out. However, the raja managed to smuggle out letters through neighbouring Jeypore state to the Governor's agent at Vizagapatam (Madras Presidency), and the Deputy Commissioner at Sironcha (Central Provinces).[5] He appealed to them both to save him. His letters are plaintive portrayals of himself as the object of grave injustice by his people: 'All the ryots of the seven parganas of my state have since eight days rebelled against me, and have been treating me with contempt in the highest degree.'[6]

---

[3] For. Pol. A August 1876, Pro. nos. 163–72, H.J. MacGeorge, Offg. Dy. Commr. Upper Godavari Dist. to Sec. to C.C., CP, 22 April 1876, NAI.

[4] The circulating branch was a common means of mobilization, a call to collective activity. The number of leaves or nicks on the branch signified the number of days in which to assemble. Guha (1983:227–46).

[5] XLVI-30-II, Statement by Lal Kalandar Singh, 26 August 1908, JRR; Thakur (1982:141-2).

[6] For. Pol. A August 1876, Pro. nos. 163–72, Raja of Bastar to Capt. C. Eastall, Acting Special Agent, Koraput, 10 March 1876, NAI.

A force of 300 Jeypore policemen equipped with muskets, and 250 of the Jeypore Raja's soldiers armed with swords and matchlocks, were deputed under two British officers and reached Jagdalpur around the 20 of March. Initial estimates of insurgent numbers by the Jeypore police put them at 30,000, which was later found to be a ten-fold exaggeration. The peasants allowed the Jeypore force to disarm them of their weapons, consisting of bows, arrows and axes, without much resistance, and even gave the British forces supplies without taking payment for it. However they would not speak without consulting with their leaders, indicating a clear pattern of organization and leadership.[7]

The Jeypore force set up camp across the river from the rebels and awaited the arrival of the Deputy Commissioner, Sironcha, under whose purview Bastar came. The stand-off between the Bastar peasants and the Jeypore police continued for a fortnight or so, but was restricted to a mutual exchange of verbal insults accompanied by the occasional stringing of bows and blowing of horns. Bastar and Jeypore had a long-standing dispute over Kotpad, a tract of land, which added to the animosity.[8] In the midst of all this, the two European police officers even got in a bit of game shooting, interrupted merely by several 'little annoyances', such as having jeering peasants follow them shouting abusively, 'See the *sahib log* run!'[9]

MacGeorge, the Deputy Commissioner Sironcha, arrived only on 5 April by which time the siege had already lasted a month. However, according to the official narrative, once the appropriate officer had arrived to dispense the blessings of British benevolence, the matter was quickly settled. MacGeorge writes: 'They all prostrated themselves before me, and said they had no quarrel with the British Government but wanted justice.'[10] He advised them to disperse by evening, except for their headmen, who were required to stay behind and present their case. Having

[7] For. Pol. A August 1876, Pro. nos. 163–72, Eastall to Goodrich, Agent to Gov-Gen, Vizagapatam, 25 March 1876, NAI.

[8] In 1862 Kotpad was finally allotted by the Governor General to Jeypore in exchange for compensation to Bastar. Joshi (1990:116–19).

[9] For. Pol. A August 1876, Pro. nos. 163–72, MacGeorge to Sec. to CC, CP, 22 April 1876, NAI.

[10] Ibid.

spent two days listening to each side, MacGeorge held an assembly attended by the raja, his officials and retainers, some 600 rebels and all the Europeans in camp. In the version recorded for posterity:

I showed them that the Deputy Commissioner of Sironcha, as the representative of the paramount power, was all powerful, and they had simply to inform him of their grievances, and a full and just enquiry would be made, but that any armed demonstration made in the future would end in their ruin and destruction of their houses and country . . . This speech evidently impressed the masses, they appeared to understand it, and all their chief men who were seated in the front rows disclaimed any idea of doing again what they had done, said they were fools for acting as they did, and that they fully trusted the 'Sirkar Bahadur'.[11]

Whereupon everyone quietly went back to their villages. Gopinath and Adit Prashad, the offending diwan and munshi respectively, were dismissed and taken to Sironcha along with Loknath, the chief advisor to the king, whose advice the peasants had supposedly sought. The British Raj had once more asserted itself to the greater happiness and benefit of all.

Interpreting the Rebellion: Colonial and Contemporary Local Accounts

As with every act of rebellion, the siege of 1876 comes to us shot through with multiple interpretations. Commenting on the downfall of Gopinath and Adit Prashad, the Chief Commissioner wrote:

the ryots may almost be said to have taken a constitutional measure for obtaining their dismissal. It is impossible not to feel astonished at the wonderful moderation which these excitable Mooreas have displayed. Their investment of Jagdalpur seems to have been a solemn demonstration; though the investment lasted nearly a month, they resorted to no violence, committed no depredations. They took food indeed from the raja's granaries, but they . . . looked upon themselves as having a right to take food. On the other hand they carefully preserved the Raja's treasure (abandoned in the first encounter) and they seem invariably to have kept the public object in view. On the

[11] Ibid.

part of the ryots this revolution or insurrection was a perfectly bloodless one, and it would be difficult to find a parallel to the conduct of these half-civilised men.[12]

While paying tribute to the maturity of the Murias, the event was simultaneously inscribed in a classic pattern central to the discourse of Pax Brittanica, that of an oppressive or weak native ruler, pitted against innocent subjects, and saved by the just British. The peasants were innocent so long as they did not practice violence against the British. In 1876, as subjects who 'had been oppressed for years', they had 'right on their side' versus a 'Raja of feeble character governing through favourites'.[13]

Yet where native rulers were involved, the 'intrigue factor' could not be far behind in any colonial explanation. In this they were assisted by the mentality of subordinate officials on whom they relied for their information. In the account given to the Chief Commissioner by Jugganath Rao, a tahsildar who was in Jagdalpur for some months after the rebellion, Rani Jugraj Kaur was said to be 'intimate' with Gopinath. As the raja himself was an 'innocent', his chief advisor, Rajguru Loknath, 'engineered' the rebellion to get Gopinath out of the way (and thus save the royal house from dishonour). Jones, the Chief Commissioner, noted that 'he certainly, if any one, ought to know what the real cause of the disturbance . . . was'.[14]

Local historians, both at the time and later, are divided in their emphases on the causes behind the rebellion. Writing in 1889, Munshi Kali Prashad, former manager of Paralkote zamindari, attributed the rebellion to a few palace malcontents who led the Murias to believe that when the raja went to Delhi, the Munshis would keep him there and rule in his place instead.[15] In Kedarnath Thakur's 1908 version too, palace animosities figure, coupled with longstanding peasant complaints against Gopinath, as the chief cause. Gopinath's failure to catch a wild elephant with the help of local *sirahas* (shamans) and his

[12] For. Pol. A August 1876, Pro. nos. 163–72, Sec. to CC, CP, to Sec. to GOI, For. Dept., 29 May 1876, NAI.

[13] For. Pol. A I, August 1876, Pro. nos. 163–72, T.H. Thornton, Sec. to GOI, For. Dept. to Governor-General, 10 June 1876, NAI.

[14] For. Pol. A January 1884, Pro. nos. 117–25, Memo by the CC, CP, NAI.

[15] *Munshi Kali Prasad ki tahrir*, Paralkote, 14 September 1889, reproduced in Shukla (1992:181–2).

subsequent action in whipping the sirahas, excited popular resentment. People blamed the incident on Bhairam Deo's father, Bhopal Deo, who was king at the time. Popular dissatisfaction with the royal family, in turn, caused a lasting division between Bhopal Deo and his half-brother, the Diwan Dalganjan Singh, and their respective supporters. Court divisions were intensified in Bhairam Deo's time, when Gopinath, a Raut who functioned as the king's valet *(kapurdar)*, was made diwan, passing over what others considered more able and educated men. Although Bhairam Deo tried his best to placate the peasants, they became convinced that only Gopinath had access to the king, and rebelled in order to have him removed.[16]

Like the British, most local historians focussed on palace politics and the actions of the diwan and munshi alone. In a rare exception, Lal Kalandar Singh, cousin of the king and a child of eleven or twelve at the time of the rebellion, attributed peasant discontent to the introduction of the malguzari settlement, and the proliferation of outside munshis to assess taxes, both of which people blamed on Gopinath and Adit Prashad. In his version, although the peasants wanted to confront the Deputy Commissioner when he arrived, they lacked the courage.[17] In general, however, the connection of these changes with the policies of the British Raj went unremarked both by the British and local historians.

A Current Perspective on Customary Rebellion

Contemporary historiography suggests that one possibility is to see it as a 'customary' rebellion, or a rebellion that was paradoxically aimed at upholding the existing order, while removing any defects. Customary rebellion, as defined by Gluckman in the African context (among the Zulu, Swazi and Bemba), signified a belief in the sanctity of the kingship over and above the defects of the particular king. Rebellion (as against revolution) paradoxically sustained the kingship, at least for a time, as rival claimants fought for the throne, thus re-affirming its centrality to society.[18]

[16] Thakur (1982:141–2).
[17] XLVI-30-II, Lal Kalandar's Singh's Note on Raj Family History, August 1908, JRR.
[18] Gluckman (1963, 1955).

In other cases, even the particular king could not be seen as doing wrong, for to admit that would be to fracture his divinity.[19] By rebelling, people believed or claimed to be acting in the name of the king, saving him from committing an injustice or having injustice committed in his land.[20]

Three factors in particular seem to support the validity of this interpretation for the 1876 rebellion: first, the fact that the raja himself was not blamed for maladministration, only his corrupt officials; secondly, the fact that it was overall a peaceful siege, and people dispersed when told the officials would be removed; and thirdly, the fact that 1876–8 were years of famine in all the areas surrounding Bastar – Madras Presidency – Nizam's dominions, Central Provinces and Bombay Presidency, following the failure of the rains and growing drought. Elsewhere the famine was marked by several attempts at seizure and distribution of food grains.[21] While there is no record of famine in the Bastar context, possibly because of the general lack of information about the period or because of a general British reluctance to acknowledge famine,[22] Ward's report does mention a failure of the harvest in 1877–8. If there was a fear of an imminent famine, such a situation may have contributed to the tribals' insistence that the raja not leave his state and thus deprive it of the protection afforded by his physical presence. The philosophy behind this is that through the performance of sacrifice and the appropriate rituals in Dussehra, the king mediates between the people and the Gods to ensure the well-being and prosperity of the land, and in that moment of sacrifice, assumes divinity himself.[23] Thus if this logic were to be followed – and the raja himself clearly desired that this be the interpretation[24] – the rebellion was intended to emphasize the divine function of kingship and demand that the raja fulfill his role.

[19] Ramachandra Guha (1989:96).

[20] Guha (1983:113); Field (1976).

[21] Arnold (1989); Baker (1993:129–42). Arnold (1989:68) notes that during this period there were a series of bad monsoons, and in Madras, difficulties began in 1875.

[22] Baker (1993:136).

[23] Coomaraswamy (1978:18); Verma (1974:187–8); Feeley-Harnuk (1985).

[24] For. Pol. A August 1876, Pro. nos. 163–72, MacGeorge to Sec. to CC, CP, NAI.

More recent studies, however, have questioned the extent to which rebellions calling upon the king to fulfill his mandate are motivated by a genuine belief in the virtues of the monarchy. Arguing for a 'not-so-naive interpretation of naive monarchism', Scott argues that struggles which appear to be upholding the kingship by appealing to the justice of the monarch represent in fact a strategic tactic to challenge the dominant order in its own idiom.[25] The question is then one of defining the existing order. In 1876, it was not kingship alone that was to be saved from itself. There were issues beyond the corruption of the two officials that tied into long-term processes connected with colonialism: their insistence on improving the finances of the state — in which the malguzari system was one element — and the introduction of new (British) judicial procedures and codes. The British seem not to have comprehended or to have deliberately ignored the colonial context of these changes. Thus, the problem was seen as one of 'weak kingship' alone. If we treat the 1876 rebellion simply as one aimed at conserving or improving a 'traditional' order, we too run the risk of succumbing to the British version of events.

The most obvious interpretation in the context seems to be that the peasants were invoking the ideal of a just king in order to protest against changes in the balance of power which were taking place at their expense. This 'moral economy approach' first popularized by Thompson[26] has been extended to embrace a variety of situations where peasants or others facing change invoke the old against the new. Ramachandra Guha uses this to explain similar traditions of non-violent resistance in the northern Indian kingdom of Tehri Garhwal. Guha portrays 'rebellion as custom' and 'rebellion as confrontation' as two styles of protest neatly matched with two styles of rule — that of the princely state and direct colonial rule. In this version, customary rebellion is a pre-colonial/pre-capitalist form, drawing on the traditional idiom of *dandak* or scripturally-sanctioned resistance against unjust kings.[27] This gave way to the harsher modalities of violent resistance when native rulers were replaced

---

[25] Scott (1990:96–103).
[26] Thompson (1993:185–351).
[27] Guha (1989:69).

by foreign powers, and traditional patterns of authority marked by 'flexible . . . claims on peasant subsistence . . . bound by a cultural and personalized idiom of reciprocity', gave way to 'legal/rational structures of authority'.[28] Guha does note that the personalized nature of kingship changed under indirect rule and there was a partial breakdown of traditional authority,[29] but his emphasis is on the distinction between a relatively harmonious relation between king and people versus illegitimate colonial rule.

Although Guha's thesis is persuasive, there are problems in transplanting it *in toto* to the Bastar case. It is quite possible to invoke an appeal to some shared norms without having to believe that those norms ever obtained in their entirety in the past. Despite the normative assumption of traditional Indian political theory that the sovereign was subject to *dharma* or the law of righteousness/duty,[30] there is no indication that all kings necessarily lived by it, and that prior to the disjuncture in people–king relations caused by colonialism, the Just King was always just. While the severity with which colonialism shattered the peasantry's milieu undoubtedly caused the frequency and intensity of rebellions to increase, not all confrontations with the colonial regime were necessarily violent either. It would be far better to treat the people's perception of the king and kingship as a changing construct, with the ideal of a Just King being selectively invoked on occasion, rather than part of some enduring pre-colonial 'culture'. How else do we explain the fact that in 1910, the king was equated by some with the colonial administrative apparatus and conversely, that in 1966 when the kingship had in fact been abolished, the king served as a rallying point for the people against the state? Although the king's lack of an appropriate response does not change the interpretation of why the peasants were rebelling, it introduces an interesting twist. The critical point about the 1876 rebellion in terms of its lasting impact is that the upholder of custom was not the indigenous monarch but the British. Indigenous paternalism did not give way to contractual relations, it gave way to a

[28] Ibid.:126–8.
[29] Ibid.:78.
[30] Verma (1974:138).

different form of paternalism. Bhairam Deo should have responded to the peasants' complaints with the impartial dispensa-
tion of justice; instead it was left to the British to take the cue.

What we should be focussing on here is not the distinction
between kingship and colonial rule, between custom and its
opposite, but the nexus between them, especially in terms of
how the British cashed in on traditional legitimacy and at the
same time attempted to upstage it through their own version
of paternalism. In this regard, it was not so much the outward
forms of rule that changed but their cultural content. On the
surface, paternalism in government persisted. However, British
paternalism had roots in various strands of political and philo-
sophical thought,[31] which were quite different from the philo-
sophical bases underlying the old Raja–Praja paternalism. The
latter was rooted in local religious custom and couched in a
familial idiom, which involved a degree of reciprocity, such as
at Dussehra. While this relation may itself have developed in
order to accommodate different groups and make the kingship
hegemonic, it subjected the king as well to certain constraints.
British paternalism on the other hand was aimed at reform and
'improvement' of the people.[32] Although the British too tried
to legitimize their rule through durbars and other occasions,
indicating their acknowledgement of the need for popular support, a position of cultural superiority was presumed. Their duty
then was to mediate between different indigenous groups.[33]

It is less easy to know how peasants interpreted or took into
account the fact of British paramountcy in their relationship
with their own immediate kings. What notion of the king's
divinity persisted when higher Gods appeared on the scene, and
these were not just distant emperors content with tribute, but
rulers who interfered with everyday aspects of existence? As the
king became increasingly ineffective in terms of being able to
limit unwelcome intrusions like forest reservation, what role did

---

[31] According to Iyer (1960:23), these included the 'Burkean doctrine of
Imperial Trusteeship, the Utilitarian theory of state activity, the Platonic
conception of a ruling elite that would act as wise guardians, and . . . Evan-
gelical zeal'.

[32] For an argument that paternalism was a product of a specific period
of British Indian history, 1858-1914, *see* Spear (1978).

[33] Lelyveld (1985).

the kingship play? As subsequent chapters show, the significance of kingship changed over time, combining elements of old and new attitudes on the part of both rulers and ruled.

British Intervention in Bastar and Indirect Rule

Following the 1818 defeat of the Bhonslas, the Maratha kingdom which was the erstwhile dominant power in central India, new treaties were drawn up between the British and the Bhonslas' former tributaries in the region.[34] Under one such treaty, Bastar's annual tribute was set at Rs 5000, a higher sum than what had been due the Bhonslas, but unlike several other states, the Bastar raja retained control over internal administration, especially judicial powers.[35] The emphasis at this stage was on avoiding confrontation. In the eyes of colonial officials, its distance from Raipur, the unfamiliar and dense jungle enroute, and the reputation of its inhabitants for 'savagery' and raids on the Chattisgarh plains below, all made Bastar eminently unfit for military intervention.[36] In 1853, following the 'lapse' of the Bhonsla state to the British, Bastar came under British paramountcy, which meant British control over its external affairs and the right to interfere in internal affairs if deemed necessary.[37] The Central Provinces (CP) were constituted in 1861.[38] In 1865, Bastar along with fifteen other princely states, was given the title of a 'Feudatory State', as against a mere 'Zamindari' or landlord estate.[39]

The assumption of paramountcy was commonly justified in one of three ways: delegation of specific rights by the princely state to the British through treaties; the inheritance by the British of 'certain residuary rights historically exercised by a superior power in a princely state'; or simply by the superior strength of the British.[40] In the case of the Central Provinces states, the second ground was the one invoked. Accordingly, British interpretations

[34] Baker (1993:41–5).
[35] Jenkins (1901).
[36] Ibid.: para 113.
[37] Low (1973:12).
[38] CP Govt. (1937:ix).
[39] Ibid.:xv.
[40] Fisher (1991:446).

of their history sought to portray them as mere dependencies administering on behalf of a paramount power (the Marathas), with carefully graded prerogatives, as opposed to the tributaries with independent sources of power that they really were.[41] Defining the exact status of the chiefs initially proved a problem. They were clearly superior to ordinary subjects yet could not be allowed to claim sovereignity.[42] But as we soon discover on reading further, the real imperative of sticking to custom lay in its profitability:

And thus tracts and districts, which have a vast area and often a wild population and which would be very troublesome and expensive if managed by British establishments, and which, if so managed, would probably not pay their own expenses, are really managed through the aid of these Chiefs, without any British establishment and yield a net profit, in the shape of tribute to the British treasury . . . To these chiefs there has been delegated a portion of the duties and responsibilities of Government, while they have been permitted to enjoy a considerable share of the public revenue.[43]

Karen Fields, writing about a different colonial context, Africa, but drawing on the same empire, sums this up succinctly as making a virtue of the necessity of 'rule on the cheap'.[44] The profitability of indirect rule was of a different order from direct financial and commercial benefits to the colonial state. The most important direct benefit was the political consolidation of a vast area through the co-optation of the local hierarchy and without the attendant difficulties or costs of administration. Economic gain was not thereby left behind, and as Fisher points out, the penetration of British business was not in any way impeded by indirect rule.[45] The subsidies or tribute extracted from princely states were also extremely profitable.[46] Yet it would not be wrong to generalize that as resources in the princely states became more valuable, they increasingly came under British purview. Right from the beginning, the British claimed independent rights over

[41] *See* for instance Craddock (1889); Temple (1923).
[42] Temple (1923:6).
[43] Ibid.:10.
[44] Fields (1985:32–41).
[45] Fisher (1991:10–12); Low (1973:88).
[46] Hettne (1978).

forest and mineral resources in Bastar and the other Chattisgarh Feudatory States.[47] As the demand for forest products including timber grew, indirect rule ineluctably gave way to direct British control over the forest establishment and, by extension, other key departments as well. In Bastar's case, long periods of 'minority administration', the colonial term for when the ruler was a minor or a woman (from 1891–1908 and 1921–1947), and 'misman-agement' (1908–1921) served as convenient occasions for the presence of British officials (or British-appointed officials) acting as chief administrators.

In the Name of the King

British administrators were nevertheless careful to consecrate their actions by frequent reference to the 'interests of the king', thus hoping to appropriate or share the legitimacy of indigenous rule. To quote Fields again, 'indirect rule was a way of making the colonial state a consumer of power generated within the customary order.'[48] This act of consumption was then tran-substantiated in what Dirks has termed a 'political economy of honour'.[49] In other words, while the British were dependent on Indian rulers for their continued existence with fewer revolts than would otherwise have occurred, they enforced the ap-pearance of Indian dependence on British rule for titles, salutes and other honours.

For the casual reader, it is hard to appreciate what the delicate political juggling and the minute administrative changes in royal nomenclature meant. But clearly, events like the signing of a treaty could be moments of high drama and emotional stress for the participants, as we discover in an account of negotiations over a bond in which the Bastar king, Bhairam Deo, was granted 'feudatory status' in return for fealty to the British empire. Unfortunately Bhairam Deo's new elevation to the status of Feudatory Chief failed to excite him. He objected to conditions in the treaty regarding conformity to British-made forest rules and the paymenu of a periodically revisable tribute. He was given until 1 December 1870 to sign, with many threats being issued

[47] Craddock (1889).
[48] Fields (1985:31).
[49] Dirks (1993:xxv).

in the meantime (from 1868–1870). His gifts were declined and he was not allowed to see the Chief Commissioner to make his case until the bond was signed. Finally, the king went to Sironcha, the regional British headquarters, to meet the Chief Commissioner, leaving his state for the first time in his life. We then witness an incredible ceremony where protocol performs the task of arm twisting:

The Deputy Commissioner went to the Rajah's camp to visit him, *but as a return visit would have compelled the chief to pass the Chief Commissioner's tent, declined to receive him in his own house until he had first been received by Col. Keatinge (Chief Commr.). The Chief held out for three days.* It was only the evening before the Chief Commissioner's departure that the paper was executed. The Chief Commissioner on this at once consented to receive the Chief in Durbar. The visit took place by lamplight in the Deputy Commissioner' house. Col. Keatinge received the Chief at the door of the Durbar room and treated him with much courtesy . . . The Chief presented the Chief Commr. with a dagger and some wild animals and received in return a revolver and pistol[50] (my emphasis).

While indigenous players were denigrated as weak and inefficient, the British were reluctant to remove most princes, especially after the revolt of 1857. Frequent annexations had been deemed one of the primary causes of the revolt, and consequently a more conservative policy was adopted in this regard.[51] According to Jeffrey:

The ambivalence of British policy regarding annexation arose from the fundamental contradiction between the imperial interests of a trading company anxious to expand and rule cheaply and the zeal of the utilitarian reformer who was often entrusted with the task of running the administration.[52]

The British attitude towards Bhairam Deo and his successor, Rudra Pratap Deo, is shot through with this contradiction. Both are portrayed as imbeciles who were incapable of administering by themselves, albeit harmless and well loved.[53] Yet rather than

[50] For. Dept. Pol. B, May 1872, nos. 41–5, NAI
[51] Hettne (1978:36).
[52] Jeffrey (1978:11).
[53] For. A Pol. I, April 1884, Pro. nos. 99–103, Chisholm, Commr. Chattisgarh Div. to Sec. to CC, CP, 26 February 1884, NAI.

take Bastar under direct management, the British authorities
contented themselves with frequent warnings to the king to
reform his administration, intermittent threats of removal,[54] and
finally as a compromise, the appointment of the raja's cousin,
Lal Kalandar Singh, as chief administrator.[55] He too was soon
removed (see chapters 4 and 5). But even in the initial period
of indirect rule it is possible to trace the impact of colonial
land and judicial policies.

Changes in the Land Revenue System

Until the mid-nineteenth century we are told, there was no
regular revenue establishment in Bastar and accounts and figures
were most imperfect.[56] Lands were divided into *khalsa* areas
(under direct state management) and *zamindari* areas, under their
own minor chiefs, who paid a fixed tribute to the king. Within
the khalsa, certain lands were given out as revenue-free grants
(muafis) to the king's relatives, retainers and temples. According
to Glasfurd, the administration of the khalsa areas, both land
revenue and judicial, was carried out as follows: under the dewan,
there was a literate manager *(kamdar)* for every few sub-divisions
(garhs). He was in turn assisted by a *negi* with jurisdiction over
a group of villages, and sometimes below the negi, a *hikmi*.
Finally there were the village headmen who collected and paid
revenue on behalf of the village, reported cases etc.[57] However
the terms and the exact structure of revenue collection appear
to have varied – in some areas, the revenue was collected by
village headmen and passed on to the pargana majhis and their

[54] For. Pol. A I, January 1884, Pro. nos. 117–25, Report on the Adminis ra-
tion of Bastar State by Lt. Col. H.C.E. Ward, Additional Commr., Chattisga. h
Division, CP, NAI (henceforth Ward 1884). This was an adverse report on
the state which advocated the Raja's removal.

[55] The rani (Jugraj Kaur) in contrast to the raja was praised by Ward for
her sound financial management. But since the British authorities were
unwilling to let a woman take charge, with or without the raja as formal
ruler, Lal Kalandar Singh was appointed. For. A Pol. I, January 1884, Pro.
nos. 117–25, NAI. As Sara Suleri (1992:70) indicates, colonial practice could
not easily admit the political independence of women rulers.

[56] Elliot (1856: para 10); Glasfurd (1862: para 172).

[57] Glasfurd (1862: para 172).

assistants, *chalkis*, who in turn deposited it in Jagdalpur. In some areas there was also a tax collector, known as *adhkari*.[58]

Land revenue as well as the salaries of officials, which were fixed, were paid partly in kind and partly in cowries.[59] In 1856 land tax varied between eight annas to one rupee on the plough, but in most places hoes were used, which were taxed between four to eight annas.[60] By 1862 rents had gone up by a quarter or half at most.[61] A plough was estimated on the area that could be cultivated by a pair of bullocks which usually worked out to ten to twelve acres. The record-keeper went to the villages and estimated the number of cattle per family on enquiry from the headmen.[62] In 1856 the amount of land under cultivation in Bastar, including penda, was estimated to be merely one-fifteenth of the total surface area, and the state treasury got more of its revenue from fines for social offences like adultery than from khalsa land revenue.[63] Weavers and other artisans such as manufacturers of brass utensils, oil pressers and distillers also paid per head taxes. Weavers for instance paid Rs 3 out of an annual income of approximately Rs 50,[64] but they appeared to have been well off due to the comparative expense and importance of cloth.[65] The grain and other revenue in kind like oil was kept in stores around the country and used to feed the Raja's household and stables as well as touring officials. The raja also issued chits against these stocks in favour of his creditors. Finally,

[58] For. A Pol. I January 1884, Pro. nos. 117–25 (Memo by CC, CP, para 12), NAI.

[59] Cowries served as money before the teak trade began to develop with Rajahmundhry in the mid-nineteenth century, and copper coins were introduced. DeBrett (1988:61); Glasfurd (1862: para 37). 240 cowries = 1 dogani; 10 doganis = 1 rupee.

[60] Elliot (1856: para 10). (16 annas = 1 rupee).

[61] Glasfurd (1862: para 172).

[62] DeBrett (1988:61).

[63] Elliot (1856: para 10). Fines brought in Rs 12,000, while land revenue in the khalsa areas brought in merely Rs 9040-14-0.

[64] 'Memo on the Administration of Bastar State' by Dewan Krishna Rao, 1886-7, JRR.

[65] In Kukanar, the weavers who today are among the poorest in the village in addition to being considered the lowest caste, were once the village money lenders.

these grain stocks could be used to help the population in times of famine.[66]

Gopinath Kapurdar, who became diwan in 1867, introduced the first *malguzari/thekedari* settlement in the khalsa lands that year.[67] Under this system, the *malguzar* collected revenue payments from the peasants and in turn paid a fixed sum (as against a proportion of the revenue collected) to the state. If the number of households or the land under cultivation increased between settlements, the malguzar kept the difference. Chapman noted that since the inception of the system, all settlements were 'exceptionally favourable to malguzars', so much so that in many villages they abandoned any cultivation of their own and lived entirely on the excess rents of their tenants or on the basis of begar extracted from them.[68]

While the peasants were supposed to give the malguzars and thekedars only 3 days free labour in the year, one each for ploughing, sowing and reaping,[69] in practice the malguzars usually extracted at least ten days labour per villager. The tenants were required to help make or repair houses, clear sites, carry grass, bamboo, and wood to the malguzar's house even if it was in another village or Jagdalpur.[70] This was to remain a problem right till the abolition of thekedari begar in 1929, under the then administrator Grigson's orders, and together with the increases in land revenue, played a major part in the rebellions of both 1876 and 1910.

Under Gopinath, the revenue paid by the peasant was fixed at the rate of two rupees and four annas in cash, two and a quarter *khandi* of unhusked grain, five *paili* of pulses, and two *sers* oil per plough. This was further enhanced in 1872 to three rupees in cash and three khandi paddy, in addition to the other items.[71] In 1884 Ward noted retrospectively that:

---

[66] Ward (1884: para 57).

[67] XLVI-30-II, Raj Family History, Statement by Lal Kalandar Singh, 26 August 1908, JRR; DeBrett (1988:62).

[68] DeBrett (1988:62-3).

[69] DeBrett (1988:65).

[70] XXII-4, Bhet Begar in Thekedari Villages, JRR.

[71] DeBrett (1988:62). Current rates (1994) are 1 khandi = 20 paili; 1 paili = 1.5-2 kg. *See also* Wilson (1940:435, 759). One approximation for a ser was 2 lb.

Gopinath's administration was certainly a financial success. The treasury was full, the Bheji and Bijapur timber trade brought in a yearly increasing income, the Revenue and Civil work was carried on with fair punctuality and there were few complaints.[72]

The peasants, however, obviously felt quite differently about his administration. The new rates of revenue on the plough were excessively steep compared to the earlier rates.[73] In the villages around Jagdalpur, the majority of lessees were Oriya brahmans, kayasths and Marathi brahmans, the clerks and accountants of the period. Bhairam Deo's passion for horses, hunting dogs and elephants had also resulted in the presence of a colony of Afghan and other immigrant traders.[74] Some of them were given leases in lieu of money owed to them. Thus Khuda Yar, who originally sold dogs to Bhairam Deo and then took to trading in cloth and brass utensils was given 234 villages of Dongar tahsil on lease by Bhairam Deo.[75] The tahsildar of Dongar itself was one Sheo Mangal Singh, a former horse dealer who had been appointed by Lal Kalandar Singh because he was 'very pressing about his claims'.[76] Similarly, the other tahsildars were also upper caste immigrants, as revealed by such names as Jaikishen Singh, Mahadeo and Sahadeo Patnaik. In some places, the malguzari was awarded to the highest bidder.[77] These groups appear to have had no compunctions about demanding excessive rents or corvée, and as officials, traders and malguzars, formed a distinct class of exploiters who ultimately became the target of attack in 1910.

What emerges in the previous account is the need to look at relative rather than absolute deprivation. In areas under Mughal administration for instance, collection of land revenue had long been commercialized and monetised. The village community had become differentiated, and as Habib puts it, 'offered a framework for "sub-exploitation" that supported as well as subsisted upon, the Mughal land revenue system.'[78] In Bastar, there was little economic or political differentiation within

---

[72] Ward (1884: para 20).
[73] DeBrett (1988:62); Ward (1884: para 33).
[74] *See* Ball (1985:617–21).
[75] I-1, Affairs, List of Leading Persons in the State, JRR.
[76] Ward (1884: para 32–3).
[77] Ibid.
[78] Habib and Fukazawa (1982:249).

villages and the domination exercised by the founding lineage, the priest and the headman must be understood in relative terms. Rates of revenue in Bastar both in the pre-colonial and early colonial periods were also negligible compared to those under Mughal and Maratha administrations, where revenue could be more than one-half of produce, and where there were different layers of intermediaries.[79] Part of the reason, of course, was that shifting cultivation in Bastar perhaps would not support greater surplus extraction, but at the same time the lack of any major attempt to interfere with it in the pre-colonial period is noticeable.

In short, heavy increases in land revenue and accompanying administrative controls were relatively recent in Bastar, even as compared to other parts of India. The parganas in Jagdalpur tahsil were the first to suffer under the malguzari system and the increased begar and consequently, the 1876 rebellion drew almost entirely upon these parganas, unlike the rebellion of 1910 which was spread across the state as more and more areas were penetrated by the new policies. If colonial nomenclature is to be believed, within these parganas, it was largely Murias who participated. But since these areas are populated mainly by Bhatras and some Dhurwas, the term Muria was apparently being used generically. Sundis, and Kallars (distillers) who were among the local elite and other artisanal groups within the city may not have been as affected by the new settlement policies. On the other hand, they appear to have been even more affected by certain changes that were taking place in the judicial system.

Changes in the Judicial System

Among the ryots' complaints to MacGeorge in 1876 were that they were:

tried and punished under the Penal code, and are heavily fined *and* imprisoned as well, that they are often punished unjustly, punished without a fair trial, and all this they say is the will of Gopinath and Adit Prashad and not of the Raja, who, they state never decides any cases himself.[80]

[79] Ibid.

[80] For. Pol. A August 1876, Pro. nos. 163–72, MacGeorge to Sec. to CC, CP, 22 April 1876, NAI.

The raja denied the charge but MacGeorge noted that the idea was widespread.[81] It is difficult to accurately know the situation in Bastar in the second half of the 19th century because accounts varied so much with official reporting. But it is clear that the people found the emerging judicial process formed from a combination of British interventions and local palace practices to be increasingly arbitrary.

Prior to Elliot's intervention in 1856, the king enjoyed complete judicial powers as did the zamindars in their respective territories. As Deputy Commissioner at Raipur, in charge of Bastar, Elliot had mandated that heinous offences should be tried by him and that appeals regarding other offences could be referred to him through the *thanedar* (police head) at Jagdalpur.[82] In 1873, Captain Scott, Deputy Commissioner, Upper Godavari District, in charge of Bastar, noted that apart from the king, his illegitimate brother and the diwan, who handled the serious cases, there were nine persons throughout the state with magisterial powers in cases of up to Rs 50. He was assured by the Jagdalpur authorities that they functioned in accordance with British laws (although the Indian Penal Code (IPC) and Criminal Procedure Code (CrPC) were formally enacted in Bastar only in 1893).[83] However, local judicial procedures continued to be woefully inadequate by British standards. Describing the administration in 1880, Mr Russell, Assistant Commissioner at Sironcha, wrote:

Apathy pervades every department, and work which in other places would be done in a few hours or days here takes many weeks and months. The day is frittered away in sleeping, gossiping & c. After candlelight the Katcherry (court) assembles and the Raja takes his seat for a short hour or so and business commences, each man with his Chirag (pipe) by his side. Then the Raja retires to his 'pani sal' or bath room, to see his favourites, males and females. Then he bathes, worships in his private temple, and again takes his seat in Katcherry to sign papers and see the seals put on. Between 9 and 10 pm he rises to go to his meals and bed, and the Katcherry is closed after less than 3 hours work.[84]

81 Ibid.
82 Elliot (1856: para 22).
83 For. Gen. A July 1873, Pro. nos. 42-3, NAI.
84 For. A Pol. I, January 1884, Pro. nos. 117-25, Memo by CC, CP, para 5, NAI.

Two years later in 1882, the situation appeared to have deteriorated further. By this time, even the limited hours of the court were devoted not to judicial cases but to the examination of horses, dogs, guns etc. brought for sale by traders, and the pacification of pressing creditors; while judicial cases were handled at the river *ghat*, where the king went to bathe. According to Russell, who visited Bastar again in 1882, the administration of both civil and criminal justice had become a 'mockery', and the king was only interested in the judicial system insofar as it was a means of raising money.[85] Sardar Rattan Singh, District Superintendent of Police, Raipur, who was sent to investigate the situation following differences between the king, queen and the Lal, painted a cheerful picture in sharp contrast to both Mr Russell who came before and Col. Ward who came after, noting that:

The administration of the country is working well. No complaint of an injustice has ever been made. . . . There is no police arrangement, but cases are apprehended by the officials of other departments and taken up direct to the magistrate. No interference is necessary in the administration of the country, as the Raja is a very good, experienced man, and it is difficult to manage the affairs of such a large illaqua (area).[86]

Col. Ward, the Acting Commissioner of Chattisgarh, who was sent to report on Bastar in 1884, to reconcile the conflicting reports of Mr Russell and Sardar Rattan Singh, was even more damning than the former, claiming that the civil courts had been closed for six months, a large number of cases were pending, and the system of verbal fines had alienated the people.[87] Ward described a system in which nominally all cases in Jagdalpur tahsil were instituted in the king's court, and then forwarded to other courts, while in the other tahsils, the tahsildar gave judgement. Apart from the king and the Lal, for cases around Jagdalpur, a Mahra named Rahpal Sirha Baiga at Bajawand who was 'possessed by Hinglajin Deo on Mondays and Saturdays', was authorised to handle cases in his possessed

[85] Ibid.: para 28.
[86] For. A Pol. I, January 1884, Pro. nos. 117-25, Sardar Rattan Singh, to Commr., Nagpur Division, 5 November 1882, NAI.
[87] Ward (1884: para 18).

state. Further, fines such as *thora banat* and *urkha chut*, customs which appeared to have been obsolete for some time, were revived in 1877-8.[88] Thora Banat was a fine on people wearing red cloth or bangles or carrying an umbrella unless they had earlier paid a premium to the raja, while urkha chut was a fine on a whole caste whenever any of its members had been detected in adultery with women of other castes. According to Ward's informants, in Shampur sub-division of Dongar tahsil, on account of three Kallar men committing adultery with Gondin or Mahrin women, thirty or forty Shampur Kallars were then brought to Jagdalpur on the raja's orders and the whole caste was fined Rs 6000. Many Kallars went to Jeypore and Raipur to avoid paying; some who recently returned were seized and asked to pay their fines.[89]

Ward also unearthed the *Gaj Baran* registers, listing decisions taken by the king at his bathing places. In the version told to Ward, the accused would be fined on complaint, sometimes even in their absence or the absence of any witnesses. At each ghat, a negi with a staff of peons would be on hand to register the raja's order and collect the fine. On the banks of the large tank, there were stocks into which the offending individual was kept till he/she paid the fine or gave security.[90] A list of the fines makes fascinating reading, giving insight into a range of minor wickedness! Not sending in a goat when required to do so, telling lies, marrying widows and carrying umbrellas without the king's permission, all could be occasions for fines. Adultery seems to have been the most commonly recognized offence.[91]

[88] It is possible that these fines were necessitated by tribute payments to the British, including the cost of suppressing the 1876 revolt. The total British expenditure on the 1876 rebellion was Rs 11,787-3-9, which was borne entirely by Bastar in 11 annual installments of Rs 1000 per annum. For. Pol. B May 1877, nos. 68-72, NAI.

[89] Ward (1884: para 23).

[90] Ibid.: para 88.

[91] Ghasia Kallar's wife went off with another man and because the raja was not informed, he was fined Rs 15; while Jurwa Lohar was fined Rs 8 for the converse — falsely reporting that his wife had gone off with a Sundi. Some suffered for the sins of their parents like Asaram, who was fined Rs 21 and his brother Rs 16 because their mother went off to live with someone else; while others suffered from the passions of their children: Ghasia Sundi was fined Rs 10 for causing his daughter to run away with Durjan Sundi.

Most of the offences seemed to have involved Mahras, Sundis and Kallars, castes living in and around Jagdalpur. There seem to be almost no cases involving even those tribal groups like Bhatras living around Jagdalpur – these would have been settled by their own village or caste panchayats.[92]

British condemnations of the indigenous judicial system, citing as evidence limited court hours, instant decisions by the king, verbal judgements on fines, and a principle of collective caste responsibility for an individual crime, can be read between the lines to evoke a picture of a judicial system well suited to a largely illiterate population, the absence of very harsh punishments, and a different understanding of judicial violations. Conceding that there were no fines on the general population of Gonds, and only on people of means, however small, and that the general population seemed quite content, Ward yet opined that the system had to be changed, as 'these were not the people who would bring about an uprising; it is the well-to-do men who have influence over the lower classes and could lead them astray'.[93] And these well-to-do people he felt, including zamindars, Muslim traders and Kallars were against the king because of arbitrary fines.

While the king and his advisors were no doubt at fault for the complaints made in 1876, what the British saw as the solution was really part of the problem, and vice versa. Ward's poor opinion of the Bastar system of justice was shared by his compatriots about the Mughal system at large, which was thought of as 'extremely venal', with its allegedly speedy disposition of cases, the direct appeal by plaintiff, and the tailoring of fines to the income of the offender. These were then seen as pointing to the absolute and arbitrary power of the emperor, rather than any rule of law.[94] British notions of justice and

---

Durjan Sundi was fined Rs 20 for running away with said daughter, and 5 others implicated in the case were collectively fined Rs 64. Brahmans were no less susceptible to matters of the heart, and braved more financially for true love: Jagbandhu Brahman was fined Rs 300 for going to Ramchand Brahman's house intending to assault him; while Ramchand was fined Rs 100 for committing adultery with Jagbandhu's wife. (Ward Report).

[92] Ward (1884: paras 48, 51).
[93] Ward (1884: para 94).
[94] Cohn (1989:139).

the alleged lack of it in the indigenous system in Bastar led to the formal legal system being gradually expanded. Those who were affected the most were the 'caste' groups around Jagdalpur, but as with every other administrative innovation, the tribal groups both near Jagdalpur and further away were gradually drawn in.

Conclusion

Indirect rule had several advantages for the British. First, it was useful for areas which were not immediately open to exploitation, like Bastar. In 1884, the Chief Commissioner explicitly concluded that Bastar was too poor to justify direct management by the state.[95] Secondly, it was cheaper. The alternative involved paying for a much larger retinue of colonial administrators and a resident British population. Thirdly, indirect rule served to deflect rebellion.[96] When rebellions did occur, they could be blamed on the king's lack of concern for his subjects rather than on unpopular policies instituted under British pressure. The impact of the British presence could be ignored, except in its benevolent aspects.

The rebellion that occurred in 1876 must be seen against this background of indirect rule, which included early increases in land revenue and changes in the administrative and judicial system. While the rebellion was aimed at defending peasant autonomy in the face of increasing encroachments by the state, it was not a 'customary rebellion' as is traditionally understood but an early stage of the new encounter between the Bastar peasants, their ruler and the British paramount power. The colonial period was a turning point in the history of rule, not because of a change from paternalism to contractual relations, but because that paternalism was couched in terms that required greater intervention in everyday life.

[95] For. A Pol. I, April 1884, Pro. nos. 99-103, NAI.
[96] For. A Pol. I, January 1884, Pro. nos. 117-25, K.W. noting by C.G., 5 November 1883, NAI.

4

How did the Land become so Bitter?

The law came to depopulate your sky
to seize your revered fields
to debate the river's water
to steal the kingdom of trees.

Your blood asks, how were the wealthy
and the law interwoven? With what
sulphurous iron fabric? How did the
poor keep falling into the tribunals?

How did the land become so bitter
for poor children, harshly
nourished on stone and grief?
So it was, and so I leave it written
Their lives wrote it on my brow.

Pablo Neruda
Canto General

The years from 1876 to 1910 marked a turning point in Bastar's history in more ways than one. Prolonged investigations into allegations of human sacrifice in Bastar from the mid-nineteenth century culminated in an enquiry in 1885–6. The sacrifices were believed to be orchestrated by the palace through a well organized system in which revenue was remitted in exchange for procuring victims. Following retractions of evidence by the witnesses involved, the legal case collapsed and in fact boomeranged on the Madras police, whose methods of investigation came under question.[1] The net effect, however, was that the state was taken under Court of Wards in 1888, with the raja compelled to listen to the advice of diwans appointed by the Chief Commissioner. The death of Raja Bhairam Deo in 1891 led to the state coming under direct British management, which continued to all practical effect even after the installation

[1] Sundar (1995:345–74).

5

of his successor Rudra Pratap Deo in 1908.[2] Direct intervention
inevitably involved a significant increase in administrative intrusions along the familiar lines of British India: schools, police,
the demand for forced labour and free supplies, and crucially,
forest management. Forest reservation was perhaps the most
drastic of colonial interventions, but it was only part of a certain
mode of colonial operation which extended to other spheres as
well, and which set in train a pattern of continued conflict over
access to forests and land. The rebellion of 1910, described in
the next chapter was merely one of the forms which popular
responses took, though it was its most extreme and immediate
expression.

Forest Policy in Bastar

In recent years, a growing number of scholars have begun
researching the history of colonial forest policies as part of an
attempt to trace the connections between imperial expansion and
the changes in local ecologies.[3] In India, debates have centred
around the degree to which the colonial period marked a radical
disjuncture with the nature and extent of pre-colonial controls
over the forest; and the compulsions propelling the development
of 'scientific' or state managed forestry. Summarizing the arguments, Rangarajan points out that while the pre-colonial period
was no age of golden equilibrium, state monopolies over specific
species of trees or the creation of hunting reserves by rulers, by
no means amounted to a complete philosophy of forest management with its attendant administrative regime. The history of
colonial forestry in India emerges out of the multiple strands of
English attitudes towards woodlands at home, the need for timber
to sustain imperial shipbuilding and railway expansion, and
colonial attitudes towards forest dwelling groups, and their cultivation practices. The latter, and to a much lesser extent commercial felling, was blamed for the denudation of forests which
in turn brought in conservationist concerns.[4] Colonial forest

---

[2] DeBrett (1988:38); For. and Pol. Dept. Sec. I, Pro. no. 20-2, NAI.
[3] *See* Rangarajan (1996); Gagdil and Guha (1992); Adas (1993:328-9); Grove
(1995); Crosby (1986).
[4] Rangarajan (1996:7, 15, 17-39).

policy was not cohesive,[5] and those involved in its creation had different views on the extent to which state right should have pre-eminence over local access.[6] However, one aspect emerges quite clearly – the fact that the colonial state arrogated to itself the right to regulate the ecological and social landscape of the country. The Forest Act of 1878 created three classes of forests – reserved forests which were generally completely closed off to the local public, protected forests in which people had 'priveleges', liable to be changed at state discretion, and in some provinces, village or nistari forests from which people could draw their basic needs, usually on the payment of commutation dues.

Prior to coming under direct management in 1891, there was no consistent system of forest management in Bastar, although under the fealty bond of 1870 the raja had agreed to abide by whatever forest rules the British might impose. As early as 1862, Glasfurd was bemoaning the devastation of the teak forests of Bheji and Sukma under the unchecked felling of contractors and state creditors, who supplied the timber market at Rajahmundhri by floating logs on the Godavari. Glasfurd estimated that in the three zamindaris of Bhopalpatnam, Kotapilly and Bheji, in 1861 alone, 30,000 logs had been cut and exported to Rajahmundhri to feed the demand from the Madras railways and the District Engineer's Department, Upper Godavari Works.[7] The timber traders who lived in the larger villages on both sides of the Godavari, employed local villagers to fell timber in return for an advance of money, cloth, tobacco or opium. The profits were shared between the trader and the logger. The latter's share inevitably went into repaying the initial loan. Apart from teak, valuable timber species like saja, bijasal, haldu and shisham were also in demand.[8] Owing to this timber trade, some of the villages in Bhopalpatnam were more developed than the capital, Jagdalpur. For instance, Muddair, 'a sort of entrepot of trade for rice,

---

[5] At the same time as the British policy of consciously encouraging rice cultivation led to the destruction of the Irrawaddy delta forests in lower Burma, they were conserving highland Burma as teak forest reserves. Adas (1983).

[6] Gadgil and Guha (1992:124); Rangarajan (1996:29–33).

[7] Glasfurd (1862: para 56).

[8] WP, South Bastar (1981:109).

lakh, wax' had two hundred houses and fifteen shops, when Jagdalpur had only two shops![9]

The raja and zamindars also looked upon the forests as their milch cow. In 1882-3 alone the raja issued drafts of Rs 86,000 against Bheji, in order to pay off his creditors. Unfortunately, due to competition by Burma teak, the value of the trade had dwindled from nearly rupees one lakh to approximately only Rs 15,000.[10] Apart from the fixed tribute, the raja also demanded from each zamindar a duty of four annas per log of teak sold, but there was no close supervision. The zamindar of Bhopalpat-nam leased out his forests for a mere Rs 700 to Bhagwandas Haridas, a Hyderabad banker and timber merchant who had already leased most of the forests on the Godavari.[11] In 1886-7, Amir Khan, tehsildar of Bheji, granted leases to three or four merchants to cut timber at one rupee or fourteen annas per log, when the going rate was six or seven rupees.[12] Under the system of contract-felling, the purchasers selected the area and the trees themselves, and logs which were unremunerative to remove were left lying about, leading to enormous wastage.[13]

The turn to developing sal in the north was justified as giving a rest to the teak forests of the south. But clearly there were other reasons too. Sal had the advantage that it was found in the more open areas of Bastar – e.g. Jagdalpur tehsil, and private trade had so far been limited owing to the distance from markets by road. Felling of sal and their use in railway sleepers began in 1897 in the Kokawada range of Jagdalpur tehsil, 65,000 sleepers being supplied to the Southern Maratha railways from there alone.[14] From 1896-9, the state made a profit of approximately Rs 30,000 on the sal sleeper operations.[15] In 1906 the state was able to contract a lease for 100,000 sleepers to the Madras Timber Co., 25,000 sleepers to Messrs Beckett & Co. and 12,500 sleepers to another company.[16]

[9] Glasfurd (1862:para 11).
[10] Ward (1884 para 5).
[11] Glasfurd (1862:para 68).
[12] AAR, 1886-7, JRR.
[13] AAR 1896-7, JRR.
[14] AAR, 1898, JRR.
[15] AAR, 1898-9; ARFA, 1898, JRR.
[16] AAR, 1906, JRR.

From unchecked commercial felling, attention turned to shifting cultivation which came to be seen as the prime source of danger, despite the occasional concession that it often got rid of over-mature and dying trees. Paradoxically the areas of shifting cultivation were also the areas of best sal growth.[17] Crump, Officiating Commissioner, Chattisgarh Division noted:

A piece of jungle after felling will contain nothing except stumps of sal and other trees cut from 4 feet above the ground, which even at the end of April are sprouting again with green leaves. Here and there is a larger tree, the trunk of which has been spared but all of whose branches have been cut off for brush wood. Such an area looks hopeless of recovery but reproduction is so fast that in four years time it is again ready for cutting for dhaya.[18]

Given the differences in scientific views regarding the harmfulness of shifting cultivation, Gadgil and Guha argue that the animosity was 'largely because timber operations competed with *jhum* (shifting cultivation) for territorial control of the forest'.[19] Here moreover, unlike the situation in Kumaun outlined by Guha (1989), it was not the introduction of new commercial species that was involved, but the competition between commercial and local uses of the same species, especially sal. As Rangarajan has shown for the Central Provinces as a whole, foresters and villagers had different visions of the forest, and different uses for the same timber. The former emphasized large logs and the latter poles.[20] This difference in vision also compelled a silvicultural orientation which managed the forests for 'major' forest produce as against 'minor', or timber at the expense of a diversity of forest products. By terming certain species and products minor, colonial forest management practices affected their future regeneration and sustainability. The 'health' of a forest in the language of scientific forestry is defined in terms of clean tree stems rather than canopy cover and density of undergrowth. At the same time, as the economic value of 'minor

---

[17] xxiii, 18, Corres. reg. reservation of forests in Kanger, Matla and Dhanpur, 1905, JRR.

[18] xxiii, 18, Note on Forest Conservancy in Bastar by H. Crump, Offg. Commr, Chattisgarh Division, 21 May 1906, JRR.

[19] Gadgil and Guha (1992:152).

[20] Rangarajan (1996:58–61, 94).

forest products' grew, the state extended its monopoly right over them, crowding out local uses.

In this context, only marginally less despised than shifting cultivation, were the practices of burning the forests to clear the undergrowth, making it easier to catch game and collect the fallen mahua; raw silk cultivation — for which tribals were alleged to cut down whole trees for the sake of a single cocoon; unconfined grazing all over the forest; girdling of trees for resin; and the 'unconstrained practice of cutting, packing and lopping all over by the ryots'.[21] Yet state responses to both shifting cultivation and these other practices were not always repressive, either in Bastar or elsewhere. In the case of shifting cultivation, it varied from a complete ban, to the creation of reserves for the practice (Baiga Chak), to the introduction of taungya systems, in which teak seeds were dibbled in between crops.[22] In the early 1900s, grazing, lopping and firing came under fresh consideration for the degree of harm they did the trees, and were eventually even turned to positive silvicultural advantage.[23] But as evidence of a certain continuity, even at the end of the twentieth century, these practices are commonly clubbed under biotic interferences and are among the first to be blamed by foresters for deforestation.

In 1896 a forest officer was appointed for Bastar, deputed from the provincial branch of the Central Provinces Forest Service, and in 1897, the forest department was separated from the revenue department and given its own staff. This led to a general standardization of operations, for instance in the issue of licenses to large timber traders. In 1898, rules for the management of zamindari forests allowing for government intervention and supervisory control were issued, but they were only merged with the forest department for the rest of Bastar state in 1944. Yet by the admission of the forest department itself, revenue rather than conservation remained the main concern throughout the period till World War Two.[24] 'Scientific forestry' and the first working plan in Bastar date as late as 1930–4.[25]

[21] ARFA, 1898, JRR.
[22] Shivaramakrishnan (1995:26–7).
[23] Guha (1989:49–55); Rangarajan (1996:89–92).
[24] DeBrett (1988:59); WP, Central Bastar (1988:146, 151–5).
[25] WP, South Bastar (1981:130).

The Trade in Minor Forest Produce (MFP)

Minor forest produce, wrote the diwan in 1889, is 'clearly the property of the state and therefore the people taking those articles from its forests are required to pay duty on them'.[26] Prior to this, most trade in non-timber forest produce had been handled by Banjaras. But there were also a few weekly markets *(haats)*. In 1909, there were twenty five haats, with eleven of them in Jagdalpur tehsil itself.[27] Ghainwa Majhi of Kokawada remembers that the only market in the area south of Darbha for a long time used to be Kukanar. The small Monday market in Kokawada stopped when the Pathans who ran it got beaten up by the villagers in 1910. From Kokawada they would leave with their loads at cock crow, and reach at noon, if they went fast. If they took children with them, it could take all day. There was dense forest all the way. Thus, people came from long distances to get a little salt or chillies, or to sell their mahua, tamarind and other forest produce. Brass utensils, cloth, earthenpots etc. were traded through barter.

As roads opened up, the number of traders increased. By the turn of the century, a few immigrant peddlers (including the traditional low caste weavers Gandas or Pankas) were selling cloth at the local markets, and buying grain and forest produce. The Thakurs of Kukanar who come from Uttar Pradesh recounted to me (without the slightest trace of embarrassment) how they used to cheat the tribals. For example, while buying clarified butter used for cooking, they would use a measuring vessel with a hole at the bottom so that while paying for only one litre, they actually got two or more. Similarly, they would count grain or mahua chanting: *Ek (1), do (2), teen (3), so, char (4), par, panch (5) . . . bara (12), hara, tera (13), mera. . . .* By using nonsensical rhyming words in between, they would coolly appropriate an extra four or five kilograms. Unfamiliar with their language, and with their system of weights and measures, the village people often did not even realize they were being cheated, and when they did, felt helpless.

Yet even being cheated in the market was perhaps preferable to not being allowed to sell produce at all. Sal resins *(dhup)*

[26] AAR, 1888–9, JRR.
[27] DeBrett (1988:57).

are a case in point. Prohibitions on girdling or tapping the tree had led to local villagers ceasing to sell dhup in the bazaars. It was only after an application by a private firm to have sal resin included in the list of MFP, that the conditions under which sal trees exuded resin came under enquiry, and people were allowed to resume sales.[28] In other cases, the state granted a complete monopoly to private firms for all manner of everyday items including firewood, bark for cordage, iron, grinding stones, poisons etc.[29] Local collection for private consumption was not prohibited but any export or even hoarding could be taxed by the licensee and the people would have to take whatever terms were offered to them for collection. In shades reminiscent of today's debates over the patenting of natural products, Mr Sinclair, of Parry & Co., pleaded for a monopoly: 'Of minor products, that which is already known to the Bastar native merchant is of little consideration. If I get the lease, I mean to take out of these forests poisons etc. that so far no native merchant has ever thought of. Without the monopoly, I start, the result will be that in six months every mother's son will be trading on free knowledge and others will soon swarm. . . . Personally, I do not think that the State or I will have much trouble in getting the wild men to sell all their goods to me.'[30] The knowledge of the 'wild men' was of course a free commodity. For some items like hurra (myrobalan), prices were determined by the London market, and the system of collection changed periodically according to whatever was most profitable for the state. From auctioning out monopolies in 1896, the forest department moved in 1906 to working hurra collection itself, advancing money to the peasants for its collection and buying it from them. As prices fell during WWI, the state decided to grant long term leases to merchants.[31]

To sum up, the new rules on minor forest produce affected local economies in several ways. The knowledge and gathering activities of the villagers had always been crucial in getting minor

[28] xxxvi, Minor Monopoly, Sale of, Correspondence between Pt. Alamchand, Diwan, BS and Political Agent, CFS, from 1890 to 1893, JRR.

[29] xxxvi, Monopoly and Sale of MFP, 1897, JRR.

[30] xxxvi, Minor Monopoly, O.T. Sinclair to E.A. DeBrett, 11 May 1910, JRR.

[31] AAR, 1898-9; WP, South Bastar (1981:129-30).

forest produce into the ambit of the market. This was now utilized in a systematic way, at the same time as their other traditional forestry practices were denigrated. The new rules severed the existing links between MFP collectors and local artisans as well as Banjara traders.[32] A greater number of immigrant traders from other parts of India now found a foothold in the state; peasant collectors were linked to the capitalist world market through monopsonist traders on terms dictated by the latter. As the volume and range of items demanded increased over the years, it set in process a motion whereby local collusion in over-extraction through market processes also increased. Finally, the rules provided one more opportunity for petty harassment of villagers. Corrupt *nakedars* or forest guards were known to demand duties from villagers on items like mahua flowers, when in fact no such duty existed.[33]

Gharpatti and Grazing Dues

Commutation or *nistar* dues were introduced for the first time in 1898, though toddy trees had earlier been taxed at two annas per tree.[34] As a revenue term the nistar right connotes the right to take forest produce for non-commercial household use.[35] We see here the beginnings of a highly detailed attempt to categorize users and regulate their access to the forests, at the same time as there was an attempt to classify land into reserved versus village forests. The nistar, or as it was known in Bastar, *gharpatti*, rate was initially fixed at two annas per tribal or resident 'low caste' household, including non agriculturists (i.e. all bonafide residents of the state), in return for personal and agricultural consumption of forest produce and unrestricted grazing. Non-indigenous residents of Jagdalpur were required to pay a fuel tax of approximately three annas.[36] In 1908, local tribal residents too began to be charged. Landless labourers, artisans and kotwars or village watchmen, who did

[32] *See also* Prasad (1994:127–8).

[33] xxxvi, Minor Monopoly, Note reporting the illegal activities of a forest Nakedar of Nelasnar in Kutru Zamindari, 11 October 1918, JRR.

[34] DeBrett (1988:29).

[35] Dwivedi (1986:755).

[36] ARFA, 1898, JRR.

only kotwari, paid two annas as gharpatti dues. Adivasi agriculturists paid four annas per plough, a plough being estimated
as twelve acres. They were allowed free grazing for four plough
animals plus one cow or bull. Non-tribal cultivators, traders
and Banjaras paid double this rate as nistar dues, but Banjaras
paid more for grazing. Certain categories of people were exempted from both grazing and nistar dues, such as Kumhars
in Antagarh, Kondagaon and Jagdalpur tehsils who were required to supply pots to officials free, and villages living along
the main highways who were required to do begar on the
roads. The blind, lame and widows were exempted from nistar
but not grazing dues.[37] Officials inevitably complained of
villagers' attempts to cheat them by undercounting the number
of cattle they possessed.[38]

Other changes were formalized in the forest manual of 1908.
Under the provisions of the village *wajib-ul-arz* (record of rights),
villagers were prohibited from cutting teak, sal, fruit bearing
trees and other specified timber trees above three feet in girth.
Shifting cultivation in areas with a preponderance of teak and
sal trees had to be applied for three months in advance, and
no one was to be allowed to remove forest produce for sale,
without appropriate licenses.[39] People now had to pay for items
which they had been accustomed to taking by right, and restrictions were placed on their access to these. Since they could not
change their lives overnight to suit the new rules, they were
categorized as 'offenders' and 'criminals'. As a forest officer once
told Elwin: 'Our laws are of such a kind that every villager
breaks one forest law every day of his life.'[40] In 1898, out of
forty-four cases of breach of forest rules, thirty-three were for
the removal of minor forest produce.[41] The number of cases
increased in subsequent years, the 'offences' including the 'illicit
removal of timber, poaching, illicit grazing', the common practice of poisoning rivers and tanks to catch fish, and even the
annual hunts, which are semi-religious affairs.[42] Old people told

[37] BS Forest Manual (1908:35-9).
[38] AAR, 1906, JRR.
[39] BS Forest Manual (1908:70-1).
[40] Elwin (1988:115).
[41] ARFA, 1898, JRR.
[42] WP, South Bastar (1981:120).

me of how forest guards would invade their homes, and examine their implements, in the hope of catching them out.

Forest Reservation

The question of forest reserves had been considered as early as 1899 by Blunt of the Imperial Forest Department who had been specially deputed for the purpose, but it was seriously taken up only in 1905. This was much later than in other parts of the Central Provinces.[43] However, as colonial rule extended itself from British India to more direct management of the feudatory states, and commercial exploitation threatened to overreach itself, it was inevitable that attention to reserves also followed. Certain basic assumptions about state ownership of forests were applied to Bastar as well, while other debates about exclusion were rehearsed afresh, evidence of the inherently dispersed nature of the bureaucracy.

The area to be reserved constituted a sweeping one-third of the total area of the state (4312 sq miles out of 13,002 sq miles) or two-thirds the total forest area of the state, excluding zamin-dari forests, which was approximately 6000 miles.[44] This was in a state where the majority of people were dependent on shifting cultivation, hunting and trapping, and the average area under cultivation per head of population was 1.75 acres. (see Table IV). Officially, reserves were selected to conserve commercially valuable forests before they were destroyed – e.g. Kuakonda contained the best teak in Jagdalpur tehsil, and Kosmi reserves among the best sal. The other aspect cited was to restore the forests (such as Gollapalli) after severe deterioration ostensibly caused by shifting cultivation. But official justifications not-withstanding, it was clear that the primary purpose was revenue generation, and the consolidation of control by the forest department to better enable this. As E.A. Rooke, forest officer, wrote to the Superintendent, Bastar State:

The main object of this reservation of these areas is the setting aside of them for the production of heavy timber for export purposes only, also for the production of smaller timber for meeting the requirements

---

[43] Rangarajan (1996:69–70).
[44] DeBrett (1988:58).

of adjoining states and British districts and local consumption of special natures, and for the supply of nomadic grazing where such will interfere with the conveniences of local residents. To gain these ends, outside destructive influences must be kept out, therefore people of the state must generally find their wants elsewhere than from the reserves.[45]

Reservation involved complete relocation of some villages — generally those which were small and which only practiced shifting cultivation. Simply being in the heart of good forest however, could also be a ground for eviction. Other villages which were allowed to stay on at the boundaries of reserves were given an additional amount of land equal to the existing cultivated amount for extension of cultivation and also twice the existing cultivated area for nistar purposes. The forest department exercised no control over this area and the village had exclusive use, subject of course to the provisions of the village wajib-ul-arz.[46] It is unlikely that this system was very accurate in the absence of detailed land surveys and given the fact that in any one year, a large portion of the land was left fallow to recuperate.[47] The total population of all villages affected by reserves was perhaps not that large — about six thousand, of which only a thousand were to be completely displaced,[48] but it was not absolute figures which mattered. Both shifting cultivation and the practice of rotating fallows would have involved more land per person than permanent cultivation.

But more important, the notion of reservation was contrary to the indigenous concept of village boundaries and sites for cultivation being 'given' to their inhabitants by the Earth. Even now, people go back annually over long distances to worship gods that were left behind when villages were deported from reserved areas. In 1914, in eighteen villages of Konta tehsil, out of 126 tenants who had deserted, 72 had returned and resettled. Yet others wished to come back and reoccupy villages in the Golapalli reserved forest from which they were turned out. The ranger's advice to them to select some other village was met

---

[45] xxiii, 18/1, E.A. Rooke, Forest Officer to Supdt. BS, 5 September 1905, JRR.

[46] xxiii, no. 18, Correspondence regarding Kanger Range, JRR.

[47].Grigson (1991:149).

[48] xxiii, 18/2, R.G. Nakhre and E.A. Rooke, Settlement Officers of Forest Reserves, to Supdt, BS, 24 June 1907, JRR.

with 'half consenting, half decrying'. He reported his conversations with the people to the diwan, 'They always said that they can't go to any other village than those in which their ancestors had lived for centuries together. They seem to be much prejudiced as they think that they would sustain a great loss of life and property if they occupied any other village than those belonging to their forefathers.'[49] Of course, local rights could not be totally ignored. The actual harm caused by shifting cultivation (dhya) was also debated:

In a landlocked state like Bastar, villagers cannot do much damage to reserves so long as there is no outside demand for forest produce. Even wanton felling except for *dhya* cannot amount for much . . . The question of rights of user is a very delicate one and every endeavour must be made by the Forest Settlement Officer to satisfy the people for to have them at enmity with the Forest Department augurs ill for the well being of the reserves.[50]

Crump had also noted that despite the low population, the whole state was divided up into villages and 'there is thus little, if any, area over which the state has full rights'. Desertion was generally temporary and such a village would be resettled by other villagers if 'a village priest can be found to lead them'. In most cases, thekedars continued to pay a nominal sum in order to retain the right to collect rents when it was resettled.[51] There were ulterior motives too in recognizing local rights. Crump remarked that if the villagers were not allowed to collect MFP from reserves, and there was no one else to do it, the state would lose that much revenue from export duty.[52] Similarly, Fisher, a Conservator of Forests who was Advisor to Bastar state, argued that both dhya and cattle grazing need not be totally prohibited within the reserves, as it would lead to flight and hence loss of valuable forest labour necessary to demarcate lines for forest protection etc. After 1910 in fact, at the same time as discouraging them from returning to their old revenue villages within the reserved forests, the state did its best to attract people to

---

[49] xxiii, 18/2, Konta Ranger to Diwan, BS, 4 May 1914, JRR.
[50] xxiii, 18, E.A. Rooke to Panda Baijnath, Diwan, BS, 14 March 1906, summarizing Fisher's proposals, JRR.
[51] xxiii, 18, Note on Forest Conservancy by H. Crump, 21 May 1906, JRR.
[52] Ibid.

forest villages. The latter were managed as sources of labour for the Forest Department and were totally under its control.[53] Indeed, Grigson later argued that if the state had had the foresight to retain villages within reserves as forest villages, the rebellion might not have happened.[54]

In the end, the debate on whether villagers should be allowed to stay in the reserves and use them for nistar purposes or be restricted to areas completely excised for the purpose gave way to compromise. Dhya, fires and the cutting of trees in reserves were to be totally prohibited, while grazing, the collection of MFP and hunting were to be allowed.[55] As the forest manual of 1908 noted, shifting cultivation was so widespread and intrinsic to local livelihood that 'it would be better to restrict certain areas from this form of cultivation rather than to restrict it to certain areas'.[56] In return for these 'privileges', each village was to be allotted a length of forest demarcation line to maintain. The villagers were to be paid a collective lump sum of one to three rupees per mile for their labour.[57] In some cases, argued the forest officials benevolently, it would be less hardship to move than to stay in such small villages and have to cope with the annual duties of clearing the forest boundaries.[58]

The peasants who were moved (i.e. whose entire villages were evicted) were given no compensation whatsoever, either for moving or for loss of property, on the grounds that they were there at state sufferance to begin with. Even here, class biases were evident. Although those who held land rent-free (muafidars) or on lease (malguzars) were deemed to have no more ownership rights over forests than ordinary cultivators, they were given some compensation if the cultivated village(s) they held were

[53] xxiii, 18, SDO Antagarh to Dewan, 12 December 1916, JRR.
[54] Grigson (1991:16).
[55] xxiii, 18/2, R.G. Nakhre and E.A. Rooke to Supt., 24 June 1907, JRR.
[56] BS Forest Manual (1908:100).
[57] But even in 1943 when the rates for forest roads had gone up to Rs 8-10 per mile, the Administrator noted that it was completely inadequate for the amount of labour required and the number of days spent. Often it was only paid much later on, and the villagers would have to walk anything up to 50 miles to get even this measly sum. xxii, i, Part 1, Extract from the Tour Notes of the Administrator, BS, for January 1943, JRR.
[58] xxiii, 18/2, Nakhre and Rooke to Supt., 24 June 1907, JRR.

forced to move in their entirety.[59] Worse, even the normal procedures of the Forest Act which provided for a preliminary three months notice were not followed on the grounds that 'the purpose of our enquiry is not only everywhere already known but is not likely to be unknown when we do commence operations'.[60] Further, the very fact of shifting cultivation was seen as grounds for the absence of any permanent right.[61]

The forest officers claimed that they had received few complaints except minor ones regarding the lack of building materials within areas demarcated for nistar and the need to resort to reserved forests. Ninety-five per cent of the villages retained within the reserves, they wrote confidently, were happy.[62] As eighty-year old Podiyami Ganga of Kankapal now remembers from his parent's accounts, it was not happiness with the arrangements that kept people from speaking: 'People were told to abandon penda and shown specific lands for shifting cultivation. The English drew the village boundary and made people settle within it. The people could not say anything in response, no answer would emerge.'[63] We know from other sources besides — e.g. the majhis' representations at the Dussehra Durbar in 1906-8, complaining about begar and bisaha, requesting remission of forest dues, questioning the proposed limits of reserves and whether shifting cultivation would be allowed, taking 'serious objection' to the prohibition of any kind of felling of timber over three feet in girth — that people were unhappy, uncertain and worried about the reservations and that in fact it was the burning issue of the day. Panda Baijnath, in reporting the durbars, felt that: 'Until a few reserves are actually formed, people will be tormented by vague fears.'[64] A letter from E.A. Rooke to the diwan describes the 'considerable opposition' to the maintenance of reserves that were recently constituted. Rooke also pointed out that as the final orders for afforestation had

[59] XXIII, 18/1, Corres. reg. Reservations in Kanger, Matla and Dhanpur, Treatment of Villages in Reserve Areas, approx 1905-6, JRR.

[60] XXIII, 18/1, Rao, Nakhre and E.A. Rooke to Suptd., 8 September 1906, JRR.

[61] Ibid.

[62] Ibid.

[63] Interviewed March 1992. Translated from Gondi by Lakshman Kashyap.

[64] XLVI, 28, Meetings of Leading Majhis and Gaitas Assembled at the time of Dashera, JRR.

Table IV: *Cultivation in Bastar, c. 1906*

Tehsil*	No. of villages	Cultivated area (sq m)	Waste Area (sq m)	Total Area (sq m)	Population	Land Rev. incl. muafis	Forest. Rev. (Rs)	Av. % Cult. Area
Jagdalpur	740	375	2505	2880	130,058	75,776	13,851	2
Kondagaon	531	103	1827	1930	47,752	25,717	20,026	1.5
Antagarh	542	100	2110	2210	39,811	14,488	11,107	1.5
Bijapur	203	51	1114	1165	21,367	10,697	13,115	1.5
Konta	114	33	927	960	7736	3356	5948	2
Total	2130	662	8483	9145	246,724	130,024	64,047	7.75

Table V: *Proposed Forest Reserves, c. 1906*

Tehsil*	Cultivated Area (sq m)	Original 'waste' area (sq m)	'Unreserved waste' (nistar) (sq m)	Reserves (sq m)
Jagdalpur	375	2505	1231	1274
Kondagaon	103	1827	916	911
Antagarh	100	2110	1194	916
Bijapur	51	1114	500	614
Konta	33	927	330	597
Total	662	8483	4171	4312

*   *Zamindaris are excluded from this table*

Source: Note on Forest Conservancy in Bastar, By H. Crump. Offg. Commr. Chattisgarh Division, 21 May 1906, JRR.

not been received even by the start of the cultivation season in 1908, despite being expected by the end of 1907, there was much uncertainty. In those villages to be displaced entirely, people were caught between the pincers of prohibition on cultivating existing fields, on the one hand, and being convicted under the Forest Act of cutting fresh penda, on the other.[65]

In the light of all this correspondence, official claims about the suddenness of the 1910 rebellion and the lack of warning seem difficult to believe. In fact, the rebellion started precisely in those areas where reservation first took place — in the Kanger forests. The Parja villages which were most active were not just those which were to be afforested but also those whose shifting cultivation was circumscribed.[66] But even after the rebellion, the authorities refused to concede that reservation had been a prime cause, attributing it to elite intrigue instead. At the same time, they were forced to take heed of popular discontent to the extent that work on reservation was temporarily suspended, and the area to be reserved was reduced to 2727 square miles — or roughly half of that planned before 1910. However, what it gave with one hand, the government took away with the other. Now all rights of nistar, grazing and hunting were officially closed in the reserved areas, though in practice, of course, people could not be totally prevented. In effect, before 1910, the forests had been protected rather than reserved forests. While reducing reserves, enforcement became stricter.

Standardization of Land Administration

Apart from the fact that it was said to cause destruction of forests, shifting cultivation presented other problems for the colonial administration in Bastar. First, the image of the shifting cultivator militated against both the Victorian and the upper caste concept of the honest toiler: productive permanent cultivators and wage labourers. Secondly, shifting cultivation

[65] xxiii, 2, Forest Officer to Suptd., 22 April 1908, Notes made on a tour through the Kanger reserve; Suptd. to Forest Officer, 27 September 1909, JRR.

[66] e.g. Elingnar, Kakalgur, Kotomsar, Kankapal, Kandanar, Chindgarh, Nangalsar, Nethanar, Kolawada, Chitalgarh, Chachalgurh, Kawapal, Tiria, Tahakwada — all in and around the Kanger range. xxiii, 18, JRR.

produced less revenue for the state than permanent cultivation. Thirdly, it made difficult the task of land revenue collection based on permanently settled villages, clearly demarcated fields, and standardized units of land and soil types. The stand-ardization of the land revenue system was important to the colonial authorities because it enabled the efficient collection of revenue and also because it was a mechanism for an increase in knowledge of the villages and people of the State.[67]

Right up to the first half of the twentieth century, the official policy remained that of spreading permanent cultivation. Con-sequently, policies designed to encourage outsiders to settle introduced shortly before 1876, were extended. This included initial remissions in land revenue,[68] as well as free grants of timber to outsiders to build houses etc., at a time when it was restricting the general right to forest produce.[69] Inviting new settlers in was not distinctive of British colonialism alone, but characteristic of all expanding agrarian states.[70] The difference here perhaps was in the scale of migration — areas like Bastar, especially in the hilly, forested and more inaccessible regions of the country, had so far been relatively free of large-scale settle-ment by alien groups.[71]

Due to the predominance of shifting cultivation, cadastral surveys were not applied to Bastar. Demarcation of villages itself was a problem as often one village had several sites within a certain area and distances between villages were too great.[72] In 1896, the diwan, Pandit Alamchand, carried out a summary

[67] LI, 13, I, Note on the Settlement Operations of Bastar State by Mr Sly, Political Agent, 1899, JRR.

[68] LI, 7/1, Establishment and Leasing of Villages, 1904; Revenue Circular no. 1, 1931, BS Revenue Manual (1931), JRR.

[69] XXIII, 23, A Corres. reg. free grant of timber, JRR.

[70] *See* Venkataramayya and Sarma (1982:681-3).

[71] The census of 1891 registered an increase of 58.4 per cent in population over 1881. While much of this was attributed to better census methods, there was also considerable immigration from other areas, especially Raipur. The majority of these would be grain dealers and other merchants, those in government service as policemen, patwaris, forest guards or schoolteachers, possibly soldiers and those in the private employ of landlords or money-lenders. CP Census Report, 1891, vol. II, Part I, pp. 56-7; CP Census Report, 1911, pp. 50-1.

[72] LI, 13, I, Settlement Note, Sly, 1899, JRR.

settlement based on the seed capacity of fields.[73] Rents were enhanced by eight annas to one rupee per plough.[74] The first regular settlement based on soil classification was completed in 1904, but for only 486 villages of Jagdalpur tehsil (out of 2170 villages for the state as a whole). The remaining 253 villages of Jagdalpur tehsil were summarily settled on rough measurement of length and breadth of each field, while the other four tehsils and the zamindaris were left unsurveyed, and settled on the plough system.[75] In short, at this point it was not an increase in rents that was sought, since that would deter cultivators, but an increase in cultivation, which it was hoped to record and tax by better survey and settlement methods.[76] In thekedari villages, the lessees retained twenty to twenty-five per cent of the total revenue, while elsewhere the rents were collected by the local headmen and paid into the state treasury.[77] After the 1876 rebellion, majhis were given first preference on the lease, and settlements (e.g. in 1896) were made on the basis of consultations with them.[78] But it is clear from Table VI that even after the rebellion of 1876, there was no significant decrease in the number of malguzars/thekedars or muafidars and they held a large number of villages.

Officially, under rules sanctioned by the Chief Commisioner, peasants could not be removed from their land so long as they paid their rents. Lands were not alienable and could change hands only by inheritance. There was only one class of tenures, although sub-leases were possible.[79] However, as the administration was to discover after the rebellion, ejection from lands

---

[73] The summary settlement involved estimating the extent of land from the amount of seeds sown, equating them to ploughs and checking the estimate against an actual count of village plough cattle.

[74] LI, I, Rough notes on the settlement of Jagdalpur Tehsil by A.S. Womack, 1902, Pol. Agent, JRR. 7.5 khandis of seeds = 1 plough in settled parts; 5.5 in forest areas.

[75] LI, I, I, Note on Settlement for the Gazetteer, JRR.

[76] LI, 13, I, Settlement Note, Sly, 1899, JRR.

[77] DeBrett (1988:63-4).

[78] LI, 1, Preliminary Report on Jagdalpur Tehsil by Settlement Officer, Jwala Pershad, 14 December 1900, JRR.

[79] LI, 13, I, Memo on the principles which should guide the Revenue officers and Courts in Feudatory States under direct management in regard to the administration of land, 22 July 1889, JRR.

which the lessee wanted to cultivate himself, overcharging of rents, demands for grains at one-third the market price in lieu of cash rents, and failure to give receipts were common complaints against lessees.[80] Flight was not uncommon in these circumstances, judging from the frequency with which malguzars surrendered their land citing inability to pay on account of desertion. From the state's point of view, the frequent change of malguzars was not a good thing, as the policy of giving each new malguzar revenue remission for a certain period led to revenue loss.[81]

Table VI: *Malguzars and Muafidars in 1892*

Tehsil	No. of khalsa Villages	No. of malguzar Villages	No. of muafi Villages	Total No. of Villages
Jagdalpur	195	225	232	752
Kondagaon	147	222	112	481
Antagarh	303	nil	170	473
Bijapur	179	4	90	273
Konta	85	5	9	99
Total	909	456	613	2078

*   Zamindaris excluded
Source: LI, 13, I, Suptd. BS, to Pol. Agent, 1982, JRR.

Famine: Eating Rabbit Shit to Survive

As part of the standardization of land revenue, rents were demanded in cash from the summary settlement of 1896–8, except for the villages around Jagdalpur whose supplies were required for the royal family. This enhanced the potential for famine as against the traditional system of keeping the portion of land revenue levied in kind in numerous local storehouses for general availability in times of scarcity.[82] In 1896–7, in 1899–1900 and again in 1906–8, there were droughts followed

[80] For. Sec. I, Aug 1911, Pro. no. 34–40, E.A. DeBrett, Officer on Special Duty, BS to Commr., Chattisgarh Div., CP, 23 June 1910, NAI.

[81] LI, 13, I, Note on Sly's Report, 1899, JRR.

[82] Int. A Feb. 1897, nos. 256–66, Scarcity in Bastar, NAI; LI, 13, I, Settlement Note, Sly, 1899, JRR.

by famine. The 1899–1900 famine seems to have been one of the worst famines to affect any part of India.[83]

Traditionally, Bastar had been relatively famine-proof because of the forests: scarcity foods included grass seeds *(jhipa)*, and the inside of the sulphi tree which was ground and made into bread. But in 1899, there was such severe drought that even the mahua did not flower and the forest died. In the more fertile areas of Jagdalpur and Antagarh, the rice crop was less than one-third the normal output in 1899–1900, while in the other areas like Bhopalpatnam, the fall was even more drastic.[84] Prices rose dramatically, from about 45–60 sers of paddy per rupee in the 1890s to eight sers a rupee in June 1900.[85] Wage rates for *kabadis* or bonded labour and day labourers, on the other hand, had remained stable over a twenty year period, especially since payment was largely in kind.[86]

The government's policy in 1896–7 of allowing free exports of grain by merchants from surrounding areas who swarmed to Bastar, while simultaneously buying up stocks at an artificially low rate to feed labourers and pay wages during the monsoons, had grave consequences in 1900.[87] Even during normal times, the monsoon months are lean, hungry months, a time when grain stocks begin to run low, and the roads become impassable. In 1900, peasants fearing that the government would follow the same policy as before, hid their grains. By October, the situation had come to such a pass that people were scared to leave their homes for fear their grain would be requisitioned in their absence, and grain riots were imminent.[88]

Lakshman Jhadi of Gangalur, Bijapur (one of the areas badly affected) told me that if any household had rice, they would pound it very softly at night lest the neighbours hear or else they would all come and compel forcible redistribution. People would tie rice in small cloth bundles, dip it into water and

[83] Baker (1993:172–235).
[84] Int. A Feb. 1897, nos. 256–66, Scarcity in Bastar, NAI.
[85] LI, 13, I, Jwala Pershad's Settlement Report for Jagdalpur Tehsil, 1900; XVII, 3, G.W. Gayer to Pol. Agent, CFS, Report on Famine as it affected Bastar state, 10 November 1900, JRR.
[86] LI, 13, I, Jwala Pershad's Settlement Report, 1900, JRR.
[87] Int. A Feb. 1897, nos. 256–66, Scarcity in Bastar, NAI.
[88] XVII, 3, Gayer's Famine Report, 1900, JRR.

squeeze it, then drink the water, keeping the rice bundle for further use. Many did not even have this. People were forced to eat rabbit shit, Dayaro Pujari of Kukanar recounted, but even they survived, while those who ate earth died.

Several large landlords (who were later to be accused of grave self-interest in the 1910 rebellion) such as the two Ranis, Lal Kalandar Singh, Murat Singh Bakshi, Bala Pershad and Abdul Rahman Khan, made personal contributions towards famine relief, as did the American Methodist Mission, which had been established in Bastar in 1893. Lal Kalandar Singh, for instance, gave each of his tenants two rupees per plough, besides remitting much of their revenue. Among the tribals themselves, people shared whatever they had. According to Gayer, 'One richish Muria practically beggared himself by feeding free the villagers of three villages.' The state itself suspended some land revenue, though less than half, and set up relief works — road and tank construction, and relief kitchens — which the tribals were reluctant to attend, owing to a general distaste for anything to do with the state, although the Maharas, Pankas, Panaras, Sundis and other Hinduized castes came.[89]

There were dispersed attempts at grain looting and related 'crime' such as cattle theft, both punished with whipping when caught. The later stages of the famine were also marked by cholera, followed by diarrhoea, dysentery and malaria; cowpox in the south and south-west; and large-scale cattle deaths due to lack of fodder and water. Human mortality was difficult to ascertain as the villagers would flee into the forests in times of cholera and not return to the same site, or else return only after it had been rid of the sickness through purification ceremonies. The famine of 1900 was compounded by the failure of the Banjaras to come because of lack of water and fodder for their cattle.[90] The growing drought from 1906–8 onwards was in many ways a repeat of the 1900 experience, with fodder scarcity and cholera, though it was not as severe as before.[91]

---

[89] GOI For. Int. A Pro. 86-9, February 1900, MN Fox-Strangways, Sec. to CC, CP, to Administrators, CFS, 14 August 1899, NAI.

[90] XVII, 3, Gayer's Famine Report, 1900, JRR.

[91] C.B. Ward to Dr A.B. Leonard, 30 June 1908 (1259-7-3:46), MRC.

The 'Punishment of Begar'

After 1876 the demand for begar increased even further as the
bureaucracy and official apparatus in Bastar grew steadily, leading
to greater demands on the peasants for food supplies and labour.
In one representative report from Kuakonda police circle, it was
noted that 123 villages were involved in making roads, carrying
loads for visiting officers from one village to another, carrying
grass and bamboo to Dantewara, repairing forest barriers, cutting
boundary lines in the reserved forests, carrying bamboos to
depots, carrying grass and bamboo to repair schools, hospitals,
forest buildings etc.[92] In addition to work on official buildings,
lessees and officials both demanded work on their personal
houses, free supplies for themselves, and fodder for their horses.
Duffadar, Darogah, Patwari, Nakedar . . . all came in turn and
people described sleeping with a stick and a bundle of rice at all
times in readiness to be called for carrying loads on tour.
Chendru, watchman of village Asna, remembered that until as
recently as ten years ago, the police would ask him and other
kotwars to sweep the police station and perform sundry odd jobs
every time they went to make their reports. Sometimes, the
officials even demanded village women, and beyond censuring
them for turning majhis and kotwars into procurers, the senior
administrators saw this purely as a problem of private morality![93]
Even traders and foreign merchants felt entitled to conscribe the
peasants,[94] and at one point a system developed of private
individuals giving their servants badges *(chupras)* similar to those
worn by state servants, in order to create the impression of
authority and thus get labour.[95] School masters, who were almost
all non-tribal, also collected supplies and subscriptions free or at
reduced prices.[96] Several old men have recounted to me how
corporal punishment was the norm in schools.

Those were also the days of extensive road building. The

[92] xxii, 4, Police Department Report, 14 September 1928, JRR.

[93] li, 25, Part i, Order by E.S. Hyde on the transfer of Revenue Inspector
R.N. Pathak, 1936, JRR.

[94] xxxviii, 25, Commissioner Fraser's Tour Notes, 1892, JRR.

[95] xxxviii, 26, Chupras, 1892, JRR.

[96] In 1886 the first 3 schools were opened, followed by schools in all the
tehsil headquarters by 1889. *See* Joshi (1990:50). By 1909 there were 58 schools,
mostly primary. DeBrett (1988:68).

Raipur–Jagdalpur road was finished in 1898; the Jagdalpur–
Chanda road in 1904; the Jagdalpur-Kotpad-Jeypore road com-
menced in 1899; while the Kondagaon-Narayanpur-Antagarh
road was completed in 1907.[97] Remembering the building of the
Darbha ghat road from Jagdalpur to Sukma over and down the
mountain, and through the Kanger forests, Chendru Murtak,
aged seventy plus, described it as a heavy task, with the people
having to bring boulders down from the mountain. Dayaro
Pujari too described working on that road when he was a child,
unpaid and surviving the whole day on only a leaf cup of mohua.
His elder sister who had also taken part, agreed — 'It was really
a punishment'. If villages were assigned to work on roads far
away, they could be away from their homes for two months,
sometimes during the prime harvesting and threshing season.[98]
Villages decided among themselves which stretch of the road to
work on, and it was then divided among households on the
basis of ploughs. Among several common complaints that
persisted almost till independence in 1947, i.e. as long as roads
were built by forced labour, was that the length of roads allotted
to a village was too high compared to the number of tenants,
and that they were made to work on both forest and PWD
roads.[99] The burden was greater on smaller families, who had
less labour to spare. These were also generally the poorer families.

In several colonial documents, we see an attitude towards
corvée as a crucial form of labour management in tribal areas,
'the only way to get work out of those lazy buggers,' even as
the pressure of notions of free labour compelled a move towards
replacement of corvée by wage labour.[100] Thus, Mitchell, Administrator of Bastar state noted that in the collective opinion
of the state officials, the system was not wholly bad.

In many parts of the state the problem is not one of obtaining labour
without wages or unduly low wages, but one of obtaining labour at
all . . . the people equally object to working for wages calculated at

[97] Joshi (1990:75).
[98] xxii, Part 4, Extract from the Tour Notes of the Administrator, BS, for
January 1943, JRR.
[99] xxii, 1/1, Part i, Corres. Reg. Allotment of Villages for annual repairs
to the PWD roads of the state, JRR.
[100] While the IPC outlawed forced labour in 1860, in Bastar it was abolished
only in the 1940s.

full market rates as they do to providing *kavad begar* (porterage) for officials. Men will labour all day to catch one rat for distribution among four or five, rather than earn 2 1/2 annas each for the same amount of labour on an adjacent road. Similarly women will spend from dawn to dusk emptying a forest pool for the meager handful of small fry which they will find in the mud, rather than undertake paid but organized work. In a society where money means very little beyond the price of a bottle of liquor and where the real bugbear is work, *begar* need not be understood to have the same unpleasant implications as it would and does in more advanced areas.[101]

The most common form of resistance to begar was, once again, flight. Routinely, villagers would desert, especially when new roads were created near their village, and along with it came the demands for begar.[102] Even in 1892, A.H.L. Fraser noted that the rents of land within a certain radius of Jagdalpur were reduced by one third to induce people to stay there.[103] The burden was perhaps not as heavy as elsewhere in India, and certainly nothing compared to the 240-70 days in a year demanded of Kikuyu squatters in Kenya.[104] But what mattered here was not absolute labour time demanded alone, but the arbitrary nature of much of this demand, which signified the petty power of the state over people, as well as the constraints of an externally imposed work discipline.[105] Literally, it was begar or labour power that sustained both the traditional and the British administrative state. Roads are a perfect example of fetishization in this context – portrayed as a great benefit of 'development' and 'civilization', they were in fact built through conscripted labour and used to exploit local resources, for the benefit of classes elsewhere.

Conclusion: How were the Wealthy and the Law Interwoven?

At the start of the colonial period, the situation was one of social and political mobility. Access to both land and forest

---

[101] XXII, I, Part I, Corres. Reg. payment for Porterage, Mitchell, 25 September 1940, JRR.

[102] XXXVIII, 25, Commissioner Fraser's Tour Notes, 1892, JRR.

[103] Ibid.

[104] Furedi (1989:13).

[105] Thompson (1993:352-403); Cooper (1992).

resources depended largely on the amount of labour power one could command, revenue demands were low, and although there was trade, there was little permanent settlement by outsiders. In the colonial period, however, all this changed with the increasing need of the state to generate revenue through agriculture, but even more importantly in areas such as Bastar, to gain income and timber from forests. Railways and ship building were essential to British imperialism by facilitating the movement of resources and troops. This in turn required controls on shifting populations and shifting cultivation, in order to ensure labour for forest logging and demarcation, or the construction of roads — all of which were necessary to take resources out. A fixed population was also required for recruitment to armies and plantations (see chapter 6).

Law played a crucial role in this process. It represented a significant site of contradiction, being both 'a maker of hegemony and a means of resistance'.[106] As one of the major cultural idioms of the British state,[107] the 'rule of law' was marketed by British colonialism as the great gift of Empire to its backward subjects and played a significant role in institutionalizing the colonial apparatus as indigenous groups too began to make use of colonial legal systems for their own ends. Yet, particular laws dealing with expropriation of land and resources away from groups which formerly controlled them were violent in themselves, and the maintenance of 'law and order' part of a coercive order rather than any law.[108]

In Bastar, by the time forest reservation was considered in the early 1900s, the principle that all forests belonged to the state was fairly well entrenched. Considerations of peasant access were voiced by certain people, but by and large the question was phrased as one of how not to alienate the locals, and how to retain their services for forest labour. Here, as elsewhere, services, first fruit offerings and gifts provided by the peasants to the raja, especially during Dussehra, which I have argued could be interpreted as symbolic assertions of their right to the produce in the first place, were re-interpreted by colonial officials

---

[106] Lazarus-Black and Hirsch (1994); Mann and Roberts (1991:35-6).
[107] Thompson (1975); Skillen (1978).
[108] Burman and Harell Bond (1979); Sumner (1979).

as returns for 'privileges' allowed them in the forest. The continuation of these 'privileges', therefore, was to be paid for in work for the new administration – making roads and carrying loads. The alternative was to have the people pay directly in the form of nistar dues, and the two, cash dues and services, were on occasion traded off against each other. In the English case, E.P. Thompson has described how through a series of cases and the establishment of legal precedents, there was a 'reification – and cashing – of usages as properties'.[109] In many of these cases, the courts relied on the legal fiction of customary rights in commons being derivative from some original grant. But there too, as Thompson notes, 'Anglo-Saxon and Norman monarchs and lords did not graciously institute but, rather, regulated and curtailed' these rights.[110]

In the colonies, however, the legal justifications for state ownership of land varied considerably. Nineteenth century Australian courts were divided on whether aboriginal ownership of land had survived the right of conquest,[111] while in India, this right was recognized only for certain classes, e.g. zamindars, and not for others, especially those who held resources in common.[112] In short, law was not just transported from England to the colonies but represented a complex mixture of imperial legislation, local administrative initiatives and the particulars of a changing agrarian history.[113] But in each case, the effect was the consolidation of the colonial state, and the recasting of existing patterns of ownership and rights in common resources. In time, these new patterns would come to be seen as 'customary' through that peculiar irony with which history is created.

[109] Thompson (1993:136).
[110] Ibid.:133.
[111] Hookey (1984).
[112] Singh (1986:15).
[113] Vincent (1989).

Map 5: *Bastar: Sites of 1910 Rebellion*

Source: Based on Index Map of Bastar in P.C. Agarwal, (1979:12)

5

In Search of Gunda Dhur:
The Bhumkal of 1910

Oh, our dark-skinned men have
pitched their tent in the Banya's
pasture lands;
Our Rajah, he is with the Whites,
and he is making war on us!

The shells from their guns
are hitting only the dust,
But oh, our guns are smashing
their camps!

Folk song of 1857 from Auwa, Rajasthan.

By 1910, life in Bastar seemed bleak to the local inhabitants, what with the reservation of forests, restrictions on penda, the introduction of grazing dues, an increase in land revenue and a greater demand for begar — all in the name of a more efficient administration. In a cosmology which held the earth responsible for everything that happened, the series of droughts and sickness were perhaps seen as an indication that the earth had turned bitter against them. People began to gather and discuss things in village councils, at bazaars and mandais, anywhere the majhis and pujaris of several villages were assembled. The rebellion of 1910 is popularly referred to as the 'Bhumkal'. The term is significant, for in its everyday usage it refers to the social solidarity of the members of a clan that binds them to each other and to their specific *bhum* (earth);[1] a pargana council meeting of all the village earth priests and clan god or ancestor worshipping priests — to settle all móral and social disputes;[2] the political authority of the village — the

---

[1] Grigson (1991:236).
[2] Popoff (1980:146).

council of elders.[3] One might read the Bhumkal then as a mode of protest juridically sanctioned by local authority, that of the elders in the name of the earth, a pitting of indigenous law against colonial law.

Planning for Protest

In 1909 some Parjas from Nethanar, one of the first villages to be affected in the Kanger reserves, met Lal Kalandar Singh, the king's cousin and one time diwan, at his estate in Tarokhi. At Dussehra that year they also appealed to the raja's stepmother, Rani Subran Kaur, his half-brothers — Kunwars Bahadur Singh and Arjun Singh — and leading town residents like Murat Singh Bakshi for help, saying that neither the king nor his advisors listened to them.[4] In January 1910, after the harvest when people were relatively more free, the Parjas met the Lal again. He pointed out that they would have to fight the English, but Puchak Parja was confident that 'they had a powerful God, and could turn missiles from guns and cannons into water.'[5] Twenty-one village and pargana headmen signed a pledge written by the Lal 'by which all bound themselves to give their life and property to secure the redress of their wrongs.' This affidavit, along with the Lal's knife and coat, were circulated through the villages as a sign of the latter's leadership. They passed through the Kanger forest from Nethanar, Elingnar, and Leda to Sukma where the items were confiscated by Jankaiyya, diwan of Sukma. Later in the rebellion, there were other letters too which circulated in the Lal's name but which were not in his handwriting.[6]

On coming back from Tarokhi in January 1910, the Parjas of Nethanar sent out messages inviting other villages to join in the rebellion. The messages consisted of mango boughs, a lump of earth, chillies and arrows. Every village contributed something to the collective expenses. According to William Ward of the

[3] Gell (1992:65).
[4] For. Sec. I, Aug 1911, Pro. no. 34–40, Confidential no. 4417, DeBrett to Commr. Chattisgarh Div., 23 June 1910, NAI. (*henceforth* DeBrett, Confidential no. 4417).
[5] For Sec I, Sept. 1910, nos. 16–17, Report on the Connection of Lal Kalendra (sic) Singh with the rebellion in Bastar State in 1910, NAI.
[6] Ibid.

Methodist Mission, 'Our Christians were compelled to give rice
and to pay from two pice to five rupees each, some gave more.'
Although the Christians were initially allowed to sit in the
committees, they were later prohibited on the grounds that they
would tell the padre, who in turn would tell the government at
Raipur.[7] Thus rebellion was organized in the same fashion as
mandais and Dussehra – through universal contribution of
people and materials, and coordinated by village heads and
pargana majhis.[8] The crucial difference here is that no women
are mentioned in the records of the time or indeed in contemporary oral histories as having taken part in the actual fighting.
No doubt, however, they were present at bazaars and other
localized events where action took place, even if they didn't
travel to fight.

The rebellion spread to other parts of the state starting from
the Kanger area. In quick succession, starting on 2 February,
the bazaars at Puspal, Chingpal, Kukanar and Karanji were
looted, and the Lal's authority cited for the act. At Kukanar
bazaar, a trader, Nursab Khan, was chased and beaten to death
by a 500-strong crowd. They came from Kokawada, Soutnar,
Chitalnar, Leda, Mudwa . . . the villages south of the Kanger
forests, and were led by Bantu Parja, majhi from Kokawara, and
Syamnath Dhakad of Mudwa, Chitulnar. The elders of Kukanar
described how the men had flowers in their bows as on hunting
expeditions. On seeing the trader, Bantu exclaimed: 'This is the
whain-chode (sister-fucker) who eats oil and grows fat and robs
us – kill him.'[9] The Kukanar people say they themselves did
not take part as their majhi was away, and the second in
command, Chamtu Chalan, refused to act in his absence. Later
Chamtu called Nursab Khan's wife to identify him, but by that
time his body had been mostly eaten away by wild animals
where it had been left in the jungle.[10]

Everywhere the houses of officials and traders, schools and

[7] For Sec. I, Aug 1911, Pro. nos. 34–40, Microfilm Acc. no. 211, William
Ward, 'The Bastar Rebellion; A Missionary's Experience', TOI, 14 March
1910, NAI.

[8] *See also* Guha (1983:124).

[9] For. Gen. B, April 1910, nos. 7–10, Sessions Case no. 1 of 1910, Bastar
State vs. Bantu Parja and Syamnath Dhakar, NAI.

[10] Ibid.

police stations, were burnt and looted and grain redistributed; in some cases money was extorted from the traders in order to let them escape; while in other cases the men from these families were beaten and the women stripped naked and turned out on the roads.[11] Recounting the episode at the Kukanar police station, Ghasi Parja of Durras described how the crowd ran to kill a woman from one of the police families coming out of her house. Beda Parja shouted that he would kill her personally and pretended to strangle her. But when the rest had gone on, he set her free.[12] Others were not as lucky, however. Three policemen in Kuakonda and one in Bhairamgarh were killed, as were a lone forester and a hapless trader who asked a Maria for the way through the forest. In Kuakonda, the overall leaders of the rebellion were thought to be the Nethanar Parjas rather than the Lal. After killing the head-constable, a mock-court was held where the local Maria leaders dressed as Parjas, the other characters acting the raja and the diwan. When Koria Majhi, alias Sukta Dhakad, was asked who would be king, he invoked a certain 'Gondu Dhurwa.'[13] Elsewhere Koria Majhi was quoted as saying that 'the former Raj had been abolished and it was now a Muria Raj.' To show his *devi-shakti* and invulnerability, he slashed himself with a sword without breaking the skin, and threatened to kill anyone who refused to obey him.

In the north of Bastar, too, government and immigrant property was attacked. The mail from Raipur, Dhamtari and places around the state was stolen, and runner's huts and mail boxes destroyed.[14] William Ward describes the phenomenon thus: 'from all directions came streaming into Jagdalpur, police, merchants, forest peons, school masters and immigrants.'[15] Some of the destruction was led by members of the royal family themselves. Kunwar Bahadur Singh supervised the cutting of the Jagdalpur–Dhamtari telegraph line, while at Bhiragaon near Kondagaon, the raja's uncle, Mukund Deo Machmara Babu apparently orchestrated the loot of Jethu Kunjam, the sole outsider there. He had been sent by the raja to bring back Lal

[11] DeBrett, Confidential no. 4417.
[12] Durras, 7 June 1992.
[13] For. Sec. I, Sept. 1910, Pro 16–17, NAI.
[14] xxII 1/9, JRR.
[15] Ward, TOI, 14.3.1910.

Kalandar Singh, but reneged and attempted to demoralize the tahsildar and other officials at Kondagaon by saying the diwan, Panda Baijnath and the rajguru, Mitranath Thakur, who were the raja's chief advisors on behalf of the British, had been killed.[16] Rani Subran Kaur called for Bhondia Majhi of Morathpal, one of the villages in her charge, and ordered him to collect men and cut off the diwan, Panda Baijnath's (writing) hand. Bhondia's subsequent actions, according to information recorded by De-Brett were as follows:

Bhondia collected 400 men, sacrificed a number of goats and started off to intercept the Dewan who was expected to return from the direction of Bijapur. This mob started on the 10th February, burnt the Marenga school, the police post, lines and pound at Keslur and the school at Tokapal (Rajur), detached a contingent to burn Karanji school and captured a head constable and four constables of the State reserve police who had been sent out to escort the Dewan and bring him in. The mob did not maltreat the guard seriously but eased them of their weapons and let them go. One party of rebels under Bhondia Majhi went off to the Koer river to block the passage there in case the Dewan left the main road. The rest went on to Dilmilli to stop the main road from Bijapur. Buddhu Majhi and Harchand Naik led the main body.[17]

Similar independent initiatives were being taken everywhere. Rora Pedda sent by the raja to save the diwan on 8 February, turned instead to organizing the rebellion, and sent emissaries like Koria Majhi to mobilize the parganas of Killepal and Mutanpal. But far from betraying the characteristics of a 'mob', there are many instances to show that, as in 1876, the people had discipline and organization on their side. Authority was, however, decentralized. The local headmen everywhere, majhis and peddas, were in charge, and whether the resistance was encouraged or stopped depended on them, although, according to Ward, the chief leaders were Gunda Dhur, Rora Pedda, Kanda Dhur, Banda Dhur, and Chaitu of Dongar. The targets were only those who had oppressed them in the past or who, by refusing to join with them, were effectively collaborators.[18] One

[16] DeBrett, Confidential no. 4417.
[17] Ibid.
[18] See Guha (1983:167–219), for an analysis of the nature of solidarity in

of these was the negi of Barsur, who thrice burnt the mango boughs sent to him, and attempted to stop the rebels. He was severely beaten with bamboo sticks, leaving him with permanent damage to his eyesight.

Violence was not the only or even dominant form in which the rebels expressed themselves. Often they made do with threats. For example, Jakari Pedda of Karli who had been despatched with twenty-five picked men to chase the diwan, passed through Tumnar and threatened to punish the villagers if they had not burnt the police outpost before he returned. He and the men went on to release the rebel accused of murdering the Bhairamgarh policeman from the lock-up. On their return, they found no action had taken place, but Jakari merely removed all state property from the police station, and gave it to the head man of Tumnar to keep, pending orders from Koria Majhi. The latter had, in the meanwhile, left for Jagdalpur with the Mutanpal and Killepal contingents.

O.T. Sinclair, employee of Parry & Co., who had a lease on MFP, and was stationed at Tongpal had the following experience as relayed by him to DeBrett.

He, found himself at once blockaded (on 1 February) by order of the Parjas of Nethanar. From that date he could only communicate with the outside world secretly. Fortunately, his own Parja workmen stood by him and brought him supplies under cover of darkness and on the 7th they faced and drove off very pluckily a crowd of rebels who, after looting Leda Bazaar, came on to rush his house. Next day he received orders from the rebel spoken of as Gondu Dur that, because of his great kindness to the people, he would be allowed to remain in safety at Tongpal and would not be put to any trouble, but that if he attempted to leave Tongpal he would be killed.[19]

Later, when he saw hundreds of men leaving for Jagdalpur with 'an arrow, chilli, bugle and axe . . . passed down the line to show that it was war,' he got uneasy, but again 'the Gondu Dur sent word to him not to be afraid and promised to give him land, bullocks and ploughs if he remained staunch.'[20] Evidently, Mr Sinclair was not attracted by the promise. He sent messages

---

peasant and tribal insurgencies.
[19] DeBrett, Confidential no. 4417
[20] Ibid.

to the British authorities, who rescued him from Tongpal after defeating the rebels at the end of February.

The Paltan Arrives

Having been telegraphed about the rebellion before the lines were cut, the Chief Commissioner sent about 250 armed police to crush it. The force was led by Gayer, former administrator of the state, and DeBrett, Political Agent, Chattisgarh Feudatory States. There was fear that the uprising would affect the Khonds of Kalahandi, and shock at both its suddenness and the moral depravity of the people in not having communicated their problems to the Political Agent when he was touring the state in January. Enroute to Jagdalpur, the *paltan* (platoon) en-countered 'crowds of fleeing Pardeshis' (outsiders) and in the jungles near Kondagaon, 'a war puja, under a mango tree':

Fresh blood, still uncongealed, of the goat that had been killed was shed before the image of Danteswari, the tutelary goddess of the State. Behind her in array were erected two miniature guns, several miniature swords, spears, etc. horses, deer, bullocks, and a rope was stretched over the lot. Cooked rice was piled over the image of the goddess.[21]

The paltan proceeded, one imagines somewhat shaken by this sight, capturing rebels along the way. When they reached Jag-dalpur on 16 February, there was an 'encounter' and five men were shot. According to DeBrett:

On seeing us the rebels got up and a great many began advancing towards us. I called upon them to send up their leaders but they would not do so. I then ordered them to move away from the ghat. This also they would not do. I then warned them that if they did not obey we should open fire. Those directly opposing us, however, stood their ground while others began creeping up from both flanks. We then tried the effect of a charge and cleared the ghat just around the motor. The rebels however would not retire far and evidently wanted to surround us . . . Mr Gayer then saw a man deliberately calling up a crowd from the rear and asked for leave to shoot him. He also warned me that it would be as well to let them have it on all sides or we

---

[21] For. Sec. I, Aug 1910, Pro. nos. 12–41, (Daily) Note of Proceedings of Officer on Special Duty, Bastar State, 15 Feb. 1910, (*henceforth* DeBrett, Daily Notes), NAI.

might be rushed . . . Even then each party only retired after it had been fired at.[22]

Retired forest ranger Gangadhar Dube who was born in 1910 to Shivram Prasad Dube, a forest ranger who took part in the process of forming reserves, and a member of the large Dube family who are landlords of several villages in the state, dictated to me in English the following version of the event:

The military force arrived in Jagdalpur in buses and trucks. This arrival of the military contingent in motor vehicles coincided with the tribals withdrawal from the police attack. They were amazed to see a vehicle moving without horses or any force. They ran to the road to observe them. The military commandant asked the vehicles to stop and the soldiers to spread throughout the groves and collect all weapons of destruction. In the meantime he engaged the tribals by showing them various parts of the vehicle. He then ordered the tribals to collect near the palace at Gol Bazaar and moved on. Towards evening, these tribals, suspecting nothing, assembled there, where they were arrested and thrashed (tied to imli trees and whipped). Thus the suppression of the rebellion started which took about 3 months.[23]

What was seen by the British as a hostile encounter, is turned through local upper caste condescension for tribals, into a benign demonstration about technical matters by the British officer to the innocent but foolish tribals. But as a good Indian he had to make his acknowledgement to the 'freedom struggle' and therefore bring in British duplicity. Perhaps it is unfair to compare a diary recorded at the time, and the hazy remembrances of old people fed on their parent's stories. But truly, there are many histories, and the victim's story can also ring with a victor's voice: 'The quarrel', said Chendru Murtak, Parja of Nandrasa, 'was with the sahibs. Gunda Dhur, through his powers, lifted the raja's bathing stone and made it fly, across the Indrawati at Kharagh ghat. All the sahibs on the other bank died. Then the sahibs got very angry and called a paltan.'[24] Chaitu Dhakad of Irikpal, was told by his father that when the paltan fired their first round, there was no noise and water came out. It was only when 'the Gora Saab took some earth and put it to

---

[22] Ibid.
[23] Jagdalpur, December 1992.
[24] Nandrasa, 1993.

his head' that the firing could start.[25] Even the foreigners then, were dependent on the earth for success.

When the paltan arrived at Jagdalpur, they found the town deserted and shut. In the words of Lt. Col. E. Clementi-Smith who accompanied the detachment of 22nd Punjabis, the palace was equally abandoned looking: 'here and there were a few figures in dirty khaki lying about, we at first thought they were bundles of clothes, but they turned out to be part of the State forces.'[26] The raja, Rudra Pratap Deo, sounded equally forlorn. He greeted his rescuers with the announcement that he had 'dedicated himself to Parmeshwar (God) and had determined to commit suicide.' This was later amended to saying that he would prefer a quiet life in Raipur to the excitement of ruling in Bastar!'[27] On DeBrett's arrival, a group of some 500 men, mostly Murias and Bhatras from the parganas surrounding Jagdalpur, collected outside the palace walls to negotiate. The leaders came forward unarmed, saying they 'had come to make representations for their stomach's sake.'[28] The 'bloodthirsty rebels' constantly referred to in the rebellion reports often turn out then, on careful reading, to be not so bloodthirsty after all.

A picture of the rebel camps was painted by Ward for the *Times of India*: 'Thousands were encamped in three circles around Jagdalpur. Rebel campfires shone beautifully at night. All night long their bison horns sounded all's well.'[29] This account, which struck a note of both romance and menace, is rendered more prosaic by Clementi-Smith's description of rebel camps:

Very primitive — nearly always situated under a tree, they consisted of boughs intertwined with no head cover. The space inside was kept quite clean and many had a small annexe. . . . In the main camps we found quantities of grain stuff of all kinds, seeds, roots and a few chickens. The grain, etc. was kept in small baskets made of palm leaves with a covering formed of some kind of large leaf pruned together with thorns. A large number of bows and arrows were also collected and here and there an axe or brass cooking pot was to be found hidden in the bushes.[30]

[25] Irikpal, 17 April 1995.
[26] Clementi-Smith (1945:248).
[27] DeBrett, Daily Notes, 16 Feb. 1910.
[28] Ibid.
[29] Ward, TOI, 14 March 1910.
[30] Clementi-Smith (1945:247).

Between 16 and 22 February, messages — written, verbal and in the form of jamun and mango branches — went back and forth between the rebel camps surrounding Jagdalpur and the British, regarding who should go to meet whom and where. Insurgent determination was sustained by passing the bloodstained clothes of those shot at Jagdalpur ghat around the camps. Although they were constantly on watch for rebel offensives, the British in fact were the ones to 'break faith' by attempting to surround the rebel camp at Gangamunda hill. They finally succeeded in doing this on the second try. The earlier attempt failed not because of strong resistance but because of British ineptitude in finding their way through the jungle. After some initial hesitation while they awaited orders from Gunda Dhur, the peasants had in fact been prepared to negotiate unarmed. Naturally, however, they refused to stack their bows and arrows as demanded, since these were crucial to their hunting and hence survival.

William Ward acted as go-between at this stage. Ward's role in the rebellion was ambiguous. He was invited to insurgent councils as a mediator, but also supplied the British with information or assumptions about their plans that were crucial in suppressing the rebellion. Before the British troops arrived, Ward claimed the rebels had cut off his wood and water supply. In further self-dramatization he added,

We ran up an American flag above our house. They compelled us to lower it because they said it would attract the *Angrezi log* who were living at Raipur. There was not a white man near to help us; we were almost helpless. That night we spent putting up a new line of barbed wire fence as a defence; we also put on top of the house two pipes on cart wheels in such a way that they appeared like cannon. When the insurgents who were guarding our back gate saw the tarred pipes and were informed that they were cannon they fell back and took up their position about two hundred vards in the jungle. Our cannon held the enemy at bay![31]

Yet after the rebellion he claimed that wherever he went touring, 'men, women and children came out from each village and with drums beating loaded me with garlands and gave me a triumphal entry into their villages.' He also claimed that after

[31] Ward, TOI, 14 March 1910.

their defeat, people had begun to lose faith in their own Gods, and turned to the missionaries instead, even though earlier they had punished and looted the Christians.[32] In a situation where 'community' is sustained through participation in collective ritual events, anyone who does not participate, whether Christians or Kumbhi Buchiyas, is often suspect.

Lal Kalandar Singh arrived in Jagdalpur on 20 February, and held conferences with the insurgents and with leading townspeople. Twenty-three majhis came in to negotiate, but others refrained. Rora Pedda and Gunda Dur assured their men that 'if there were four times as many troops here they would not be able to do anything; that the troops will be taken and they and the Sahibs thrown into the tank.'[33] At noon on 22 February, the British were told that the Lal had ordered mango boughs to be sent to all the ghats to block them as the sahibs were running away, and soon it became 'obvious' to DeBrett that unless Lal Kalandar Singh was arrested, nothing could be done. The arrest apparently made Subran Kaur so angry with the raja that she terrified him into asking for a guard of fifty reserve police. This, however, the unsympathetic British refused to provide.

Soon after another reinforcement of troops arrived, the rebel camp at Nayamunda tank was surrounded on 26 February and 511 men captured. Describing the attack, Clementi-Smith wrote:

in a few seconds the whole jungle resounded with weird cries gradually getting fainter and fainter as the alarm spread from one rebel camp to the other. . . . We could see here and there groups of the rebels running about in a wild state of alarm; they apparently had not realized the possibilities of any movements at night being made against them, but beyond this and making a great noise nothing happened.[34]

After some heavy firing by the police, the rebels surrendered in batches and the remainder were captured in searches. By describing the rebels as alarmed, tame, depressed, frightened, astonished and hoping to escape detection,[35] the British helped to create a

---

[32] W.T. Ward to Rev. A.B. Leonard in New York, 10 March 1910; W.T. Ward to Dr Benton, 14 June 1910, (Acc no. 74-11), MRC.

[33] DeBrett, Daily Notes, 24 Feb. 1910.

[34] Clementi-Smith (1945:246).

[35] Ibid.:247.

picture of people with limited intelligence who had been misled into rebellion rather than planned for it consciously. They were flogged, in the hope that it would have a ripple 'demonstration effect'. By early March, the leading town residents suspected of complicity were arrested. Slowly, the rebels around Jagdalpur began to surrender, pargana by pargana: Kachorapati, Nawagaon, half of Chitapur, Marpar, Amorapati, Agarwara, Killepal, Muttanpal, Renkhera, Jaitgiri, Baragaon and so on. In some cases, they responded to messages sent out by Ward telling them the government would cede their demands.[36]

But long after the rebels around Jagdalpur had been caught, the rebellion continued in different parts of the state — limited only where the zamindars or others took action against them, e.g. in Kutru, Bhopalpatnam and Sukma. Reactions varied in the South-West. In Jagargunda, the assembled crowd dispersed on hearing about the whippings in Jagdalpur, but resistance continued in Chintalnar and the Balond bazaar in Kuakonda was looted. A Bihari trader-cum-moneylender had his skull fractured. In Usur, as late as the middle of March, a police official and his wife were murdered, and the houses of several outsiders burnt.[37] In the north around Chote Dongar, a police force was attacked twice in early March by a large group of rebels, numbering in the hundreds. One constable was killed with a matchlock. Reinforcements were summoned, and in the hundred and forty-four rounds fired in retaliation, twelve rebels were killed and several wounded. The rebels left after taking all edibles from Chote Dongar, but were pursued by Gayer who burnt four villages, 'admonished' eight Marias, and spared those villages who 'came in'.[38]

But the last battle had yet to be fought. A member of the malguzar family of Nethanar reported that five hundred men from the parganas of Agarwara, Tirathgarh and Nethanar had gathered at Nethanar Gehupadar 'to decide how best to arrange for their stomachs'. They said that if DeBrett wished to see them he should come to Nethanar with the Lal Sahib. The real plan, as relayed by spies (servants of Ward and Sinclair), was to take

[36] W.T. Ward to Rev. A.B. Leonard in New York, 10 March 1910; W.T. Ward to Dr Benton, 14 June 1910, (Acc no. 74-11), MRC.
[37] DeBrett, Confidential no. 4417.
[38] DeBrett, Daily Notes, 19 March 1910.

Jagdalpur five days after the full moon, i.e. on 30 March.[39] But before this could happen, at 2 a.m. on 27 March, six hundred fighters asleep in an opening in the jungle of village Alnar, were surrounded on all sides. Alerted by their sentry, they fought back killing one soldier and wounding eleven others: 'The arrows in the ground all around each of our men were as thick as the quills on a porcupine's back,' wrote DeBrett. In return however, at least twenty-one rebels were killed, and probably about a hundred more injured.[40] A Bhatra song blames the debacle on betrayal. The traitor, Sonu Majhi, got the fighters drunk on two huge drums of liquor. When they were sleeping, with their bows and axes lying unheeded by their side, he went and told the padre. And the padre brought the paltan to catch them unawares.[41] But once again, it is not clear who really won, since memories survive and take on lives of their own. Chendru Murtak narrated the battle:

On the people's side, were the big elders — Mille Mudaal of Palem, Soyekal Dhurwa of Nandrasa, and Pandwa Majhi. All the pargans camped in Alnar tarai. The paltan surrounded the people in a flash. Gunda Dhur had flying powers and flew away. But what could those with bows and arrows do? As many people died on the paltan's side as died on ours. The battle took place at night. The people hid in murtand shrub, tendu shrubs and crawled away. The paltan also ran away. All those who remained alive (of the rebels), somehow found their way home to their villages. Then in honour of having won, they sacrificed chickens and pigs and ate them. Some died and some were saved.

After this final encounter, columns of police went out and 'secured' the countryside — marching through the jungles around the Kangeir and Kolab rivers, through Katekalian, Kuakonda and Dantewara parganas, fining, trying and punishing those who had taken part. They often found the villages deserted. The elders today vividly recall being told by their mothers of the flight into the jungles, the terror lest a child's cry alert the troops to their presence. And eighty years later the most striking thing

[39] DeBrett, Daily Notes, 20th March, 1910.

[40] DeBrett, Confidential no. 4417.

[41] Bhumkal Geet, sung by Supal Dhurwa of Niyanar, collected and translated by Lala Jagdalpuri, M.P. Adivasi Lokkala Parishad (1988:1-3).

that hundred-year-old Hirma Kumhar of Kukanar remembered of this time was that: 'In the English period there were a lot of soldiers. English noses were very big.' This may seem inconsequential to us but clearly represented the face of oppression to him.

Punishing the Rebels

By the beginning of May, the bulk of the troops had been sent back, and only DeBrett remained, with forty men and three *sowars*. The rebel 'rank and file' were whipped and sent back, on the grounds that summary justice rather than long imprisonment was better suited to wild men. They were to learn that they 'could not with impunity flout the overtures made to them, not only by their chief but also by the officers of the British government deputed to deal with them'.[42] In fact, it was claimed, the punishment was 'just, necessary, and in the interest of these forest people generally, in the truest sense humane'.[43] Individual cases of leaders were tried under law, including that of Bantu Parja and Syamnath Dhakad for the murder of the trader at Kukanar market.[44] Some were hanged and others deported. Chendru Murtak in his accounting of victors and losers said:

There was a Sicklel (Sinclair) Sahib during the Bhumkal. During that time the English paltan would come and beat and harass all those who had come back from the Bhumkal. Sicklel prevented them and answered for them. At that time the English were searching all over for Gunda Dhur. He was hiding. Sicklel wouldn't allow anyone to be beaten or sent to jail. He took the risk for his pargana. Then all those who won were given Bhumkal muafi land and land titles.

Others in Kukanar, e.g. the elders of Bokadabadar, corroborated Chendru Murtak on 'Sicklel Sahib's' role in the enquiry. They said that Chamtu revealed all and the Kukanar people were saved. But many were scared by the enquiry and fled to Korra. Several of the 78 Bastar prisoners sent to Raipur fell seriously

[42] DeBrett, Confidential no. 4417.

[43] For. Sec. I, Aug 1910, Pros. nos. 12–41, B.P. Standen, Chief Sec. to CC, CP, to Sec. to FD, GOI, Confidential no. 60, 29 March 1910), (*henceforth* Standen, Confidential no. 60), NAI.

[44] For. Gen. B, April 1910, nos. 7–10, NAI.

ill, with accusations and counter-accusations being traded back and forth between Jagdalpur and Raipur jails about lack of proper treatment.[45]

All of Lal Kalandar Singh's estate was confiscated by the state, and he was exiled to Ellichpur in the Berars with an income roughly one-twelfth of what he was used to.[46] The other large landlords involved were also exiled to various parts of the Central Provinces for their complicity in the rebellion. Except for Machmara Babu, most were allowed to return after a few years. Rani Subran Kaur died that year itself, sparing herself further trouble.[47] Their muafis were resumed by the state to pay part of the cost of suppressing the rebellion while the rest was to be met by an Imperial loan, since the state could not afford it.[48] Heavy punitive fines, totalling approximately Rs 85,000 were also imposed on the over 65 villages which took part. In other words, all the rebels, whether elites or villagers, had to pay the costs of their own defeat. Those who had resisted the rebels, such as the Barsur negi, the dewan of Sukma, zamindar of Kutru, Chamtu Challan of Kukanar; Koppa Pedda and Husseini Pedda of Massenar and Dinbandhu Jaya of Dantewara – were rewarded, according to their status. For instance, the Barsur negi got a muafi village and a silver medal; the zamindar of Kutru, Nizam Shah, was given the title Sardar Bahadur, and Chamtu Challan was given acres revenue-free within Kukanar.

William Ward was later accused by the British of double-dealing for not informing them of the rebellion which he was said to have known about beforehand, and later pressurizing the raja to be given some of the Lal's or the rani's sequestered villages. His aim, apparently, was to make the Methodist Mission one of the biggest landlords in the state.[49] He was sent out of the

[45] XII 1/5, State prisoners sent to Raipur jail, JRR.

[46] For. Sec. I, Sept 1911, Pro. 16–17, NAI.

[47] XII 1/4, JRR.

[48] The cost was estimated as approximately Rs 58,437-11-0. The annual revenue of Bastar state in 1911 was only Rs 387,739 and its expenditure roughly equal to that. Annual tribute to the British government (apart from the costs of contributing to the Political Agent's office) was Rs 20,000. AAR, 1911, JRR.

[49] For. Sec. I, Aug 1911, Pro. nos. 34–40, CC, CP to FD, GOI, 16 December 1910, NAI.

state, with the full support of F.D. Campbell, who succeeded him, and who saw Ward's role as damaging the prospects for missionary expansion.[50] Ward defended himself by saying that the administration feared that he would make public his knowledge of the police shooting (under orders) of unarmed wounded tribals after the Alnar battle.[51] The position of the American Methodist Mission in Bastar was a delicate one. C.B. Ward, father of William Ward, had been granted land by Commissioner Fraser when the raja, Rudra Pratap Deo, was still a minor, in contravention to normal Government of India orders forbidding this. The mission's continued presence was against the raja's wishes.[52] As the 'dominated fraction of the dominant class,'[53] the missionaries were dependent on the administration for permission to operate, but the success of their operations depended on their relations with the people, even if it meant going against the administration if necessary.

In many cases the context of the rebellion makes the primness of the law appear ridiculous — when the whole countryside is up in arms it seems odd to try people for 'being members of an unlawful assembly' (Sec 142 IPC). Yet, to have all acts, including the surrounding of the rebels at Alnar, and the burning of their villages duly authorized and footnoted by law, was of the essence in British self-understanding.[54] The other side of reducing insurgent politics to crime was exalting colonial crime to law. The contrast with 1876 was also constantly made — the present effrontery of the rebels in not falling at British feet seeming all the blacker against the background of their behaviour then.

It was not as if they were mere armed demonstrators, as in the 1876 rising only asking for the redress of reasonable grievances. Had they been so they would have first petitioned the Political Agent who had just toured through the whole state before the rising broke out; they would have fallen at the feet of the British officers on their arrival as

[50] F.D. Campbell to Dr Leonard, 19 September 1911; 19 December 1911, MRC.
[51] W.T. Ward to Rev. A.B. Leonard, Malaysia, 6 June 1912 (Acc no. 73-43), MRC.
[52] F.R. Felt to Dr Leonard, 21 October 1908, MRC.
[53] Comaroff and Comaroff (1992:209).
[54] DeBrett, Confidential no. 4417.

in 1876 and welcomed them as their saviours from oppression. They did none of those things . . . the outburst was accompanied by murder, arson, looting and general savagery, it was a regular revolt against civilization, against schools, against forest conservancy, against the opening up of the country by Hindu settlers. In short it was a movement of Bastar state for Bastar forest dwellers.[55]

Interpreting the Rebellion: Secondary Reflections

The rebel list of complaints included the reservation of forest lands, petty oppression, excessive demands by officials and malguzars for free labour and supplies, and interference with the right to manufacture liquor, a right which had been outlawed by a new excise policy. Some rebels asked for the lessees to be ousted, and to be allowed to pay their forest dues and land revenue directly into the state treasury.

The British were willing to accept the complaints against the subordinate officials but not against the rules themselves.[56] In fact the former was entirely consistent with their own views on the condition in native states – with their native rajas, native diwans and native officials. The diwan, Panda Baijnath, was unfavourably compared with English officers in terms of his strength and authority to administer, control subordinates and dispense immediate justice. DeBrett asserted: 'A native cannot do this as effectively as an Englishman and that is the long and short of it.'[57] Some efforts were made to 'reduce the establishment to the smallest proportions consistent with that style of administration suited to a primitive country,'[58] for example by abolishing seventeen out of thirty six police stations, reducing the number of schools and abolishing a separate touring department for their inspection. In the case of schools, this was paradoxical as people positively wanted education, and objected only to extortionate demands by schoolmasters. They had apparently told Ward that they wanted one person in every

[55] Standen, Confidential no. 60.
[56] Ibid.
[57] DeBrett, Confidential no. 4417. *See also* Grigson (1991:16) for this view.
[58] For Sec. i, Pro. August 1911, nos. 34–40, B.P. Standen, Chief Sec. to CC, CP, to Sec. to GOI, FD 16 December 1910, (*henceforth* Standen, Confidential no. 175), NAI.

household to read and write so that they could explain rules to the rest.[59]

The practice of subletting out-stills, which was introduced in 1905,[60] was to be abolished and efforts made to lease them out only to locals, rather than to a single large contractor like Kalika Singh. This man had leased many stills in Jagdalpur tahsil and charged extortionate fees from his lessees, who in turn used to water down the liquor considerably to make profit. But at the same time it was considered 'fatal' to allow people to distill their own liquor as they had wanted. DeBrett opined: 'They are far too much addicted to liquor as it is, and are perfectly savage and not in the least responsible for their actions when under the influence of drink. It is unsafe even for an Englishman to go into a Maria village when the inhabitants are indulging in a carouse.'[61] It is difficult to know where to draw the line between class and race prejudices such as manifested above, which perhaps couldn't be helped, and a more cynical refusal to perceive a genuine problem.

Not surprisingly, the most burning issue for the insurgents, the reservation of forests, 'did not amount to much' in the eyes of the administrators writing about it. To quote DeBrett's claims again,

As a matter of fact, great care had been taken over the demarcation of reserves . . . and the people had been disturbed as little as possible. But those who had seen some of their villages taken into the reserve, such as Lal Kalandar Singh, Mukund Deo Machmara Babu and Murat Singh Bakshi, resented a measure which was likely to prevent them making money out of the forests and they worked on the people to make a grievance of the affair.[62]

The town elites were thus easily dismissed as motivated by money alone, while the villagers' anger over the issue was dismissed as due to the 'superstitious reverence in which the aborigines hold their village sites'.[63] And despite the need for

[59] DeBrett, Confidential no. 4417.
[60] The outstills system replaced the old system of having families of Sundis and Kallars in each village to distill liquor for festivals, on the same terms as other village servants like the raut and atpahria.
[61] DeBrett, Confidential no. 4417.
[62] DeBrett, Confidential no. 4417.
[63] Standen, Confidential no. 175.

caution engendered by the rebellion, DeBrett opined that there could be no question of stopping reservation. 'Bastar must always rely largely on its forests to provide funds for the work of administration and it is most important that this valuable property should not be destroyed.'[64] One measure of this importance was that by 1911, forest income alone accounted for roughly one-third of the total income of the state.[65] In any event, the British heavily discounted the possibility that any of their own policies could have been responsible for the rebellion. The fact that they did not make representations to DeBrett who was touring a few days before the rebellion began 'is one of the surest proofs that the grievances themselves had not strained their patience to the breaking point, and that if there had not been the incitements from the Lal, the Bari Rani, and the knot of Hindu intriguers inside Jagdalpur, there would have been no rebellion'.[66] Palace intrigue, in short, was the crux of the administrative explanation for the rebellion, viz. the rani and Lal's resentment over the loss of power they had faced with the coming of the British administrators, compounded by the latter's alleged fear that with the birth of a child to the raja in 1910, his last chance at succeeding to the throne would be lost. Standen, Chief Secretary to the Chief Commissioner, CP, pithily summed up this official interpretation: 'The whole of this rebellion owes its origin to the jealousy of a childless widow and the ambition of a disappointed man.'[67]

Tertiary Reflections: A 1990s Anthropological Understanding

It was probably true that participation by the local elite was motivated in part by anger over having their forest access withdrawn, their muafis resumed, and their influence on the administration reduced. No doubt their sympathies with peasant complaints were enhanced because in this instance they were not directed against themselves but against the British. But it is also likely that they had old feudal-paternalist links with the

[64] DeBrett, Confidential no. 4417.
[65] AAR, 1911, JRR.
[66] Standen, Confidential no. 75.
[67] Standen, Confidential no. 60.

people as evidenced by their behaviour during the famine of 1900. L.K. Mahapatra points to a special relationship between the senior rani and the tribals in the Orissa states, in which the latter looked upon the rani as their 'Mother'. She in turn supported them against oppression by officials or the king's harmful policies.[68]

It also seems unlikely, even disregarding local historians who portray the Lal as a father-figure to the whole state,[69] that he had engineered the rebellion to coincide with the impending royal birth. It was the Lal who arranged for the third marriage of the raja's father, Bhairam Deo when the latter had been childless from his first two wives. Finally, since by Standen's own admission, 'the rough outline of this conspiracy has been gathered from rumours, hints and statements,' there seems little reason to give it the central place the colonial authorities did. There was indeed plenty of evidence of Lal Kalandar Singh's complicity — the letters in his name and his circulating knife and coat. The raja complained that the Lal abused him for calling in the British. Rebel statements that they wanted the Lal to be present at negotiations; the information relayed by spies that they were going to blockade the road to prevent his removal to Raipur after his arrest; letters addressed to him as '*Shriman 108 Maharaja Lal Sahib*,' the 108 appellation generally being reserved only for the king; and a statement allegedly made by a Muria to the Lal of Bamra, that 'our Raja is wandering in the jungle and other people are here in comfort' — all indicated that in the eyes of the people at least, the Lal was a more legitimate king than the actual raja whom they supposedly referred to as 'the dumb man'.[70] The Lal had in addition admitted to 'being a member of the Arya Samaj and a believer in the Swadeshi propaganda.'[71]

But in the matter of assigning culpability or leadership, the people are divided today. According to Hirma Kumhar, the Kukanar centenarian, the fight was between two brothers and the common people were independent. Mundra Majhi of Pharaspal,

[68] Mahapatra (1987:25-26).
[69] Thakur (1982); Narmada Prasad Srivastav, Interviewed Jagdalpur, 1992.
[70] For. Sec. I, Sept. 1910, nos. 16-17, NAI; Standen, Confidential no. 60.
[71] For. Sec. I, Sept. 1910, nos. 16-17, NAI.

Dantewada tahsil, claimed that the 'English came before 1900 to
get the alchemist's stone from the raja. The raja told the English
not to beat him, but to beat the people. . . . People gathered at
Nethanar, and the English shot them. Gunda Dhur wandered
the bazaars with chillies and a mango bough. The Bhumkal
happened because the English snatched Bastar.'[72] Podiyami Ganga
of Kankapal, whose father Podiyami Tokeli took part in the
rebellion, was more willing to excuse the raja, whose sin, if at
all, seems to have been inaction:

The British came and started taking land, though they came straightforwardly and without force. When the raja realized this he called all his
supporters. War started. His staunch supporters died and the rest were
whipped. My father, Podiyami Tokeli suffered many strokes, escaped
and survived. It was a movement to get rid of the British. The British
used to tie them to horses and pull them. From every village two or
three people went to Jagdalpur: Gargideva and Michkola of Chidpal,
Dole of Markamiras, Adrabundi of Markamiras, Vadapandu of Baleras,
Unga of Palem — all Gond Muria. Lots of Dhurwas also took part
but I don't know their names. The raja did not himself give the order.
Raja didn't pay attention to things happening around him, so seeing
the situation of land being taken, his supporters gathered people. And
people voluntarily went. People went for one week continuously.[73]

If the accounts of 1910 that have been handed over from
generation to generation are considered, it is clear that the real
hero of the rebellion was not the Lal, not even if he is viewed
as a 'consenting party' or figurehead for the people who took
their own initiative, the 'Bahadur Shah of Bastar'.[74] It was
Gunda Dhur, ultimately, who was crucial to the Bhumkal. As
Podiyami Ganga went on to say, 'Gunda Dhur sat in prayer,
preparing for war. At that point, the British pretended to flee.
So Gunda Dhur thought what was the point of praying —
leaving the ritual unfinished — he thought it would be best
to chase them out. At that point, the British turned around,
surrounded people and killed them.' Had Gunda Dhur been
able to complete his prayer and been filled with devi shakti,
they would not have lost.

Who was this Gunda Dhur and what happened to him? The

[72] Pharaspal, 1990.
[73] Kankapal, April 1992, translated from the Gondi by Lakshman Kashyap.
[74] Sept. 1910, Pro no. 16-17, NAI.

1. *Calling to others, Kukanar hunt*

2. *Annual Community Fishing in Bhimsen Tarai, Kukanar*

3. *Grinding mandia*

4. *At the Kukanar market (Photo: Siddharth Varadarajan)*

5. *The Palace at Jagdalpur*

6. *Dussehra chariot*

7. *Lallu Pujari arrives at Kumdakote with Danteswari (umbrella)*

8. *Bystanders at the Dussehra festivities*

9. *Devi in costume at Bodaras jatra, supported by another Devi
(Photo: Siddharth Varadarajan)*

10. *Pravir Chandra Bhanj Deo and Vedvati
soon after their marriage, c. 1960s*

11. *Baba Bihari Das in his ashram*

12. *Dayaro Pujari in front of his gudi in Bodaras*

13. *Meeting at Bodaras to discuss government plans to resettle oustees from the Maolibhata steel plant project in the village, 1993*

British were never sure whether he was one person or many. When some of the people from Chitapur pargana surrendered, 'they were ordered to bring in Puchak (one of the Gundu Dhurs) or take the consequences.'[75] 'No one is able to say who this Gondu Dhurwa is, by some it is thought to be Puchak, a Parja leader, by others it is thought that the term referred to the Lal.'[76] Different accounts given to me today suggest many things. A mundane version is that he was a Parja of the cobra clan called Puchak from Guppapadar, a hamlet of Nethanar Gahupadar. In the wake of the repression, half the lineage went to Talurnar in Orissa, while others who remained were too scared to confess to any association. But he was clearly more than that. Some say he was a powerful shaman. He got his name from his ability to make ropes of sand (in Parji, *gunda* means sand, or dust) as well as bend iron into ropes *(gunda* also means bend). It is also said that he could turn bullets into water, and that he could fly in the sky. According to some, he was *Dev Dhur* (a Devi inspired Dhurwa) from Nethanar, who came with an axe. According to others, he was the ancestor of Boda Dhara who was nominated MLA after independence.[77]

For one year after the rebellion, the British searched for him, sending horsemen everywhere. In Kankapal, they say, such a horse died when it crossed the village boundary. Some think he was hanged, and others that he was crucified — but the majority are certain that the British never caught him. He changed his clothes and went into hiding. In June 1911, a group of Kumbhi Buchiyas (members of a religious sect), who were said to be looting bazaars around village Jaitgiri, had an encounter with the police, in which their leader Bhadu was shot. They claimed that they were 'children of Nethanar' sent by Gunda Dhur and said that by beating up the head constable of Jaitgiri outpost in the Karpawand bazaar, they had defeated the 'children of the king'.[78] Whether he was captured or escaped, whether he was one person or several, it is certain that he lived on, for what is flesh when the memory is alive?

[75] DeBrett, Daily Notes, 9 March 1910.
[76] For. Sec. I, Sept. 1910, nos. 16–17, NAI.
[77] Field Notes, 1991–93.
[78] XII. 3, JRR.

Conclusion

How does one conclude the description of an event that is continually re-enacted? At most, one can point to a process that had just begun. The following extracts from three different periods, including the present, indicate the persistence of the tension between the right to livelihood and notations of state property.

Some villagers from (the revenue villages) Chikpal and Parcheli have re-inhabited the forest villages of Kudumkhoda and Mundenar on the grounds that the lands belonged to their forefathers, and that even when they had shifted to (the) revenue village they would return to worship the Deo of that village and that if they didn't do so they were attacked by calamities. Now having come back to the original village, they say death is preferable to shifting out again. *(C.F.O. Daver, to Asst. Settlement Officer, 29 September, 1936)*

On the road from Tetam to Katekalyan I found general dissatisfaction at the restriction of penda cultivation. I was unable to convince them of its evils. Podiyami Bandi Peda of Tumakpal has to get his son married and for this purpose he wants to cultivate penda in the prohibited area. I told him that he should not do it. He replied plainly that he would cultivate it and go to jail as he had to get his son married. I think the Officials of the Forest Department and the patwaris should keep an eye on him and prevent him damaging the forest for penda cultivation. *(Extract from the Tour Diary of the Assistant Administrator, BS, for the month of January 1939)*

Yesterday, we visited Badri Mur, a recent settlement of about 30 landless families straddling the Kanger national park and reserve forest. It is the site of an old village that was included in the reserve boundary. For three years the forest department tried to remove them. Accompanied by the police, they would pull down the houses and break the bunds. The women would come out waving poles and sticks, and each man in the village has been arrested 20 times. Badri Mur is one of many such villages fighting court cases about what the state defines as 'encroachment' and what the people define as their 'right to cultivate land to satisfy their hunger'. *(Extract from the Tour Diary of the Anthropologist, for the month of December 1992)*

The rebellion of 1910 bears continuity with not only previous struggles, but also those that have succeeded it. At the same time, the specific legal and political traditions and ecological contexts from which the Bhumkal drew its significance have now been considerably weakened or changed. In 1996, several hundred encroachers in reserve forests are due to get title deeds under the latest regularization scheme of the Madhya Pradesh government.[79] Under the vastly reduced amounts of land left over from development projects, forest reserves and settled agriculture, penda may no longer be the ecologically viable option it once perhaps was. Co-operation with the forest department in the form of joint management agreements may be a better option for gaining some control over forests than open confrontation. Under the expanded shadow of the state, communities are increasingly differentiated and collective rebellions harder to organize. But, so long as the children of the king live, so too will the children of Gunda Dhur.

[79] *Madhya Pradesh mein Dinank 24 October 1980 tak Atikramit Vanbhumi ke sarvekshan avaim somankan hetu disha nirdesh*, MP. Govt. Forest Department, Vallabh Bhavan, Bhopal, 25 January, 1995.

6

The 'Tribal Question', 1927–1950

*At a conference in Ranchi, one of the Development Commissioners
present got up and asked plaintively, 'How can we develop the tribes
along the lines of their own genius when they haven't got any genius?'*

Verrier Elwin, *The Tribal World of Verrier Elwin.*

The anthropological attempt to classify tribes within a
certain taxonomy has inevitably resulted in the compliment
being returned. Describing the Saora reaction to outsiders,
Elwin recorded: 'After any outsider had been to the village,
they made special sacrifices to purify the place from any possible
magical defilement. In one area I found a regular tariff: for a
Forest Officer they sacrificed a goat, for a Sub-Inspector of
Police a fowl, and for an anthropologist a large black pig.'[1]
Anthropologists may well feel chagrined at being associated
with swine, but the connection of certain kinds of knowledge
with power is by now well established. The first part of this
chapter examines the connections between anthropology, colonialism and indirect rule, a matrix in which 'reform' and
'custom' were seen as inextricably linked. After the Bhumkal,
a series of anthropologist–administrators argued for a change
in policy towards tribal populations in Bastar. Drawing on the
African experience of indirect rule, they put forth proposals
that they thought would lead to the preservation of tribal
culture. The most important of these was the attempt to codify
and apply 'customary' civil and criminal law to tribal groups.
In the process, a particular vision of 'tribes' or the 'tribal' was
constructed. The second part looks at how some of these early
debates and their practical implications fed into broader academic and political issues related to tribal policy as it developed
in independent India.

---

[1] Elwin (1988:189).

'Anthropologically-Minded Administrators'

Writing about W.V. Grigson, administrator of Bastar (1927–1931) and author of *The Maria Gonds of Bastar*, which remains an authoritative text, J.H. Hutton noted, 'it is the very high privilege of that altogether too rare individual the anthropologically minded administrative officer, that he can often bring practical benefits to the subjects of his studies as well as informative benefits to the readers he instructs.'[2] In trying to locate the anthropologically minded administrators within a broader, comparative milieu, it is necessary to turn to two bodies of material – the ideologies of rule that came to prevail at different points in time across empire, and theoretical orientations within the discipline. Neither of these can be understood in isolation from each other.[3]

Bastar was perhaps unusual in that from the late 1920s upto independence, the administrators associated with it had a broadly common vision of what was to be done – which they defined as coming from an anthropological perspective.[4] While not an administrator himself, Verrier Elwin was a strong influence on, and supporter of, the policies followed in Bastar, both through his writings and his personal friendships with the Bastar administrators. His position as Honorary Ethnographer and Census Officer of Bastar State (1941) in turn facilitated his ethnographic explorations. Unlike J.H. Hutton and J.P. Mills, two other anthropologist–administrators who went on to teach anthropology at Cambridge and London respectively, none of the Bastar administrators – W.V. Grigson, E.S. Hyde, and Norvall Mitchell – were professional anthropologists. Indeed, Elwin too was not an anthropologist by training, although he was to go on to become one of the most prolific ethnographers of his time, a leading authority on tribal affairs and an occupant of various positions in the Nehru government. He studied English literature at Oxford, came to India as a missionary, but broke with

---

[2] Hutton (1991:xv). Hutton himself, as former administrator in the North-east, Census Commissioner, author of *Caste in India* and Reader of anthropology in Cambridge, might be said to fall within that category.

[3] Asad (1973a:12); Vincent (1990:63–70).

[4] The administrators in the period under study were: W.V. Grigson: 1927–1931; D.R. Rutnam: 1931–1934; E.S. Hyde: 1934–1940; A.N. Mitchell: 1940–1942; K. Radhakrishnan: 1942–1943. GOMP (1950).

the church and set up his own 'ashram' for social service among tribals in the Central Provinces. Thus he too came to his anthropology through his practical work.[5]

The 'anthropologically minded administrators', whether formally trained or not, were definitive in influencing the course of anthropology in India. They used the standard tools of the trade — *Notes and Queries*, attended anthropological conferences and communicated extensively with each other, as well as with some Indian anthropologists, albeit to a much lesser degree.[6] The emphasis on fieldwork, even if at second hand, through information collected by subordinates or through official encounters, was also a means whereby they established their authority on the tribal question.[7] At the same time, any history of anthropology's colonial encounter which aims to avoid Eurocentrism and reductionism, must take into account several personal and intellectual histories. The first departments of sociology and anthropology were set up in Bombay (1919) and Calcutta (1921) respectively. There were several noted Indian anthropologists/sociologists, such as S.C. Roy, who founded *Man in India* in 1921, N.K. Bose, K.P. Chattopadhyay, D.N. Majumdar, Iravati Karve, G.S. Ghurye, M.N. Srinivas and others. Although some of them trained at British universities, such as Chattopadhyay, Majumdar and Srinivas, and the general trend during the period (1920s–40s) continued to be tribal studies, with a fair share of anthropometry thrown in, their relation to the discipline was somewhat different. Some like Chattopadhyay and Bose were involved in the nationalist stuggle, suffering breaks in their academic careers in the process.[8]

[5] *See* Elwin (1988).

[6] The views of this group of anthropologist-administrators have been pieced together from their published works and letters: Hutton (1941); Grigson (1993, 1991); Archer (1984); Hyde's private papers deposited at the Cambridge South Asia Centre contain letters written to him by Elwin and Grigson, among others. The number of administrators with an interest in anthropology was considerable. Even by 1900, nine per cent of the membership of the Anthropological Institute in London comprised of colonial civil servants, most of whom had worked in India. Vincent (1990:69).

[7] Grigson (1991:xxi–xxii).

[8] For one account of anthropology's trajectory in India, *see* Vidyarthi (1978:1–29).

Both professional anthropologists and administrators-cum-anthropologists shared a common field, which was, broadly speaking, the study of social structure. Yet they had quite different positions with respect to the overall administration, and often quite different theoretical frameworks. To start with the former, this was not just a simple distinction between Indian and British anthropologists. Despite efforts by the Royal Anthropological Institute from 1900 onwards to gain recognition from the Colonial office for the practical uses of anthropology, patronage of 'practical anthropology' took a while in coming.[9] Even when the administrative value of cataloguing local cultures was accepted, providing administrators with anthropological training was seen as preferable to hiring professional anthropologists, whether native or British.[10] The latter were seen as potentially subversive. For instance, following Elwin's work on the Baigas containing passages which were seen as critical of the forest and land revenue administration in British India, there was some discussion as to whether he should be allowed access to official records for his Muria ethnography.[11]

The 'anthropologically minded administrators', too, had differences with mainstream administrators as to what the colonial authorities should be doing, though they did not doubt the necessity of colonialism itself. In arguing for the isolation of tribal groups from the corrosive influences of mainstream India, the anthropologist-administrators came up against both the upper echelons of the British administration and the Indian nationalists. The senior administrators were keen on the extension of administration and to give one example, further restrictions on shifting cultivation to increase the scope for commercial exploitation of forests. The nationalists, for their part, saw the policy of protecting tribals from other Indians as a policy of divide and rule and favoured assimilation as a way of 'uplifting' the tribes. The upper ranks of the Government of India (GOI) were also more pragmatic about a peaceful deal with the Congress,

[9] Vincent (1990:116–21).

[10] Moore (1993:8–9); Adas (1995:301).

[11] VII, Census 1, Part XXIII, Major Burnett, Pol. Agent, Chattisgarh States Agency to A.N.Mitchell, Admin. BS, 27 September 1940; reply from Mitchell defending Elwin, 4 October 1940, JRR.

which required a move away from paternalism and towards eventual partnership. This was resented by many of the junior officers.[12] As Norvall Mitchell, Hyde's successor as Administrator of Bastar State (1940–42) wrote to him:

> The difficulty is to grasp firmly the anthropological principles of administration and not to let higher authority or outside influences loosen one's grasp . . . though I cannot say how long the Administrator, whoever he may be, will be able to stand between the State and the subversive forces which are continually getting at it. It is really tragic that the GOI and their representatives should be the chief of these forces.[13]

In other words, the anthropologist–administrators often saw themselves and like minded colonial officers as the only hope for the people. There could be differences of opinion among them as well, for instance between Elwin and Hyde over the latter's alleged support for Roman Catholic missionaries in Mandla. But the 'anthropology' which they espoused was one which would enable 'better government' through knowledge of tribal culture and customs. They almost all subscribed to a functionalist perspective. While there is very little explicit theorizing even in Elwin, the only full-time anthropologist of them all, it is clear from all the talk of 'integrated wholes' and 'degradation' following contact with Hindus and others, that societies were seen as bounded wholes, with each aspect, religion, performance etc. contributing to this.

By contrast, some of the earliest thinking on the issue among professional sociologists/anthropologists showed a keen awareness of the problems involved in dealing with the tribal question in this way. The work of G.S. Ghurye, Bose, Srinivas and others on pan-Indian links, although in some cases coming out of a nationalist perspective, predates many of the later critiques of the concept of 'tribes'. Similarly, the work that came out of the Rhodes-Livingston Institute (RLI) in Northern Rhodesia in the 1940s — on urbanization, migration, 'customary' political institutions and law — was, in its awareness of the impact of colonialism and capitalism, far in advance of the 'anthropology'

[12] Spear (1978:185).
[13] Norvall Mitchell to Hyde, Deputy Commissioner, Mandla, 28 September, 1941, Hyde Papers, Box 8 File C.

professed by Elwin and Hyde. One of the more novel features
of the RLI's work was the focus on the present, rather than a
reconstruction of the past. Despite their protestations, this is
what the functionalists were implicitly doing.[14]

The well-known mutual symbiosis between functional anthropology under colonialism and the policy of indirect rule is also
relevant here. Anthropologists supported indirect rule as a way
of maintaining native customs. Indirect rule built on small-scale
units such as tribes and villages, which anthropologists had
constructed as the basic building blocks of society.[15] As Asad
has pointed out, a picture of an integrated, consensual polity
could only be achieved by leaving out the presence of colonialism as the ultimate arbiter of local power.[16] In addition,
Adas lists several different factors that went into the revival of
indirect rule in the early twentieth century. This included the
need to economize on resources and manpower; a growing
admiration for tribal societies as a result of earlier anthropological work; a faith in social evolutionism leading to a belief in
the need for different types of governance for people at different
stages; the example of earlier traditions of indirect rule as regards
princely states in India; and finally, the need to shore up
indigenous elites and potential collaborators in the face of
growing democratization at home and in the colonies.[17]

Indirect Rule as a Form of Protection

In the period between 1927–47, several reforms were introduced
in Bastar aimed at ameliorating the factors responsible for the
rebellion of 1910. Some administrators were more critical than
others of their own government's responsibility for the plight
of the Indian tribes in general, which was one of poverty and
landlessness. Hutton for instance, wrote that, 'far from being
of immediate benefit to the primitive tribes, the establishment
of British rule in India did most of them much more harm
than good.'[18] Grigson was even more alive to this fact. He noted

[14] Vincent (1990:276–82).
[15] Anderson (1968); Banaji (1970); Feuchtwang (1973:99); Stocking (1984).
[16] Talal Asad (1973a:108).
[17] Adas (1995:291–307).
[18] Hutton (1941:417).

that nistar and grazing grievances had generally arisen due to so-called reforms introduced into zamindari areas under courts of wards administration. Abolishing the zamindaris was therefore hardly an answer.[19]

But even when the problem was recognized as one of the government's doing, the solution was also seen as requiring further government action, and preferably a British government with experience and capability, which could balance the different groups in India against each other. An Indian government, it was feared, would only impose the values of the mainstream, which was defined in terms of a 'Hindu' or a 'Muslim' culture, sharply distinguished from 'tribal' culture. In the process, the large number of scheduled castes who took an active part in community life in areas like Bastar or Chotanagpur were written out of existence. Groups like Pankas, Maharas, Rauts, Ghasias, Kumhars etc. would define themselves as Hindu, or Kabirpanthi — yet they too worshipped the same village Gods, celebrated the same festivals, and suffered from similar problems such as lack of access to forests. In proposing his reforms for Bastar, Hyde argued that:

These primitives have more in common with African tribes than they have with people in other parts of India such as the plains of Bengal, the Punjab or Maharashtra . . . I do not think that 'self government' outside the village or tribe has ever entered their heads. It is obvious that what is needed here is a form of protectorate and this can only be achieved by a benevolent autocracy.[20]

He examined various options — representative assemblies as had been introduced in other princely states (Praja Sabhas and Praja Mandals), tribal self-rule and rule by the (British) government. Of the three, according to him only the last would work. The more 'cunning' among the tribals would dominate representative bodies, the majority would not be interested in or able to cope with formulating broad policy and 'the first demand of such a body would undoubtedly be for the right of unrestricted felling of trees, the abolition of forest reserves and the encouragement of shifting cultivation.'[21] Part of Hyde's distaste for representative

[19] Grigson (1993:365).
[20] Hyde to Major Webb, Pol. Agent, Chattisgarh States, 23 March, 1939, Hyde Papers, Box 8, File A.
[21] Ibid.

institutions stemmed from his extreme hatred for the Indian National Congress, which he once described as a Nazi party with Gandhi as its dictator.[22] In part, his objections were due to the Congress refusal to co-operate with the British war effort after 1942. The Congress was not the only culprit in this; British elementary school teachers, trade unions and socialists also suffered his ire for their pacifism and opposition to empire.[23] Hyde was perhaps extreme in his views, but his attitude towards the war and towards Congress was quite common among the British civil servants of his time.[24] In short, the British position on elections among tribes was partly a defensive measure against the inroads of the nationalist struggle. The same feature underlay indirect rule in Africa.[25]

At the same time, there was also a specific belief in the inability of tribals to handle representative institutions. Grigson argued that 'anything that smacks of formal election by voting should be avoided like the plague'. He described his experience of tribals voting in the Central Provinces as 'pathetic processions of bewildered aboriginals into the polling booths, of the meaning of which they had not the foggiest conception. Some came because it was the Sirkar's order, some 'to worship Gandhi'. None of the voters went from the forest villages in some districts, because they said they had had no order to do so from the Ranger.'[26] Elwin, likewise, added his voice to the general chorus of disapproval regarding tribal suffrage and instead agreed with Hyde and Mitchell that protection was the need. But he too despaired of the prospects: 'All our efforts and love and knowledge will be swept away in a few hours when the Nationalist Hindu governments come back to power.'[27] In short, there was

[22] Hyde to Commr. Jubbulpore Division, 28 December, 1940, Hyde Papers, Box 8, File E.

[23] Secret and Personal letter from Hyde to a Brigadier, Longlech, 17 June 1943, Hyde Papers, Box 8, File E.

[24] Hunt and Harrison (1980:179-226).

[25] Roberts (1990:34); Chanock (1985:27).

[26] Grigson, Note on Political Reforms, Chindwara, 20 July 1940, Hyde Papers, Box 10, File 5. There was a limited franchise under the Government of India Act, 1935, allowing for elected provincial legislatures and some elected local government bodies.

[27] Elwin to Hyde, November 6, 1940, Box 2, Hyde Papers.

complete unanimity on the fact that the tribals must be protected, and only by the British. Casting about for a suitable
model of administration, Hyde argued that the American model
of reserves would not do 'as so much penetration had already
taken place before we took charge of the administration'.[28]

The idea of having a special class of area for tribal people,
with a different framework of laws from that in the rest of
the country had first been espoused in the Scheduled Districts
Act of 1874. This was followed by the Montague-Chelmsford
Report of 1918, the GOI Act of 1919, and the GOI Act of
1935, each of which successively refined the categories and
modalities of exclusion.[29] More specifically, under rules framed
for the Santhal, Kol and Paharia areas, civil and criminal
offences were to be handled by tribal headmen, provided of
course that they did not violate British norms of morality and
justice.[30] As such, these experiments were the direct precursors
of the Bastar panchayat policy of 1932. Strangely, however,
these were never mentioned by Hyde, Grigson or for that
matter any of the other administrator–anthropologists of the
time. Suggesting the Manipur administration as a model, J.P.
Mills, then Secretary to the Government of Assam, asked if it
might be possible to 'give fairly 'advanced' reforms to the
civilized areas of the State in return for maintaining paternal
rule over the less civilized?'[31]

Attempting to show how different Bastar was from the rest
of India, Grigson asserted that 'for conditions in Bastar the real
parallel is England before the Roman Conquest and not India
in the twentieth century'.[32] For Hyde, however, the African model
of indirect rule seemed the obvious choice and Lugard and
Huxley were his inspirations:

There is as far as I know in India no suitable administration on which
to model Bastar. . . . Conditions in Bastar are in many ways more

[28] 'The Administration and the Aboriginal', Note for a talk by a ES Hyde,
Hyde Papers, Box 8, File A.
[29] Rao (1968)
[30] Ghurye (1963:70-9); Jha (1987).
[31] J.P. Mills, to Hyde, 15 April 1940, Hyde Papers, Box 10, File 5.
[32] Grigson, Note on Political Reform, 20 July 1940, Hyde Papers, Box 10,
File 5.

similar to Africa than to other parts of this country. British administrations in Africa are generally held to be very much more superior and
better suited to primitive peoples than those in India. The most notable
feature in the African Colonies and Protectorates is the principle of
indirect rule.[33]

As applied to Bastar this meant retaining the Raja as a figurehead
and working through tribal headmen and 'moulding' them into
'channels of progressive change'.[34] Yet Hyde recognized that the
African model could not be entirely duplicated in Bastar since
various aspects of administration (land revenue, forest, excise,
education, police) were centralized and he believed that they
should remain so in the interests of greater efficiency. Moreover,
the tribals were not to be trusted with forest or excise matters,
except for some control over their village forests. Finally, differences in the population, the distances, and lack of education,
all required that 'agencies of indirect rule should be in relatively
compact localized areas, such as parganas'.[35] This really left only
the judicial administration, and Hyde's major efforts towards
reform of the administration therefore boiled down to supporting the panchayat scheme that Grigson had proposed, and that
his successor, D.R. Rutnam, had introduced in 1932. How these
worked in practice will be dealt with in the next section.

   To sum up thus far, in defining their vision of 'anthropologically minded administration', the Bastar administrators drew
upon the experience of the British empire. The ideal was mostly
conceived in terms of the preservation of indigenous culture
and the emphasis was on forms of administration that could
ensure this. Some variant of indirect rule was therefore inevitably
popular with them, which in Bastar took the form of reviving
'indigenous' councils, viz. village and pargana panchayats. The
connection between the creation of customary law, indirect rule
and the gesture towards anthropology in administration was
common to Africa and to certain parts of India, basically those
which had been designated 'tribal' like Bastar and the North
East. However, as Chanock notes for Africa,

[33] Hyde, Note on the Proposal to Introduce Administrative Reforms in
Bastar State. Hyde papers, Box 8, File C.
[34] Grigson (1991:297).
[35] Hyde, Note on the proposal to introduce administrative reforms in
Bastar state, Hyde Papers, Box 8, File C.

Both administrators and anthropologists were conceptually ill-equipped to realise that by then the African legal conceptions that appeared to be current had been formed out of forty years of conflict with colonial government, by the economic and social transformations resulting from the colonial law and by new divisions in African society.[36]

In some ways, the experience of countries like Brazil would have been more appropriate to the situation in India as perceived by Hyde et al, than the African situation. In the latter, the 'tribes' are not distinct from any 'mainstream'. In Brazil, as in India, the debates over policy towards 'Indians' formulated the issues of protection or integration in terms of a 'mainstream' versus indigenous groups who need to be 'developed'.[37] Since Brazil had never been part of the same empire, however, these debates did not enter into colonial arguments about India.

The Codification of 'Custom': Village and Pargana Panchayats

By the 1920s, the judicial system whose early beginnings helped to prompt the 1876 rebellion, was well entrenched. The panchayat reform, touted as the major instrument of indirect rule in Bastar, involved depriving the regular courts of jurisdiction over seventeen sections of the Indian Penal Code, and giving village panchayats the power to impose fines in such cases up to Rs 25. The sections dealt with simple assault, theft etc. and civil disputes arising out of marriage, adultery, and tribal and caste customs, so long, of course, as they were not 'barbarous'. Appeals against the decision of the village panchayats were to be made to newly formalized pargana panchayats, consisting of a pargana majhi and four village headmen. The village watchmen were to report the decisions on a regular basis to the police, who would have the power to decide that any particular case be re-tried under regular courts. In such cases, the courts would take the panchayat's decision and fine levied into account and reverse the panchayat's order if necessary. The fines

[36] Chanock (1985:49).
[37] Davis (1977:2).

levied were to be spent on village improvement works.[38] Grigson justified his reforms in the following words:

It seems to me that some such system would at once preserve the best features of tribal political organizations, give us full knowledge of tribal feelings and practices with respect to offences against the community, save the people the harassment of protracted trials by the regular Courts at great distances from their villages, as well as the harassment of police investigation and would ensure decisions being taken which would command the confidence of the people. At the same time by insisting on all decisions being reported to the police, and retaining the reserve power of ordering retrial by the regular Courts, we could prevent the Panchayats from ordering barbarous or tyrannical sentences, and persuade them gradually to reform anything that is wrong in traditional tribal customs.[39]

The reform would also financially benefit the state by saving the police and courts extra work. In order for the panchayat scheme to work, however, the existing confusion of custom, the absence of pargana heads in some places, inconvenient pargana boundaries and similar problems had to be smoothened out. Parganas themselves did not exist on a uniform basis throughout the state. As Grigson noted: 'The parganas of modern Bastar include some obvious former garhs, some obvious barhons . . . and some obvious old tribal clan units'.[40] Some parganas on the other hand, he acknowledged that he had created himself, with the result that 'the word pargana is now used of any sub-division of a tahsil or zamindari in which villages are grouped under a group headman or pargana majhi.'[41]

Among the Hill Marias or Abujhmarias, the parganas were clan areas. The hereditary clan headman or pargana gaita was formally appointed by the state as pargana majhi, but he could only work through consultation with the village headmen and elders of his area. Tasks, whether for the state (e.g. road building, setting up officials' camps) or for clan festivals, were distributed among villages by common consent, rather than orders given.

---

[38] xxvii-4 A part i, Note from Grigson, Administrator, BS, 19 December 1929, JRR.
[39] Ibid.
[40] Grigson (1991:33).
[41] Ibid.

Any attempt to abuse that authority was resisted.[42] In the south, among Bison Horn Marias, Dhurwas and Dorlas, as against clan areas, parganas represented 'former petty kingdoms or garhs of forgotten chiefs, or divisions of the early medieval Telanga kingdoms of Barsur, Dantewara or Bhairamgarh.'[43] The pargana majhis in these areas were possibly descendants of the original chief or his appointed headmen, or as in the case of Hamirgarh pargana, displaced the original headman for reasons of the latter's unfitness (*see* chapter 1). The pargana headmen in the Bison Horn areas, did not have the same authority as in the Abujhmarh hills, and village headmen exercized more immediate authority. In some places, like Bijapur or Kutru, there was no tradition of pargana panchayats at all, or anything other than village panchayats. The new appellate powers given to the pargana majhi by the state, it was hoped, would change all this.[44]

In the drive towards 'custom', change was necessary. For one, the selection of pargana heads was standardized. Pargana headmen were visualized by Grigson and Hyde as an important link between the state administration and the tribes. They were to be chosen, subject to confirmation by the state, by the village headmen, i.e. elections took place annually in the tahsildar's presence. Under Hyde, it was proposed to make their term last three years. The office was generally hereditary and 'fully recognized by the State which gives its holder remuneration and the right to attend and take a prominent part in Darbars etc.'[45] Thus the participation of majhis in Dussehra was formalized into a 'right' conferred by the administration, rather than an intrinsic contribution to the legitimation of the polity, as in pre-colonial days. Secondly, the pargana boundaries had to be fixed to correspond as far as possible with *patwari* circles, forest ranges and police station circles so that the pargana majhis had to deal with only one functionary.[46] However in Abujhmarh (where parganas were constituted on the basis of clan boundaries) the attempt to reorganize boundaries was strongly resisted, with the

[42] Ibid.:289.
[43] Ibid.:290-1.
[44] Ibid.:291.
[45] Hyde to Major Webb, 23 March 1939, Hyde Papers, Box 8, File A.
[46] LI, 6A part II, Memo on Boundaries of Parganas, 3 June 1930, JRR.

Marias stating that if a village was transferred to another pargana, the people would not obey their new majhi.[47]

The question of overlapping constituencies between village and pargana headmen also had to be sorted out if the pargana was to function as a true appellate body. For instance, in cases where pargana majhis also worked as headmen and revenue collectors in the villages where they lived, the latter function had to be taken away. But since commission from this provided their income, alternative remuneration had to be found.[48] Rules were framed to ensure that pargana majhis did not hear cases in which they were interested parties, either as a member of the original panchayat or as one of the persons named.[49] But this is unlikely to have been of much value, since it would have been rare to take a majhi to panchayat. More importantly, decisions could generally be enforced only when the headman backed them. Inevitably, there were a few instances of people getting confused about the exact appellate structure, and taking their cases to the pargana majhi first. Grigson seems to have been aware of this fact:

It is no use expecting formalism from such unlettered tribal tribunals; the rules as issued perhaps err a little on the side of formalism, and the panchayats must not be expected to follow them too strictly or blamed if at times they exceed their nominal powers, so long as rough, ready and cheap justice, within the comprehension of the villagers, results.[50]

But at the same time, there was an implicit assumption that what the panchayats would deliver was 'customary law'. In fact, however, while jurisdiction over some cases was given over to 'customary' institutions, these institutions were themselves transformed as far as possible to resemble the structure of the formal legal system. As Fallers noted, 'Customary law is not so much

[47] LI, 6A part II, Settlement, Corres. reg. the settlement of boundaries of parganas in each tahsil, Note by E.S. Hyde, 21 January 1937, JRR.

[48] In the khalsa portion of the state, pargana majhis and their assistants got Rs 24 and Rs 18 p.a. In Sukma zamindari, the majhis got paid Rs 12 p.a. and the assistant majhi in Chindgarh, known as Chalki, was paid Rs 6 p.a.. LI, 6A, JRR.

[49] XXVII Judicial, 4 A part II, Memo No. 2701, 29 July 1935 — Sec. C, Rule 1 of BS Panchayat Gen. Circular no. 9 ; XXVII, 4A, Part II, Sec. I Amendment, JRR.

[50] Grigson (1991:297).

a kind of law as a kind of legal situation which develops in imperial or quasi-imperial contexts in which dominant legal systems recognize and support the local law of politically subordinate communities.'[51] Chanock, Sally Falk Moore, and others have extended this observation to show that the local law itself was created anew under this situation.[52] But 'custom' itself did not exist as some 'authentic' or historically static pre-colonial practice before its colonial encounter. As the pargana example shows, the concept was shifting and was linked to state formation even prior to the British.

'Customary law' is also notorious for its gloss over 'local servitudes of gender, age and status', and its assumption that because it is 'customary' it is thereby acceptable to all.[53] In Bastar, there were two important consequences of the limited nature of the reforms: first, the introduction of deception and uncertainty at all levels of the legal process; second, a further change in the balance of power between local groups and outsiders accompanied by the depoliticization of the existing system of pargana majhis and village headmen.

The Reforms in Practice: Domination and Deception

As a system of indirect rule, one creating trust between the people and the administration, and as a method of saving people from the police and courts, the codification of pargana panchayats did not have all the intended effects. In part, the lack of desired results occurred because reality did not match rhetoric. The devolution of jurisdiction was limited — only seventeen sections were transferred and minor ones at that. Thus in 1943, Elwin described:

... the remarkable, but not unusual picture of tribesmen still deeply attached to their own ethical and penal system, still regulating their lives by their own laws of ownership, partition and inheritance, but unable to invoke any sanctions to enforce them and compelled in time of need to turn to a foreign code that was made without reference to their traditions and the conditions under which they live.[54]

[51] Fallers (1969).
[52] See Starr and Collier (1989); Vincent (1990:383).
[53] Anderson (1990:165).
[54] Elwin (1977:36).

This picture of the bewildered native dealing with the formal colonial legal system is a common but evocative one. As Grigson argued, the presence of the police was counterproductive. The pressure of having to feed them when they descended on villages for investigations, the labour involved in transporting supplies to the police station and performing additional work there and the time and expense involved in lengthy judicial proceedings far away from the village, all led to a greater concealment of cases than otherwise.[55] Elwin records cases where people committed suicide rather than face the police, regardless of whether they were innocent or not.[56] Hyde noted of several cases he tried that the matter had initially been concealed by the village panchayat, including the pargana majhi, and that some cases of murder had also been compromised. In one such case, he noted disappointedly that the pargana majhi's actions 'are clearly not compatible with the position he holds.' Witnesses turning hostile, especially when the case involved someone powerful within the village, remained a common occurrence.[57]

Even today, where villagers report cases to the police, it is not because they genuinely think that this is the proper sphere to refer them. Rather, it is out of fear that if the cases are not reported, the police will harass them. They collectively make choices — reporting the case if it seems to be the lesser evil, otherwise concealing the crime and settling the case among themselves. Cases come to light, however, when one of the parties is unhappy with the decision and wants to use the court to override it. Thus the authority of the panchayats is gradually eroded, but without the authority or legitimacy of the courts being increased. Not surprisingly, there is now increased scope for deception in intra-village relations as well. One such case told to me by the women of Kumargaon village in 1993, illustrates the complicity of the kotwar in suppressing cases:

One summer night, a woman left her sleeping husband outside and went in to sleep. In the middle of the night a man slipped inside, locked the door, and made love to her twice. Somewhat later, her

[55] Grigson (1991:284-5).
[56] Elwin (1977:193-6).
[57] Descriptions of cases tried by Hyde, Hyde papers, Box 1. *See also* Elwin (1977:174, 185-94).

husband knocked on the door asking to be let in. She called out sleepily, asking who it was. He replied: 'Your husband', whereupon she asked in surprise, 'Then, who is this man snoring next to me?' When she got up to open the door, the fake 'husband' rushed out. There followed an exciting chase in which the fake husband hit the real husband with a stick, but the wife managed to whack him back.

While the husband was convinced that his wife had suffered a genuine mistake, the other village women were loudly sceptical: 'How could she not recognize her own husband,' they asked, 'that too — twice!' The couple tried to call a panchayat, but the intruder had bribed the kotwar, and he obligingly sabotaged it by not informing anyone. With the result that the panchayat was called three times, but no one attended. Eventually the couple reported it as rape to the police. The village women may have been rightly doubtful, especially if the intruder was a better lover. But the point is that the woman would not have got a fair hearing in the village. The notion of truth invariably emerging in village arenas in the light of face-to-face, long-term social relations, as opposed to the litigiousness and lies induced by the formal legal system, has long since become invalid, if it ever existed. The panchayat is not the first or only occasion when the case is aired — there is always much spadework and behind-the-scenes canvassing by the parties involved.

It is not uncommon for entire hamlets to wrongly accuse other hamlets in order to avoid police harassment themselves. In another case, a man hung himself on a tree outside Chevaras, a hamlet of Kukanar. In such situations, including accidental death, it is common for the police to demand money from the villagers, threatening to arrest them all with conspiracy to murder. The elders of Chevaras therefore untied the corpse and hung it up on a tree outside Bodaras. The Bodaras people in turn untied him and buried him in another village two km away. Although these are two recent examples, they bear enough similarity to cases mentioned by Elwin or Hyde in the '30s and '40s to doubt the functioning of the reforms even then.

The use of fines presents another problematic issue. When the reforms were first introduced, the panchayats rarely spent the fines levied on village improvement works as they were supposed to, much to the dismay of the administrators. Instead panchayat funds were commonly spent on village festivals or used by the panchayat members *(panchs)* for drinking or holding a feast, with some of the money being given to the complainant. In a list of 11 cases decided in different villages of Konta tahsil, the panchs 'misappropriated' the fine in all of them.[58] The village panchayat of Narainpur, on the other hand, took their new . judicial powers too seriously. They spent the nearly fifty rupees collected in fines on purchasing Hindu Law books instead of digging wells or repairing roads, to the irritation of the tahsildar, who could not see the use they had for them. But perhaps in a situation where the courts practiced Hindu law and the number of immigrants had increased, this made eminent sense.[59] Today, the fines levied for social misdemeanors such as marrying out of caste or criminal offences, including murder, range in the thousands, (up to Rs 10, 000), but the amount reported as levied is nominal.[60]

In short, since village and pargana panchayats existed in the 'shadow of the law', they could not function as significant alternatives to the formal legal system.[61] Under the pressure of police harassment, economic compulsion and local power politics, village panchayats do not automatically guarantee 'justice', even in relatively egalitarian places like Bastar. People continue to pursue their own agendas in order to negotiate local village politics, sometimes using the state in order to do so, and at other times, maintaining a degree of autonomy from it.

Changing the Balance of Power:
Tribes and the Mainstream

By assigning the Majhis carefully specified powers, the political structure of village and pargana majhis which had been crucial in organizing the rebellions of 1876 and 1910 was reduced to a mere cog in the judicial system. As in other adivasi regions, in the process of subordinating the political power of the local people to that of the British government, they were also subordinated to other classes. Land laws allowing for commodification and alienation of land, excise laws allowing liquor outstills and

---

[58] xxvii, 4A part ii, Village and Pargana Panchayats, JRR.
[59] xxvii, 4A part ii, SDO, Jagdalpur to Administrator, 18 March 1935, JRR.
[60] Sharma (1990:xxi); M.A. Iqbal pers. com.; Field notes, 1991-93.
[61] Galanter, quoted in Anderson (1990:171).

making home distillation a crime, forest laws allowing for commercial exploitation of forests – all benefitted certain classes and communities against others. The restriction of judicial powers that could be applied by panchayats to outsiders, played the same role.

A critical problem was caused in Bastar by the presence of immigrants who refused to be bound by custom. Officials were exempt from the panchayats, while traders, especially in places where they were concentrated, preferred to go directly to the administrator rather than the village panchayat. In such rare cases as they did apply to the village panchayat, they only accepted the decision if it was in their favour.[62] The administration eventually decided to withdraw village panchayat jurisdiction for non-aboriginals in such villages, on the grounds that traders took advantage of village courts to obtain decrees for claims which were either time-barred or in which extraordinary rates of interest had been charged. The result of this was that while the administration may have been able to provide protection towards tribals in such cases, it also meant that the authority of village panchayats was set aside in cases where the formal legal system did not recognize a fault, but which was nevertheless a violation of community law. The restriction of cases tried under IPC Sec. 494, 497 and 498 concerning bigamy and adultery, only to aboriginal or semi-aboriginals, and the exclusion of state servants from the purview of village panchayats, meant that local communities were powerless to resist this major source of exploitation in their own way. Even where informal panchayats were convened, they had no effective sanction, and sometimes the solutions proposed were inadequate to the changed circumstances.[63]

In sum, the tribals' own means of protecting themselves, their own political organization was rendered toothless. They were cast in the role of perennial victims vis-a-vis the mainstream culture. Protection by the British government or the Indian state

---

[62] XXVII, 4A Part II, Application by the Head Panch Thadgu of Geedam, to Tahsildar, approximately 1930s, JRR.

[63] *See* for instance B.D. Sharma's attempt at holding panchayats to restore conjugal rights to adivasi women abandoned by employees of the Kirandul mines. Sharma (1979); PUCL (1989:19). *See also* Mohanty (1987), for the theme of tribal girls being lured and abandoned by outsiders.

which followed, was thus seen as the only solution to their problems. The role of colonialism in changing the balance of power between different communities was ignored in the process.

Administration in Bastar: Overall Appraisal

The anthropologist–administrators left their mark in other ways as well. Shifting cultivation was a hotly debated issue. Grigson and Hyde were opposed to any forest reservation or restrictions on shifting cultivation in Abujhmarh on the grounds that the degradation of the forest due to this cause was much overrated and that the traditional way of life of the Abujhmarhias must be preserved. In this they were opposed both by the Bastar Forest Officer, for whom it was 'a moot question to decide whether the preservation of Marias should take precedence over the reservation of valuable II and III quality sal forest,'[64] and by other administrators of the state, such as Mitchell who felt that too great an isolation left aboriginals with no preparation for inevitable intrusions.[65]

Some valuable schemes were started during this period, such as the Ulnar Nistar Forest scheme, which provided for the protection of village forests by the villagers themselves (who paid watchmen among themselves to do the job), in return for the exemption of begar.[66] The Ulnar scheme, though very successful, and a precursor to the current Joint Forest Management schemes, was dropped after the 1950s. Bisaha or the practice of obtaining supplies compulsorily from villages by touring officials, either free or at less than the market rates, was prohibited. Efforts were made to standardize the system of purchase and to reduce the incidence of begar, though the peasants still had to pay for public works through increased cesses. The kabadi or bond service system was made illegal.[67] The thekedari system which introduced alien thekedars/malguzars was also abolished under Grigson, and

[64] xxiii 18 E, Part iii, Chief Forest Officer, to the Admin., BS, 21 July 1934, JRR.

[65] Norvall Mitchell, 'Memoirs: Years That have Ended,' written in 1975–76, IOL Mss Eur D 944.

[66] xxiii, 31/B part i, WP, Ulnar Nistari Forest, JRR.

[67] BS General Manual, 1932, Jagdalpur, General Circular no. 3 (Bisaha), Supplement to no. 3 (Begar and Bisaha), no. 7 (Kabadi).

efforts were made to restore the task of revenue collection to the local headman.

The net outcome of these reforms, however limited, was that the resulting system of administration was considerably less intrusive than in other parts of India. Bastar was often cited by anthropologists and administrators as a success story of the isolationist or protectionist position. While comparing the Bastar administration's effect on its tribal population to that of administrations in other parts of India, Elwin wrote:

Among the Bastar Gonds, tribal life and organization still retains its old vitality . . . (it) is an integrated whole, it makes sense, there are no gaps in it, it has no insulated spots, everything is regulated and functions in its proper place. But go to a semi-civilized village in Mandla or Balaghat. The people might belong to another race. Servile, obsequious, timid, of poor physique, their tribal life is all to pieces. . . . The souls of the people are soiled and grimy with the dust of passing motor buses.[68]

He goes on to attribute this situation to Bastar's administration being conducted on anthropologically sound grounds and quotes 'an intelligent Bastar Gond' as saying, 'in Chattisgarh, the people are ruled by the District Council which is full of our oppressors, the banias and money lenders, but here we are protected and loved by the Dewan Saheb who saves us from our enemies.'[69] As late as 1981, Haimendorf noted that the economic independence and cohesion of the village community in Bastar still compared favourably to that of the Gonds and Kolams in Adilabad district to their south. He explained this as due to

the long tradition of a liberal tribal policy in the erstwhile princely state and the one-time involvement of high-powered and anthropologically minded British administrators such as Sir Wilfred Grigson, followed by equally dedicated members of the Indian Administrative Service such as Dr B.D. Sharma.[70]

Certainly people in Bastar seem to have retained a more 'traditional' lifestyle compared to other parts of India, an

---

[68] 'Note by Verrier Elwin written at the request of the Administrator, Bastar State, on the effects of the present policy of administration of BS on the tribal population', Hyde Papers, Box 8 File A.
[69] Ibid.
[70] Furer-Haimendorf (1982:202).

impression given largely by the remaining forest cover, unlike many other regions in India where people have to go long distances in search of fuel, fodder and water, and the fact that people still worship their own Gods. At the same time, it is essential to note that this 'preservation' does not indicate an untouched nature but was itself a product of a conscious policy. As Nicholas Thomas puts it in the context of Fiji:

Indentured labour and the paternalistic insulation of native society from the market were, in terms of the colony's socioeconomic structure, two sides of the same coin; hence the logic of the shocking gulf between the violent punishment in plantations and coolie lines, and the indirect and paternalistic discipline in the villages over which (the administration's) net was being cast.[71]

Moreover, a realistic appraisal of the extent to which these administrators were able to make a difference in the overall structure of colonialism would have to take several factors into account. In their desire to portray Bastar as a paradise of primitivism, the anthropologists and administrators ignored or underplayed several features which bore the unmistakable footprints of colonialism. It could be argued though, at least in Grigson's case, that this was strategic and part of his battle to wrest protectionist policies from the higher administration rather than wilful blindness. For instance, he was conscious of the rapid changes, including the heavy labour recruitment that sent people from central India to the Assam tea plantations. The economy of the nearby state of Jashpur was said to be largely dependent on remittances from tea garden coolies.[72] In the mid-1920s the Political Agent noted that due to the activities of the recruiters in Bastar, 'no less than 28 villages in the Kutru Zamindari and 6 villages in the Bhopalpatnam Zamindari have become entirely depopulated.'[73] In 1938, the administration decided to legalize the process by setting up a recruiting depot for the Assam Tea Gardens at Jagdalpur. One of the considerations that had delayed the formal depot, was that it would open up state subjects to

[71] Thomas (1990:158).
[72] Grigson (1991:18); Report on the Constitutional Position of the States of Bihar and Orissa and Central Provinces, by Sir A.C. Lothian, Acc no. 206, CRR, NAI.
[73] Bates and Carter (1992:228).

foreign and disruptive ideas about electoral self representation.[74] In 1941, when the initial contract for the depot was renewed, 661 adults were recruited and 87 agents appointed. By 1946-7, the number of annual recruits had increased to 1300.[75] In Kukanar alone, there were at least four families which had come back from Assam, and one young man spoke to his mother in Assamese!

Similarly, the two World Wars had an impact on the local economy, even in 'remote' Bastar. In 1942 a state branch of the National War Front was set up and 'recruiting officers from British India were given every assistance'. There was an even more massive movement of materials. In his memoirs, Mitchell records in passing the common sight of 'the endless lines of bullock carts and lorries carrying north to Raipur the varying sizes of teak and sal for railway sleepers or for jetty piles in the Persian Gulf.'[76] A recent Forest Department Working Plan for Bastar noted that 'during the Second World War particularly after the occupation of Burma by the Japanese forces, there was a liberal supply of teak timber from all over the State. No marking or felling rules were observed for this supply.'[77]

Despite the efforts of the higher administration to shield aboriginals from land alienation or corrupt contractors, land transfers continued to take place. This was particularly common in Jagdalpur tehsil where the number of immigrants was higher and the land had greater value. The usual procedure was to have the tenant surrender his land to the headman, who would then reallot it to the purchaser, often through the revenue courts, and usually for some commission.[78] The felling and sale of teak trees on tenant lands during WWII, was another example where practice belied intent. On the grounds that shade or falling leaves would damage standing crops, tenants were allowed to apply to the revenue department to cut down teak trees on their lands. These were then sold to contractors with nominal payoffs to the forest department. Once a tenant's teak trees had been

---

[74] F. No. 443-P/38 of 1938, Pol. Dept. Pol. Branch, NAI.

[75] AAR, 1941, 1946-47, JRR.

[76] Mitchell, 'Memoirs', IOL, Mss Eur, D 944.

[77] WP, Central Bastar (1988:150).

[78] Ramadhyani (1942:24-5).

depleted, he/she was encouraged by contractors to colonize fresh lands, and repeat the process.[79]

Finally, Bastar's relative happiness needs to be placed against the background of the intense agitation in the neighbouring feudatory states of Orissa (e.g. Nilgiri, Dhenkenal) under the aegis of the Prajamandals.[80] Complaints common to the whole belt included high rents, arbitrary cesses, begar, monopolies on everyday items like salt, kerosine, betel leaves, the absence of a right to sell produce like lac or tendu from their own trees, or the hides of their own dead cattle to whomever they pleased, the large number of reserved species which limited nistar rights, high grazing dues etc.[81] Echoes of these occasionally found their way to Bastar, though they were generally dealt with quickly by the local administration. For instance, there were several Halba meetings in Antagarh and Kondagaon tahsils in March 1939 to protest against grazing dues, after they had been abolished in Kanker.[82] More importantly, the Orissa struggles and the overall nationalist context prompted a series of enquiries into conditions in the feudatory states and khalsa zamindaries including Bastar. In most cases, the reports emphasized the lack of clear rules and the arbitrary powers of the zamindars and local village lessees, and recommended a standardization of the legal and administrative system.[83]

To sum up, the differentiation of princely states from British India served two purposes during this period. While elsewhere in India, the British sought to portray their rule as 'advanced' compared to the backward princely states, in places like Bastar, that very backwardness was put to advantage as a success of indirect colonial rule — innocent tribal oases in contrast to rapacious Hindu dominance elsewhere. However, the domain of 'custom' was limited and even within that limited sphere, represented not a form of non-intervention or isolation but a

[79] WP, South Bastar, (1981:128-9).

[80] Pati (1993:108-31).

[81] Ramadhyani (1942).

[82] Fortnightly Report of the Agent, Eastern States Agency, March 1939, CRR, ESA, Acc. No. 352, NAI

[83] Ramadhyani (1942); Kamath (1941); Report by Mr J. Bowstead on the administration of the Orissa States, File No. 22 (4)-P(Confidential) of 1940, S. no. 1-25, Pol. Dept., Acc. no. 206, CRR, NAI.

different form of intervention in the shape of 'preservation'. This too was under threat from wider economic compulsions and impending political change.

The Debate over 'Tribes': Recapitulating Positions

The debate on tribal policy in India was initially defined in terms of two broad positions: isolation or protection, and assimilation. These were broadly associated with British administrators and anthropologists and Indian nationalists respectively. In the 1950's a third and middle position was articulated — controlled integration — which came to be the official Nehru policy. Right from the beginning, however, various participants claimed the moral high ground of the middle policy, and accused the others of wanting either total isolation or total assimiliation. In practice obviously, several people who were assigned to one or the other camp had much more nuanced views. Despite their differences, I club Grigson, Elwin, Hyde, Hutton, Mills and the other British anthropologist-administrators together in one group as supporters of protection, even isolation, and discuss this position under the umbrella of Elwin's writings. Elwin's position changed over time in its emphasis, and in fact it was he who drafted Nehru's tribal *panchshila* in the 1950s, advocating a non-intrusive administration that would help tribals to 'develop along their own lines'.[84] But the essential concern that a tribal 'way of life' not be submerged, remained a constant with Elwin. The nationalist position is represented through Ghurye and the debates in the constituent assembly on tribal policy.[85]

In a 1940 letter in response to social worker A.V. Thakkar's letter proposing an Aboriginal Association to help the cause of tribal welfare, Elwin divided the field up between 'Protectionists' and 'Interventionists', and distinguished between the two thus:

The Protectionist regards the aboriginal with love and reverence. He does not see him as a being on a lower level. . . . The Protectionist

[84] I thank Ramachandra Guha for alerting me to this fact. Nehru (1959); Singh (1989).
[85] See Grigson's (1993:451–2) bibliography on the isolation vs assimilation debate.

does not want to keep the aboriginals 'as they are' for ever, least of all as specimens in an Anthropological Zoo. He is keen on progress, but his problem is how to adjust the progress so that the Indian aboriginal does not suffer the disasters that have been witnessed in other lands. He would have education, but of a special kind. . . . The Interventionist on the other hand, is all for 'uplift'. . . . He has cut and dried ideas about what is good for people and he applies these indiscriminately. . . . The Interventionist has very rarely lived among the aboriginals so as to understand what they really think, though he has often visited them in order to do them good. . . . Wherever the Interventionist policy has been followed, there has been decay and degradation.[86]

His own position, as is obvious from this letter, was that of an 'out and out protectionist'. Elsewhere, Elwin divides up the tribals into four classes with reference to the degree and manner of integration into mainstream society. At one end were the most isolated groups who had retained their communal egalitarianism, while the majority were those who had lost or were losing their culture, religion and social organization under external impact, and had consequently suffered a 'loss of nerve'. Elwin's line-up of the various solutions to this 'loss of nerve' are as follows: the 'political solution' — isolation through the creation of excluded areas; the 'geographical solution' and the 'missionary solution' — both of which would result in the assimiliation of the forest and hill tribes to the plains economy and absorption within either Hinduism or Christianity. Finally there was his own protectionist solution, which was termed the 'scientific' or anthropologically certified solution. In this last, 'every tribe and every district has to be considered as a problem in itself.'[87] Unfortunately, even as chairman of the Multipurpose Tribal Blocks Committee (set up in the 1950s to appraise and channel development in areas of tribal concentration) and advisor to the North East Frontier Agency (NEFA) under the Nehru government, Elwin was able to do little to change the overall trend in the country. For instance, the new government

---

[86] Elwin, 5 October 1940, in response to a printed letter from A.V. Thakkar (Gen. Secy., Harijan Sevak Sangh), 12 September, 1940, Hyde Papers, Box 7, File D.

[87] Elwin (1943).

proved to be even more against shifting cultivation than the old, and voices like Elwin's were rare.

Ghurye differed in his formulation of the problematic, and on its solution. His book, initially titled *The Aborigines, So-called and their Future*, and later changed to *The Scheduled Tribes*, is a cogent exposition of all the various debates and constitutional provisions dealing with tribes, argued from the assimiliationist or as he later preferred to call it, 'integrationist' position.[88] In his schema, Elwin was worse than an 'isolationist' or 'pre-servationist'. Elwin, according to Ghurye, was a 'no-changer' and 'revivalist'.[89] Ghurye's own position on the problem was that it was not one of cultural submergence but a problem faced by 'backward, ignorant and exploited people' in general, and was caused not just by a Hindu takeover, but by several factors — including land laws introduced by the British, 'improvidence and ignorance of the people', and 'passion for land and higher powers of intelligence, thrift and chicanery of the money-lending classes.'[90] As far as Ghurye was concerned, the 'so-called aboriginal' was better termed a 'backward Hindu'. He points out the migrations by different tribes, the similarities in many customs between tribes and low castes, and argues for the consequent impossibility of distinguishing between the two on grounds of religion or of assigning a greater antiquity to one as compared to the other. The solution to the problem, according to Ghurye lay in 'strengthening the ties of the tribals with the other backward classes through their integration,' which was a 'matter for practical administration'.[91]

Ghurye's position has as much to commend it as to condemn it over Elwin's. Ghurye recognizes the commonality of class, exploitation and several cultural features between tribals and low castes, but the problem of cultural imperialism which Elwin and others were alive to is neglected. But rather than culture being something (a sort of treasure) that people 'have' and which they 'lose' by being overwhelmed by more powerful forces (as Elwin portrays it), people make choices about why and what they present as their 'culture'. However, what Elwin recognized

[88] Ghurye (1963:x).
[89] Ibid.:173.
[90] Ibid.:207, 126.
[91] Ibid.

and Ghurye did not was the fact that this happens in a situation of economic and ideological inequality, and hence cannot be treated as a free and unproblematic 'assimiliation'. Finally, as we saw in chapter 2, *contra* the implicit assumption in both Ghurye and Elwin, assimilation has never been a one-sided process, and what is assumed to be a given 'Hindu' culture has been created by the multiple borrowings and conscious alliances of its various practitioners — from Mother Goddess cults, from Islam or Christianity.

The debate on isolation versus integration was complicated by the fact that it took place within a specific historical and political conjuncture. Intentions and actions acquired meanings beyond their immediate context. Anything that threw doubt on the concept of India as a nation was interpreted by nationalists as a slur on the capacity of Indians for self government, and as a colonial attempt to hold on to power through a policy of divide and rule.[92] One such hotly contested issue was the policy regarding backward areas (Sec 52-A(2) of the GOI Act, 1919) and excluded areas (Sec. 91 and 92 of the GOI Act, 1935). Under the 1935 Act, certain areas (with a tribal majority) were wholly excluded from the normal purview of provincial legislatures, which by this time also had Indian members, and placed under the personal rule of the governors of the provinces. In other 'partially excluded areas', while ministers could initiate policies, governors had special powers to make, modify or repeal legislation for these areas. Whether the policy of excluded areas was fuelled by an unwarranted distrust of Indians, or whether, as Grigson argued, it was a genuine remedy to the absence of past protection,[93] needs to be seen against the background of the ideology and policy of independent India.

The Policies of Independent India

At the dawn of independence, the situation regarding policy towards tribals was a complex one. On the one hand, there was the potential for change built up by the long history of popular resistance to colonialism, the serious concern shown

[92] Ghurye (1963:129); Elwin (1943:23-4).
[93] Grigson (1993:424-8).

by several public figures to improve the plight of tribals, and the drive towards a welfare state, at least as embodied in the preamble to the Constitution and its Directive Principles. On the other hand, the class structures and the party system that would determine the existence and form of the future nation-state were already firmly entrenched, and colonial policies on the maintenance of 'law and order', basic land and forest rights were continued, but now in the name of a new 'Indian state'. The focus here is on the Constituent Assembly debates on the Fifth and Sixth Schedules of the Constitution in order to bring out how 1947 was indeed a critical moment in Indian history.

The Fifth Schedule deals with the administration of scheduled areas and scheduled tribes in all parts of the country except for the North-East, and makes provision for a Tribes Advisory Council and certain laws to prevent alienation of land to non-tribals and exploitation by moneylenders. The Sixth Schedule deals only with the states in what was formerly undivided Assam. These required a different set of laws, owing to the fact that these areas had been isolated by government policy to a greater extent than other tribal areas in the country, the tribals were in the majority and their culture was deemed quite different from that of the rest of India. The Advisory Committee on Fundamental Rights and Minorities set up by the Constituent Assembly in turn designated three sub-committees in 1947. One, chaired by Gopinath Bardoloi, was to examine the tribal and excluded areas in Assam; another, chaired by A.V. Thakkar, was to study the excluded and partially excluded areas 'other-than-Assam', while the third was to consider the 'tribal areas' in the North West Frontier Province. The proposals of the first two committees were incorporated in the draft Constitution of February 1948.[94] These committees had assigned much more power to the Tribes Advisory Council as against the merely consultative role that it later acquired in the version finally adopted by the Assembly. Partly, this emasculation of the council was due to the feeling of both the drafting committee and members of the Constituent Assembly that given their state of 'backwardness', tribes would not be able to cope with complicated legislation or administration, and hence should not be given decisive powers,[95] and partly due to

[94] Rao (1968).
[95] Ibid.:580.

the sustained objections raised by several members of provincial legislatures, who felt their powers were being circumscribed.

To a large extent, the debates on the schedules, which took place on 5 and 6 September, 1949, followed the parameters set by the protection versus integration controversy. But aboriginal advancement was no longer seen in terms of preserving a sphere of 'custom' — now the central problem that exercized the minds of the Constitutent Assembly was one of reconciling the diversity of custom with the 'national life of the country'. The point that the tribals were not one homogenous whole as compared to the rest of India, but differentiated by many factors — geographical position, language, religious and social practices, and economic mode — was reiterated. There was also discussion on the appropriate term to be used for tribals, and whether adivasi (original inhabitant) would give the erroneous impression of greater antiquity than other groups.[96] A crucial difference in these debates was that government responsibility for development was widely recognized, i.e. a positive duty to ensure sufficient funds for education, health etc. rather than simply the negative duty of protecting tribals from exploitation or alienation, which had been the hallmark of the earlier excluded areas policy. Hence, stress was laid on the leading role of the central government, which alone would have the funds to initiate such development.

But at the same time as the Schedules and the discussions that accompanied them were motivated by practical considerations, the debates also reveal some startling displays of condescension, if not virulent racism, especially towards the people of the North East, of whom there was little knowledge or care. There is little to chose from between some of the views expressed there and the kind of debates on the issue that occurred in the British parliament. One common viewpoint is reflected by the following words of Professor Shibban Lal Saksena (UP: General):

. . . the existence of the scheduled tribes and the scheduled areas are a stigma on our nation just as the existence of untouchability is a stigma on the Hindu nation. That these brethren of ours are still in

[96] The term 'backward tribes' was first used as an official category in the Government of India Act, 1935 and changed to 'Scheduled Tribes' in the Indian Constitution (1950). 'Scheduled Castes' was also coined by the Government of India Act (1935) and has remained in official usage to this day. *Census of India* (1988:168).

such a sub-human state of existence is something for which we should be ashamed . . . I only want that these scheduled tribes and scheduled areas should be developed so quickly that they may become indistinguishable from the rest of the Indian population.[97]

In reaction to the 'zeal which several people of this house profess to have for promoting the interests of Adibasis', Jaipal Singh, a Munda tribal himself and leader of the Jharkhand party retorted:

If however, your mission of amelioration of the lot of the Adibasis is of the kind that the British professed to have, coming to India over all this distance of six thousand miles, I would ask you mercifully to leave us alone, and quit the Adibasi regions. I would remind such people of the adage 'Physician, heal thyself . . . [98]

In response, there were several snide comments regarding Jaipal Singh's inability to represent the tribals on account of his education (Oxford University) and his personal lifestyle. One representative exchange is as follows:

Jaipal Singh: I am very sorry to disappoint him that, in supporting the Fifth Schedule, I did not dress in my bows and arrows, the loin cloth, feathers, ear-rings, my drum and my flute . . .

Biswanath Das: May I know whether the Honourable Member has ever put on clothes like that?

Jaipal Singh: What makes Mr Das think I never wear the clothes that my people wear? . . .

Biswanath Das: I would not compare my Friend Mr Jaipal Singh with Shri Thakkar Bapa . . . . A person, from his residence in the second or third floor of the Hotel Imperial, ill compares himself with a person like Thakkar Bapa.[99]

A tribal who had made good, and could no longer be 'uplifted', and simultaneously one who had his own views on what should be done about the tribals, was suspect indeed. The historical existence of tribal polities, for example, the Gond chiefs of Garha Mandla in Central India, was now deeply buried. But it is in the discussions on the Sixth Schedule, that we get the worst

[97] Constituent Assembly Debates, vol. 9, New Delhi, (30 July – 18 September 1949), p. 979.
[98] Ibid.:993.
[99] Ibid.:993–5.

displays of chauvinism. Kuladhar Chaliha (Assam: General), advocated that administration in District and Regional Councils in the North East should be made subject to directions by the State Legislature. He argued that there should be restrictions on complete self-government by the tribals:

Nagas are a very primitive and simple people and they have not forgotten their old ways of doing summary justice when they have a grievance against anyone. If you allow them to rule us or run the administration it will be a negation of justice or administration and it will be something like anarchy. . . . In the subsequent provisions of this Schedule you will find that an Act of Parliament cannot be imposed on them unless they consent to it. *Have you ever heard that an Act of Parliament cannot be applicable to any people unless they agree to it?*[100] (italics mine)

There were others who drew upon the authoritarian traditions of utilitarianism with more skill than even their colonial teachers. Brajeshwar Prasad (Bihar: General), a strong advocate of centralization, declaimed:

I may be confronted with the question 'What will you say to the tribals if they come and tell you that they want political autonomy . . . ?' I will never concede this demand. I believe in the principle of the greatest good of the greatest number. I will not jeopardise the interest of India at the altar of the tribals . . . [101]

It was also in the sixth schedule that nationalist resentment at the policy of Excluded Areas found the most prominent expression. Rohini Kumar Chaudhuri (Assam: General), arguing that the North East Hill areas had been segregated by the British for their own ends said:

When the ICS officers came to India, their first concern was to find out some territories in the Province of Assam where there were no mosquitoes, there were no lawyers and where there were no public men. . . . Do you want an assimilation of the tribal and non-tribal people, or do you want to keep them separate? If you want to keep them separate, they will combine with Tibet, they will combine with Burma, they will never combine with the rest of India, you may take it from me.[102]

[100] Ibid.:1007–8.
[101] Ibid.:1009.
[102] Ibid.:1014–15.

Although the concern for a united India and territorial safety was perhaps understandable in the wake of partition and fears of Chinese aggression, it is also clear that the roots of many of today's problems may be traced back to the anti-democratic and authoritarian impulses of some of the Constitution's makers. Of course there were other voices of caution, such as Gopinath Bardoloi (Assam: General), Rev. Nichols Roy (Assam: General), Dr B.R. Ambedkar and Jaipal Singh. To them may be ascribed the fact that the Schedules were in place at all. J.J. M. Nichols Roy pointed out that rather than expecting the hill tribes of Assam to rise to the standard of plains Hindus, there were many respects in which the latter should emulate the former as being more civilized, for instance in the level of equality that prevailed among them. Jaipal Singh's speech is also particularly illuminating. He noted that the tribals had been persuaded to accede to the provisions of the Sixth Schedule of the Constitution with some difficulty, and on the explicit understanding that the provisions would be honoured. He outlined two solutions:

One was the power solution, the other was the knowledge solution. The vehement language of some of our Members inclines towards power solutions. They want to force the tribal people of Assam to do things against their wishes and expressed will. I suggest that is no solution at all. If you do that you are certainly going to bring about what you fear. You are not going to obviate, but you are going to bring about a further disintegration of India.[103]

Conclusion: Relevance to the Present and the Future

Today, when one of the most hotly contested questions in Bastar is whether the Sixth Schedule should be applied to it too, these old debates are strikingly resonant. In each period it seems, when one is on the brink of something new, we are condemned to repeat ourselves. Today, the traders accuse the administration of a policy of divide and rule, upsetting the old harmony between upper and lower castes or tribals. The administration accuses activists of wanting to keep tribals as artefacts, of celebrating a communitas, egalitarianism and harmony with nature, which does not in fact exist. The activists, on the other hand, accuse

[103] Ibid.:1017.

the government of sacrificing tribals at the altar of a 'development' which serves only the rich. Debates about forest policy question the wisdom of excluding villagers from reserves and sanctuaries versus involving them through a scheme of joint forest management.

In the post-colonial state, however, the different conditions under which the debate takes place gives the same positions different connotations. To argue for integration or assimiliation today can no longer have even the limited anti-colonial connotations it once did. Today, it is the assimilationists who are in power, and any further assimilation of peripheral groups can only mean further proletarianization under capitalism. Thus, in some ways, the anthropologist-administrators were proved right. But even in the 1930s–50s, when the debates were first taking place, there was a certain blinkered reluctance on all sides to accept the already advanced operation of capitalism. This was amply evident in the commercial orientation of the forest department, mines and plantations which drew precisely on the labour or resources of 'tribal' areas. Moreover, any attempt by adivasis to seize their own rights was crushed — whether in the Prajamandal struggles in the Orissa states in the thirties, or the CPI-led armed struggle of peasants and tribals against the oppression of landlords and the state in Telengana in 1948-49.

Eventually, as we shall see in the next chapter, the policy followed by independent India did not differ substantially from that of the colonial state, either in its benevolent or repressive aspects. A policy of reservations in jobs and the legislature was set up, money pumped in under various development programmes, and laws against land alienation retained. However, the Tribes Advisory Councils became practically defunct.[104] In fact, if anything, the pace of exploitation has increased post-1947, as improved communications and the growing demand for timber brought more outsiders into areas like Bastar. Any honest attempt to address the 'tribal question' must therefore eschew the idea of harmonious pre-capitalist village communities which are as much of a myth as the notion that activists are motivated

[104] For a history and analysis of development programs for tribal areas, *see* Sharma (1984).

by a desire to keep tribals in museums. The question today is one of the effects of capitalism and the struggle for democracy at large, which is fought in culturally specific ways. In the process, culture too is created anew.

7

The Congress and the King

It is the logic of our time
No subject for immortal verse
That we who lived by honest dreams
Defend the bad against the worse.

C. Day Lewis

As the nationalist movement gained prominence and the role of the native states as supports of the British empire acquired new importance,[1] the history of the central Indian states was correspondingly re-written. They were seen as having been given increasing independence and status by the British rather than having lost it:

the Central Provinces States have grown out of zamindaries, owned to a large extent by illiterate and in several cases debauched zamindars . . . into States ruled by comparatively young men, brought up as rulers of States should be . . . That the time has now come still further to develop the powers enjoyed, is creditable alike to the Chiefs themselves, and to those who have watched over them from the beginning.[2]

But this new development did not in the least signify autonomy. By this time, the native rulers (whether Indian or African) had been remodelled to fit the requirements of the British system of indirect rule. The ideal prince, as Jeffrey puts it, was one who was 'progressive but not too progressive; taking part in the administration, but not too big a part.'[3] But for the rare female ruler, training was directed at making the right marriage.

[1] Jeffrey (1978); Hettne (1978:36).
[2] F. no. 423 - Pol (Sec) 1932 For. & Political Department, Note by HE Sir Montague Butler, Governor of the CP on the Report on the CP States prepared by Mr A.C Lothian, 21 July 1932, p. 6.
[3] Jeffrey (1978:18).

On Bastar king Rudra Pratap's death in 1921, the British reluctantly acceded to public request, as expressed by village and pargana headmen, zamindars, and Jagdalpur notables, and appointed his daughter, Prafulla Kumari as ruler. They made it clear, however, that it was a question of 'expediency rather than right'.[4] When she turned fourteen, the question of the Rani's marriage came up. The CP Administration fixed a match with Prafulla Kumar of Mayurbhanj, despite the objections of the Rani's step mother *(Patrani)*, and her own disinclination. The Patrani was exiled, the Rani was kept under close surveillance and finally 'persuaded' to marry Prafulla Kumar in 1927. The dispute attracted much attention in the local newspapers and even a question in the British House of Commons.[5] The Rani died in 1936 at the age of twenty-six, following an appendicitis operation in London.[6] To this day, rumour in Bastar has it that she was killed at the behest of the British. There was popular discontent, and the people, through the majhis, demanded the immediate return of Pravir, her son and successor, from London.[7] However, the return of Pravir also meant the return of Prafulla Kumar, the Rani's husband. For several reasons, the energies of the Administrator and the CP Government which had been invested in ensuring that Prafulla Kumar married into the state, were now invested in keeping him out of it.

Prafulla was described as a 'coward' and a 'vicious rake' for among other things, having infected his wife with syphilis, and made her repeatedly pregnant despite medical warnings to the contrary.[8] But the real problem was his alleged nationalist tendencies, evidenced by a single newspaper article he wrote on the impotence of Indian princes under British rule, and the

[4] 1922 For & Pol File 319–Int., Report by W.E. Ley, Political Agent, 7 January 1922, NAI.

[5] For. & Pol. F. no. 305–P, 1924-7, NAI

[6] F. no. 84–P(S)/1936, Microfilm Acc no. 353, CRR, India Office, London, to Sir B.J. Glancy, Pol. Sec to F & P Dept., 2 March 1936, NAI

[7] F.no. 84–P(S)/1936, Telegram from Resident, ESA to Pol. Sec, For. & Pol. Dept., GOI, 4 March 1936, NAI

[8] F. no. 84–P(S)/1936, Acc. no. 353, Reel 2, CRR, ESA, Confidential Notes on Diary and letters by Pol. Sec. GOI; Burton to H.A.F. Metcalfe, F&P, GOI, 25 June 1931, NAI.

stupidity of the education they were provided.[9] Although Prafulla later tried to explain this away as a desire to win the left votes
when standing as Secretary at the Cambridge Union,[10] he was
eventually prohibited from entering the state. He was given an
allowance to complete his studies in anthropology at Cambridge,
while the state assumed sole guardianship of his children.[11] In
this period too, as after 1876, we see the same tension between
direct control and the need to preserve monarchies. The conse-
quence was complete control over princely families, who were
thus placed in 'impossible situations'.[12] Many of them paradoxically revived their political careers only under the electoral
system of independent India.

In 1936, at the time of his mother's death and his installation
as ruler, Pravir was seven years old, the second of four siblings.
He was apparently a 'highly strung child, very difficult to handle, . . . subject to violent fits of hysterical weeping and screaming
which are sometimes very difficult to stop.'[13] An English child
psychologist in Calcutta who eventually treated him, felt that if
his 'severe anxiety' was not treated, it could develop into in-
sanity.[14] The root of this behaviour and that of his siblings,
allegedly, was early cruelty by their father, Prafulla Kumar.[15]

The four children appear to have had a rather insular upbringing, almost entirely under English governesses. Their contact with

[9] F. no. 617-P, 1934, For. & Pol. Dept., Acc. 357, CRR, ESA, Article in
The New Statesman and Nation, The Weekend Review, 1 September 1934.

[10] F. no. 84-P(S), Confidential Note by Pol. Sec. , B. Glancy on meeting
with Prafulla, 20 November 1936.

[11] F. no. 84-P/36, F.V. Wylie, Pol Sec. For. & Pol. Dept., to Lt. Col A.S.
Meek, Agent to Gov. Gen., ESA, 11 June 1936.

[12] Jeffrey (1978:18). The classic formulation of Gluckman regarding the
dilemma of African chiefs also comes to mind here — caught between their
obligations to their people, and the demands placed by the British.

[13] F. no. 23 (3) - P/40-(Sec) of 1940, Pol. Dept. Pol. Branch, Col. Barton,
Res., ESA, to C.G. Herbert, Pol. Advisor to Crown Representative, 27 November 1940, NAI.

[14] Ibid.

[15] File no. 17-P 1941, Supplementary Report of the ESA for the second half
of October 1941; F. no. 13-P (sec) 1944, Acc. no. 353, NAI. It is beyond the
scope of this study to examine the psychological implications resulting from
Indian children being evaluated and treated within a British cultural framework.
No doubt, however, this was an important issue in their upbringing.

the state was largely limited to making occasional appearances at Dussehra.[16] After leaving Rajkumar College, Raipur, in 1940, due to a nervous breakdown, Pravir completed his schooling at Daly College, Indore. His term reports there indicate nothing more serious than a weakness at mathematics.[17] However, a course at the Indian Military Academy, Dehradun, had to be abandoned before the usual two years due to negative reports by his commandant regarding his 'defeated and disinterested attitude' and 'physical weakness together with lack of concentration and will-power'.[18] The public explanation for his leaving was his coming of age (18 years). Since Rudra Pratap's death in 1921, the state had been under direct British management. The Political Department now decided to invest Pravir with 'full powers' in July 1947.[19] Pravir's early childhood is relevant to the extent that it explains some of his later behaviour. It is also interesting to note how adverse reports on his capabilities, which might in earlier times have kept him from being given full powers, were ignored when it came to the transfer of power in 1947.

Accession and After: Post-1947 Bastar

Coming barely a month before independence, and at such a young age, Pravir's investiture was regarded with some suspicion by the new government. It added to the prevailing tension regarding the integration of the Indian princely states. While the British and the princes argued that with lapse of paramountcy, full sovereignty was to be restored to the Indian princes, the Congress disagreed.[20] This was exacerbated by the plans to grant a mining lease in Bastar to neighbouring Hyderabad state, whose ruler had declared independence from the Indian Union.[21]

[16] F. no. 17-P 1941, Pol. Dept. Pol. Br., Extract from the tour impressions of the Political Agent, Chattisgarh States, 1942, CRR Microfilm Acc. no. 352, NAI.

[17] Resident, ES to Fitze, Sec. to Crown Rep, 16 January 1942; Progress Reports, Daly College Indore, 1942–4, Microfilm Acc. no.*203, NAI.

[18] F.no. 25-P/47 Pol Dept. Pol Br., Company Commander's Report in the case of 624 G.C. Pravir Chandra Deo, Minor Maharaja of Bastar, NAI.

[19] F. no. 25-P/47 Pol Dept. Pol Br., NAI.

[20] Fisher (1991:453–4).

[21] Menon (1985:155).

Pravir himself was warned by Sardar Vallabbhai Patel, Deputy Prime Minister, of the serious consequences of acting against India's interests and granting a lease to Hyderabad.[22] In any event, he, along with the other rulers of CP and Orissa states acceded to the Indian union in December 1947, and the mines issue was temporarily shelved.[23] The former states of Bastar and Kanker were merged into the district of Bastar in the state of Madhya Pradesh. Apparently, Pravir never reconciled himself to the loss of power.[24] Despite Bastar's accession, the Indian Government continued to express anxiety over Pravir's behaviour. The ostensible reason was fear that he would spend all his money, which included a privy purse of Rs 2 lakhs, in 'debauchery' and charity.[25] One Samir Kumar Gupta, who came to work on the Dandakaranya refugee project for a few years, and lived in the palace compound, gives an adulatory account of a typical scene:

I found a stream of human heads, busy in receiving gifts being distributed by the Maharaja. Heavily garlanded by the public, the Maharaja was still busy in distributing currency notes which were of the denomination of Rupees one hundred to rupees ten. . . . It was more than pleasing to my eye to see the Maharaja with a perpetual smile on his lips while distributing his wealth . . . [26]

Eventually, in 1953, the Madhya Pradesh government succeeded in taking Pravir's property under Court of Wards on the grounds that he was mentally ill and incapable of managing his own affairs.[27] In 1951 Pravir had started training in tantric practices.[28] When the rains failed in 1955, he attributed the drought to divine anger at his estate being taken under Court of Wards, and started a *yagna* (fire sacrifice) to invoke rain. Contemporary

[22] Ibid.

[23] F. no. 161-PR/47, 1947, Ministry of States, Political (R) Branch, NAI.

[24] Joshi (1967:120).

[25] File no. 161-PR/47, 1947 Ministry of States, Political (R) Branch, NAI. Privy purses for the ex-rulers had been fixed at a certain proportion of their state incomes at the time of accession. Bastar's income was 18 lakhs, and approximately 11 per cent of this was to go annually to Pravir.

[26] Gupta (1965:55-7).

[27] F. no. F.24 (40)-PB/53, 1953, Response by Mr K.N.V. Nambisan, Council of States Secretariat, 29 August 1953, to Question raised in the Council of States by Prafulla Chandra Bhanj Deo, NAI.

[28] Joshi (1967:120).

news reports say this increased his popularity among the people, but it did not find any favour with the government. Pravir's general policy of cultivating the villagers, rather than the traders and government officials of Jagdalpur, also offended the latter greatly.[29]

One result of the merger of the princely states into India, was the holding of elections on the basis of universal franchise. Excluding Kanker, Bastar had seven seats in the state assembly and one seat in the Lok Sabha in New Delhi. The combined district now has eleven Vidhan Sabha and two Lok Sabha seats. Administratively too, there were several changes. The structure of the Political Department with a resident Administrator, Political Agent, Chattisgarh Feudatory States and Resident, Eastern States Agency, was replaced by the more standardized Indian administrative system. Larger states like Madhya Pradesh are divided into several divisions (headed by Commissioners) comprised of several districts. Till 1981 when it came to form a seperate division of its own, Bastar was part of Raipur division.[30] Post-1947, while there was an increase in expenditure on schools, roads, and hospitals, as well as on police stations, the extraction of resources from Bastar also increased. The post-merger period, particularly the 1960s, was therefore, a time of rapid inflow of outsiders. From 1951–61, there was an increase in population of 27.7 per cent, and from 1961–71, a record increase (taking the period 1901–71) of 29.85 per cent, caused mostly by migration from other parts of India.[31]

Two projects in particular contributed to this, the Dandakaranya refugee resettlement project (DNK) set up to resettle displaced persons from former East Pakistan, and the commission of the Bailadilla iron ore mines, which started exporting to Japan in 1966. Paralkote and Pharasgaon in Bastar and Umerkot in undivided Koraput district were selected for resettlement because of their vast forest areas. Approximately 58,000 acres of land were released to 7330 families.[32] At least twenty-five per cent of the benefit of the DNK project was to have gone

[29] *DS*, 14 August 1960.

[30] GOMP (1984:28). The district then consisted of 8 tahsils out of which 3 more were carved in 1982.

[31] Census of India, 1981, Bastar District, Part XIII-B, p. xxv.

[32] *DS*, 14 August 1960.

to local tribals, including land and employment but eventually they got very little out of the project, and only 495 landless tribal families were given land. On the other hand, the massive felling of trees created consternation, the Paralkot sirahas predicting that it would lead to some disaster.[33] The Marias of Dantewara who were displaced for the mines also got no employment from it or from the Bailadilla–Kottavasla railway line. Labour was imported from Andhra Pradesh and Orissa instead.[34] In subsequent years, both the initial tension about Hyderabad taking over the lease, and the Bailadilla mine itself, were to acquire new dimensions in the popular imagination as some of the issues against which Pravir Chandra fought. In 1992, during the steel plant protests, Dayaro Pujari told me that the Raja was killed because he spoke out against iron leaving the district and organized people to break the railway.

As for welfare measures, which should have increased the legitimacy of the state, the officials who were responsible for implementing them had, at best, an immensely patronizing attitude as signified by the word 'uplift', and at worst, a contemptuous and exploitative attitude. As Elwin noted in 1960 about the staff of the Multipurpose Tribal Blocks:

There is still all too common a tendency for officials to regard themselves as superior, as heaven-born missionaries of a higher culture. They boss the people about; their chaprassis abuse them. . . . Any failure is invariably placed at the tribal door; in report after report, we have found the Block officials blaming everything on the laziness, the improvidence, the suspiciousness, the superstitions of the people. Altogether too much fuss is made of the hardships of living in a tribal area, and officials seem to regard themselves as heroic martyrs who are carrying a burden far heavier than anything the white man had to bear.[35]

Land and Forest

Access to land and forest continued to be the major issues of the period, as they have always been in Bastar, where a majority of the people are dependent on both. Since independence, there

[33] *DS*, 29 May 1960; 13 November 1960.
[34] Pandey (1967:para 55).
[35] GOI (1960:20–1).

has been both change and continuity in forest policy, with ownership and control of forests continuing to vest in the state, but with indigenous commercial-industrial interests replacing imperial needs as the main determinant of policy.[36] In addition there were other schemes of industrial expansion and hydro-electric projects all of which involved massive destruction of forests.[37] Between 1956 and 1981, 125,483 hectares of forest land in Bastar were transferred to development projects. This accounted for a third of the total forest loss in the district.[38]

A significant post-independence innovation was that people were given full rights, including that of felling and sale, over timber and fruit trees standing in their fields (*bhumiswami* rights). Earlier they had been prevented from cutting teak or fruit bearing trees. But the new system also proved to be a major source of exploitation of the tribals, as businessmen bought trees from them at a fraction of their actual price, leading to massive denudation. Eventually, the MP Protection of Scheduled Tribes (Interest in Trees) Act, 1956 was passed, under which the price at which trees were sold had to be sanctioned by the Collector and she/he could direct that the payment be done in her/his presence. However this did not really check the problem, as businessmen managed to find ways of circumventing this.[39] A legal change in the position of *nistari* forests into protected forests in 1949 meant a shift in management from village panchayats to the forest department. Procurement of daily requirements thus became more difficult. In 1976, nistari 'concessions' as well as commutation dues were abolished and nistari fair price depots set up, from where villagers are required to buy their small timber, firewood and bamboo on concessional rates.[40] Nationalization of major NTFPs did not help in the manner it was meant to (*see* introduction).

By the late 1950s, both legal and illegal felling in protected and reserved forests had increased dramatically, often with the complicity of the forest department. Even when trucks were

[36] Gadgil and Guha (1992:185).
[37] WP, Central Bastar (1988:287)
[38] CSE (1985:87).
[39] Pandey (1967:122-3).
[40] WP, Central Bastar (1988:7, 51).

initially seized, the large contractors were usually let off. Petty cases were however dealt with severely.[41] Legally, according to forest department records, prior to 1958, Rs 15 crore worth of trees had been felled. From 1958–75, the figure had increased to Rs 35 crores worth of felled trees, signifying a dramatically increased volume as against a mere rise in timber prices.[42]

However the forest department and concerned officials and politicians continue to portray the 'forest problem' in Bastar as primarily one of encroachment by cultivators in reserved forest areas.[43] To some extent this is a problem of definition: in the absence of proper registration of cultivation in the past, many people become illegal encroachers on land they have been cultivating for several years, and which was subsequently declared reserved.[44] At the same time, one cannot doubt that it is a serious problem and one which has been exacerbated in recent years. For instance, in Jagdalpur forest circle alone, 32,531 ha or 32.5 sq km out of 11,600 sq km were encroached upon from 1976 to 1980.[45] But the problem must also be looked at in terms of an unproductive agricultural base, the lack of other employment opportunities, and the collusion of the forest department in making money through illegal bribes. Approximately 27.5 per cent of the total area of Bastar is available for agriculture,[46] only 2.9 per cent is irrigated (see table II) and for every iron plough in use in the district, there are 2610 wooden ploughs. The small pockets using tractors, pumpsets and fertilizers are concentrated in villages around Jagdalpur, and are usually limited to the richer castes like Brahmans and Sundis.[47]

[41] *DS*, 14 August 1960.

[42] CSE (1982:47). Some production figures are given in CSE (1985:86).

[43] *DS*, 30 October 1960, Statement by Forest Minister of M.P., S.N. Shukla; conversations with forest officers in Bastar, 1991–93.

[44] Draft Article by Dr B.D. Sharma on encroachment, n.d., ca 1992.

[45] Figures provided by the Jagdalpur Forest Circle, August 1995, Conservator's Office, Jagdalpur. The settlement of encroachments has been going on, on a regular basis from the 1950s. In 1965, the MP State government passed orders to settle all encroachments till 17.7.1962, in 10 districts where heavy encroachment had taken place, including Bastar. GOI (1984:A-99–100).

[46] GOMP (1984:103–4, 106).

[47] PUCL (1989:2).

Pravir's Political Activities: Members and Membrins

Faced with a situation of greater outside penetration, the destruction of forests due to commercial exploitation and unsated land hunger, Pravir Chandra Bhanj Deo represented an alternative around which the masses of Bastar sought to mobilize against the government. In 1955 Pravir set up an organization called the Adivasi Kisan Mazdoor Sangh. Apart from trying to mobilize popular support to get Pravir's estate back from the Court of Wards, the organization also took up village issues — advising the villagers not to pay government dues and to occupy government land.[48]

An attempt was made to create an organizational structure that reached down into the villages. Pravir titled his leading workers, male and female, members and membrins respectively, and gave them membership cards and a distinctive attire. He also appointed his own majhis, chalkis and kotwars in a system that paralleled the government system. Pravir's appointees were called raja majhis and given blue turbans, as against the red turbans that the state gave pargana majhis every Dussehra. Membrins were given red sarees. It is difficult to say if the appointment of parallel figures caused dissension within the villages. Some of the majhis who testified at the Pandey Commission suggested that they were kept out of affairs due to their affiliations with government, but possibly this was motivated by a desire to distance themselves from Pravir and the movement in the aftermath of the 1966 firing incident. In 1992, when I talked to the pargana majhis, the impression I got was that there had been different spheres of operation.

Pravir's functionaries — members/membrins and majhis — worked for him by spreading his messages, both verbal and through written pamphlets, at village markets, and organizing meetings or processions.[49] They also went in turns to the palace for duty and lived there for a few days or a week, till the supplies which they had taken from home were exhausted. Their duties involved helping Pravir to carry out all his rituals, such as the rain invoking yagnas; co-ordinating all the people who came there; or redistributing the supplies that were collected. The

[48] Joshi (1967:121).
[49] Pandey (1967:para 57).

traditional atpaharia system also continued with certain villages contributing people to clean the palace floors and wash the dishes. The palace has large grounds, and village visitors would often camp out there.[50]

Budri Bai, a woman from Matkot described in 1992 how she became a membrin, painting the king as someone who was always kind to his people, even if he was belligerent to the government. For women, who had to face an otherwise hard life, this sense of caring was no doubt important. She had once gone to the palace to see the king, and had reached just after the daily distribution of charity. The Raja had noticed her. Budri Bai narrated their conversation, imitating the Raja's kind tones and her own humble responses:

Raja: Bai, where are you from? Are you scared of me?
Bai: No, Huzoor, I am not scared of you.
Raja: When did you come?
Bai: Just now.
Raja: I just distributed lots of money. Why didn't you come then?
Bai: I didn't come for money, Maharaj. I came just to see you.

And then because she came regularly, he made her a membrin. She went on to remember: 'Raja used to say: Don't get lost at night, *bai log*. Don't drink tea in the hotels. Or the police will say, these are Raja's membrins and will hit you on the legs. You will get hurt, *bai log*.' No doubt this remembered paternalism is enhanced by nostalgia. But coupled with it is also a sense of pride in working for a cause, and in having responsibility and collective decision making power which hitherto had been confined to men. Pravir no doubt realized this and sought to utilize this spirit in his own movement.

Electoral Politics and Congress Opportunism

Having failed to supress Pravir's growing popularity, the Congress now decided to make use of it. He was given a Congress ticket for the 1957 State Assembly Elections, and was also made president of the District Congress Committee. Pravir too was happy to make use of any alliance that might help towards his goals, although he later justified his own opportunism by

[50] Interview with majhis and membrins, Dussehra 1992

reference to that of the Congress.[51] The election results showed
that the Congress party's faith in the ex-king's popularity was
not misplaced: Pravir Chandra and all his nominees won. In
one incident, the people told a Congress candidate who was
campaigning against Pravir's candidate that, 'they did not care
about the merits and demerits of a candidate. All they cared
was that he should be Maharaja's candidate.'[52]

However, Pravir was still unable to get his property released
from the Court of Wards, and resigned from the assembly in
frustration, claiming: 'I could have benefitted the society far
better with my own economic resources instead of deceiving
people and wasting public money like the other Congress
M.L.A.'s.[53] Consequently he was warned against 'inciting the
adivasis', and one of his main workers, Bira Majhi, was arrested
under the Preventive Detention Act of 1950.[54] Pravir, in turn,
threatened the administration with his 'supernatural powers'
and popularity with the people. By this time he had started
another party called the Adivasi Seva Dal. Here again, local
issues were meshed with district-wide issues and the people's
grievances and Pravir's personal grievances both came to be
symbols of Congress corrpution and the government's support
for certain groups at the expense of others.[55]

One such instance concerned Bastar village, 16 km north of
Jagdalpur, which was also the home of Suryapal Tiwari, District
Congress Chairman. The villagers accused Suryapal of misap-
propriating the money from the local co-operative society and
running a government fisheries scheme as his own personal
fiefdom. In June 1960, under the leadership of the Adivasi Seva
Dal, fish were removed from two government (co-operative
society) fish tanks and divided up among the people. An-
nouncements had been made on market days in the area to
gather for the event and about 1500 people turned up. Suryapal
Tiwari reported the incident and had sixteen people arrested,
which further increased the resentment against him in the

[51] Bhanj Deo (1965:59); election pamphlets, Lallu Pujari's collection.
[52] *DS*, 7 June 1959
[53] Pravir Chandra (1965:62).
[54] Pandey (1967:para 47)
[55] Pamphlet titled *Bastar ke Rajniti ke Aadh Zor, Zulm, Zabardasti,* Jagdalpur,
1958.

village.[56] A local reporter, describing popular reactions to Surya-pal, naively concluded:

Queer as it may appear, inspite of Shri Suryapal's years of contribution to upgrade the social and economic standard of the villagers, his inherent urge to work for the village, a great majority of the people of the village in which he lives, belong to the opposite camp.[57]

Like many Congress politicians from upper castes and landed families who claimed to be social workers, Suryapal Tiwari was alien to the people he claimed to represent.[58] Under the leadership of the Adivasi Seva Dal, he became an object of popular opprobrium. In November, Raghunath Mahapatra of the Adivasi Seva Dal was arrested for making 'obscene and threatening utterances' in front of Suryapal Tiwari's house. The Oriya Brahmin surname, Mahapatra, suggests that not all Pravir's supporters were tribal; but the large majority were. The day following his arrest, a mass meeting was held in Bastar village, presided over by Pravir and attended by one thousand people, after which again several of them gathered in front of Suryapal Tiwari's house and shouted abuses.[59]

In the meantime, meetings and mass actions were taking place all over the district, under the aegis of the Adivasi Seva Dal. The felling of trees, the taking over of government land and land owned by upper castes, moneylenders or traders began to grow in scale.[60] The nascent district branch of the Communist Party of India was also becoming active in land occupation and the closing down of liquor shops.[61] The government for its part, portrayed land grabbing as nothing more than lawlessness, claiming that it was doing its best to solve the land hunger, and that 22,000 acres of land had been distributed to landless tribals.[62]

Public meetings held in Jagdalpur, as well as the bigger villages

---

[56] *DS*, 12 June 1960.
[57] *DS*, 26 June 1960.
[58] For the class basis of the Congress in MP, *see* Baker (1979:128-31).
[59] *DS*, 13 November 1960.
[60] *DS*, 12 June 1960.
[61] *DS*, 13 June 1960; 15 January 1961.
[62] Interview with R.P. Noronha, Commissioner, Raipur Division, 25 June 1960, *DS*, 3 July 1960.

and small towns in both north and south Bastar attracted crowds of up to 5000 people and more. In general, Seva Dal workers would speak while Pravir would merely preside over the meetings. The target of attack was apparently not the government but the Congress, and particularly, Suryapal Tewari.[63] On occasion, other parties joined their platform to criticize the Congress, ranging from the Praja Socialist Party to the Ram Rajya Parishad. There were negotiations to merge the Adivasi Seva Dal with the rightist Swatantra party.[64] In the meantime, Pravir also declared his intention of forming a Chamber of Princes that would demand the restoration of the former Princely States.[65] The government responded by arresting the main workers of the Adivasi Seva Dal, strengthening the popular feeling that the government sided with Suryapal Tiwari and not with them.[66]

Pravir's Arrest and the Lohandiguda Firing

In view of the activities of the Seva Dal, Pravir's continued warnings that the corruption and oppression of the local Congress in Bastar was forcing the potential secession of Bastar, and the possiblity of violence,[67] a detachment of the Special Armed Forces was stationed at Jagdalpur and several key points in the district. There were also rumours of Pravir's impending de-recognition as ex-ruler, with the concomitant loss of privy purse priveleges, which finally occurred following his arrest under the Preventive Detention Act on 11 February 1961.[68] He was taken to Narsinghgarh jail. His younger brother Vijay Chandra Bhanj Deo was declared ex-ruler in his place.[69] The official justification was that Pravir was a source of disorder and had threatened an armed rebellion as in 1910.[70]

[63] *DS*, 20 November 1960.
[64] *DS*, 27 November 1960; 18 December 1960; 25 December 1960.
[65] Mentioned in the President's order of derecognition, *infra*, n. 70.
[66] *DS*, 4 December 1960.
[67] Undated printed open letter to Prime Minister Nehru from Pravir Chandra (pamphlet collection of Lallu Pujari); *DS*, 11 December 1960.
[68] Pandey (1967: para 50).
[69] *DS*, February 19, 1961.
[70] President's Order Derecognizing Pravir, 12 February 1961, Pandey (1967: para 50).

In Bastar itself there were several meetings and processions demanding Pravir Chandra's release. People were not prepared to accept Vijay Chandra as the king and the raja's workers made plans to resist the government in every way.[71] Various acts of protest began in March 1961. In several local markets across the district, e.g. in Lohandiguda, Tokapal, Deora and Karanji, people refused to pay bazaar taxes and asked the non-tribal merchants to leave the market, bringing them into conflict with the police. There was stone throwing on the one side, and *lathi* charges and tear gas on the other. The infamous Suryapal Tewari was threatened at Narayanpal and had to be rescued by a police force.[72] The liquor shops in Sirisguda and Ghotiya and the school in Barsur were burnt, mango boughs were circulated in bazaars and large groups of people were seen marching to Lohandiguda, approximately thirty kilometres from Jagdalpur. Several school teachers flooded into Jagdalpur, fearing what seemed to be a potential repeat of 1910.[73]

Following a decision to stage mass demonstrations in Jagdalpur to demand Pravir Chandra's release, people began to gather at Bailabazaar and Kharagghat on the outskirts of Jagdalpur late on the night of 28 March. Police harassment the next day resulted in a clash between the police and a crowd of five hundred people. Two further busloads of police were rushed in and about a hundred people arrested and then later dumped on the roadside a long distance away, in what was a common police method of dealing with protestors.[74]

On market day, Friday, 31 March 1961, there was a large meeting at Lohandiguda attended by over 10,000 people. Vijay Chandra was brought to try and disperse the crowd but they refused to leave. The police burst tear gas shells and when the crowd still continued to advance, they opened fire. Thirteen people were killed and several others were injured. The people had been told that the bullets would turn to water but once the firing started and they saw men and women falling, they began running away. Those who stayed were lathi-charged by the police.[75]

[71] *DS*, 26 March 1961.
[72] *DS*, 2 April 1961.
[73] Ibid.
[74] Ibid.
[75] *DS*, 9 April 1961; 17 March 1963 (court hearings reported).

206 Subalterns and Sovereigns

The atmosphere in the state continued to be tense, with people apparently under the belief that if Pravir was not brought back to Bastar, there would be drought and famine. Police patrolling in key villages and major bazaars no doubt added to the tension.[76] Sec 144 of the Criminal Procedure Code (CrPC), prohibiting public meetings, was imposed in Jagdalpur and surrounding areas till 11 April 1961. The Maharaja's party and all the opposition parties (PSP, CPI and Jansangh) demanded a judicial enquiry into the firing.[77] This was consistently ignored and on the contrary, fifty nine people were prosecuted for rioting and being members of an 'unlawful assembly with intent to murder'.[78] The case against them was eventually dismissed by the Additional Sessions Judge at Jagdalpur, who found no provocation for the firing or evidence that the assembly had been in any way unlawful or aimed at murder.[79] The Congress then tried to regain legitimacy by sending a 'good-will mission' into Bastar.[80] At its recomendation the government made an ex-gratia payment of ten thousand rupees to the families of six persons killed. It is evidence of the popular fear and alienation from the government, particularly the police, that in the beginning no-one came forward to identify their dead.[81]

1962–1965: Protesting the Court of Wards and De-Recognition

Pravir Chandra was released in April 1961. He returned to Bastar in August to the jubiliation of his supporters, and the consternation of the Congress and the administration, some of whom apparently asked for transfers. The reaction of the other political parties, barring the Communists, was opportunistic, as they were all hoping to form alliances with Pravir for electoral purposes.[82] With Pravir's return, and its own growing unpopularity, electoral prospects looked bleak for the local Congress. There was also

[76] *DS*, 16 April 1961.
[77] *DS*, 9 April 1961.
[78] Sections 148 and 307/149 of the IPC.
[79] Pandey (1967:para 51).
[80] *DS*, 28 May 1961.
[81] *DS*, 20 August 1961; 23 July 1961.
[82] *DS*, 30 April 961.

inner factionalism.[83] Several influential candidates who had previously sided with the Congress, withdrew rather than risk losing prestige by being identified with the Congress, or appear to be standing against the Maharaja.[84]

Pravir had by now formed yet another party — the Akhil Bharatiya Maharaja Party, which he claimed was intended to revive India's ancient heritage. He campaigned actively for the 1962 state assembly elections, going on foot to several places, and publicly declared that he would support those candidates who worked towards an enquiry into the Lohandiguda firing.[85] Once again, Pravir's candidates won by large margins. The Congress even forfeited its security deposit for the Lok Sabha seat and for three assembly seats.[86] Pravir himself had to stand from Kanker, (having been disqualified on technical grounds from contesting from Bhanpuri, within ex-Bastar state),[87] where he lost against the former ruler of Kanker.

A new phase of the movement now started, lasting from 1962–5. In July 1961, Pravir had married Shubhraj Kumari alias Vedwati, princess of Patan, but pleaded poverty in bringing her to Bastar, on account of his de-recognition and loss of privy purse. Consequently his followers, who were keen on seeing the new maharani, collected money for a grand reception. With Vedwati's presence, women became even more active in the movement.[88] Their demands were that Pravir be re-instated as ex-King, his property be released from the Court of Wards, and that he be allowed to sit on the Dussehra chariot. At a large public meeting held in the palace on 3 August 1962, Member of Parliament Lakhmoo Bhavani was asked either to work for Pravir's re-recognition or resign.[89]

The campaign to obtain a judicial enquiry into the Lohandiguda firing also continued. In 1962, a subscription drive for

---

[83] *DS*, 7 May 1961; 2 July 1961; 19 October 1961.

[84] *DS*, 10 December 1961; 7 January 1962; 21 January 1962.

[85] *DS*, 31 December 1961.

[86] *DS*, 31 December 1961; 4 March 1962 — election results.

[87] *DS*, 28 January 1962.

[88] Joshi (1967:126). Pravir already had a mistress, Subhadra, who left her husband in 1960 to join him. She stayed with him till his death in 1966, despite his marriage to Vedwati and his occasional mistreatment of her. *DS*, 6 March 1960, 8 October 1961.

[89] *DS*, 5 August 1962.

the Maharaja party was accompanied by the distribution of a booklet titled *Lohandiguda*, which kept alive the memory of the incident and the fact that justice had not been done.[90] Action took the form of hunger strikes by individual members of the party, signature campaigns, periodic demonstrations and memorandums to the government.[91] In one instance, on 6 May 1963, a group of people hoisted the flag of the former Bastar state on top of the Court of Wards office, broke open the locks of the old palace and paraded through the town shouting slogans, demanding the return of the king's property. This was followed by a confrontation on 8 May between people inside the palace and the police who were trying to force them out, resulting in one policeman being wounded with an arrow. A few days later, the administration cut off water and access to the palace, forcing about sixty-one tribals inside to come out and surrender.[92] Nine leaders were arrested for being the principal agitators and sentenced to jail for periods varying from six months to five years.[93]

In the meantime, continuing public alienation took some gruesome forms. In September 1963, two police constables went to village Bhejripadar to arrest one Hirma, who was charged with stirring up the agitation in the palace between 6–11 May. They were beheaded by the villagers, their bodies abandoned in the forests adjoining Bhejripadar, while their heads were found in a stone quarry pit near Pandripani some miles away. Hirma and his comrades were found outside the Raja's palace the next morning giving rise to the rumour that the heads were being carried as trophies to Jagdalpur.[94] The killings caused widespread alarm, particularly to police and other state servants posted in the interior. On the other hand, police patrols started at Tokapal after the Bhejripadar murder led to police excesses on tribals. Several villagers, including the women of Telimarenga, complained to the Police Superintendent that the police were beating them.[95]

[90] *DS*, 16 September 1962.
[91] *DS*, 22 September 1961, *DS*, 14 April 1963; 5 May 1963.
[92] *DS*, 12 May 1963.
[93] *DS*, 19 May 1963; 18 April 1965. The leaders included Mangal Majhi, Mata Maria, Budoo, Mahadeo, Ramdhar, Sudoo, Lakhmoo.
[94] *DS*, 1 September 1963. Hirma Maria and six others were given life sentences, and four others were released. *DS*, 15 March 1964.
[95] *DS*, 28 September 1963.

In November 1963, Pravir cut off the hand of a rickshaw puller, Motilal, with a sword. His 'excuse' was that Motilal had tried to trick him by lining up for charity twice. Pravir was arrested under Sec 326 IPC (causing grevious hurt by dangerous weapons), but released on bail. Two police constables who were to serve as prosecution witnesses were threatened by Pravir's men. They were told that if they deposed against him, they too would be beheaded and their houses burnt.[96] However, Pravir had the case transferred to Jabalpur, pleading bias on the part of the local magistracy, and much of his time during 1964 and 1965 was occupied with appealing his prison sentence in successively higher courts.[97]

The Government finally released the property held under Court of Wards on 25 July 1963, whereupon it became embroiled in legal disputes, which continued throughout 1965. Pravir's younger brother, Vijay Chandra, claimed right to it, as the official ex-Maharaja.[98] In July 1965, when Pravir was away in Jabalpur he took away some articles including items used for the worship of Danteswari.[99] This led to protests by crowds of women upto 10,000 strong, who eventually got the prayer items returned.[100] Vedwati, Pravir's by now estranged wife, also laid claim to some of Pravir's property.[101] But other issues apart from the property still remained unresolved. In 1964, several of Pravir's men such as Mangal Majhi, Mata Maria, Lakhmoo Dual and others, started a campaign to recall the sitting MLAs and MPs. They were accused of serving no useful purpose in parliament, and not working towards solving any local problems, such as nistar facilities, land or even the re-recognition of Pravir as ex-king.[102]

Here was a king with illusions about his own greatness, but

[96] *DS*, 15 December 1963; 22 December 1963.
[97] Pandey (1967:para 54).
[98] *DS*, 6 October 1963; 24 May 1964.
[99] *DS*, 4 July 1965.
[100] *DS*, 28 November 1965, Pandey (1967:para 54).
[101] *DS*, 24 April 1964. Vedwati had filed for separation on the grounds of cruelty and because of his mistress Subhadra's presence in the palace. She also applied for a court order to restrain the sale of property by Pravir till her maintenance suit had been decided.
[102] *DS*, 21 June 1964; Aug 23, 1964.

who nonetheless had the vision to pick up on the genuine demands of his people. The various political parties he formed were successful because they combined both these aspects. What is particularly interesting is the manner in which the organizations campaigned for a judicial enquiry into the Lohandiguda firing, and insisted that their elected representatives fulfill their mandate. In many ways it seems as if the movement embodied genuinely democratic ideals despite its overall leadership by a king.

Dussehra as Political Statement

From 1949 until after Pravir's death, Dussehra once again emerged as a significant site of confrontation, with both the administration and Pravir recognizing its symbolic importance. Immediately after independence, the question of ex-rulers being permitted to hold Dussehra Durbars became a political issue as it was feared that this would help them retain their hold on the people.[103] Pravir had been absent from Bastar in 1948, but in 1949 he relinquished his role in the political aspects of Dussehra, such as the chariot procession, and said he would continue to take part only in his religious role as priest of Danteswari.[104] By 1960, however, in the wake of his growing popularity – and also his own claims to rulership – the notion of his riding on the chariot was reactivated. In the 1960 Dussehra, a deputation of tribal leaders, including ex-MLAs Boda Dara and Dora Dokka, raised the issue with the Collector and were told to petition the government for the following year. But they proceeded to make their point in other ways. The newspaper description of what happened is dramatic:

Hundreds of pullers ready to move the 'rath' suddenly dropped the siyari rope on the ground as a number of blue turbaned tribal leaders mixed up with the huge crowd were seen to elbow their ways to them and whisper something in their ears. The Police band ceased to play, the large number of police constables, to accompany the Rath procession stood at attention and thousands of tribal processionists, men, women and children, halted in pouring rains, curious and eager to move with the movement of the chariot.[105]

[103] F. no. 10 (85) – P/49 1949, Ministry of States Pol. Branch, NAI.
[104] Ibid., (proclamation by Pravir Chandra Bhanj Deo in 1949 Dussehra).
[105] *DS*, 9 October 1960.

The leaders were asked to reconsider their decision, which they said they would do on consulting with the maharaja. However there was no response, and the authorities resolved the situation by taking the Danteswari umbrella around in a jeep instead.[106] The Congress, rather hypocritically, now began to oppose holding Dussehra as a state festival (i.e. having state funding, a guard of honour etc.) on the grounds that it violated the secular and democratic nature of the country and strengthened the king's position. However, the leading towns-people in Jagdalpur insisted on continuing with the event, so as not to hurt adivasi sentiment.[107]

In 1961, for the first time since 1948, Pravir as the '*Mati-Pujari*' or Earth-Priest of Danteswari, sat on the chariot with four attendants behind him. Both in 1961 and even more so in 1962, when Pravir's wife, Vedwati came to Bastar for Dussehra, there was a record attendance of several hundred thousands of people. In both years, the government declared it a non-official function, and all expenses were borne by the people, with contributions organized from every village, as in the pre-colonial days.[108] Throughout these years, the Administration imposed Section 144 for the duration of the festival.[109] Attendance declined somewhat in 1963 and 1964, following a separation between Pravir and his wife, poor rains, and a bad harvest in 1964.[110] The presence of both a king and queen signified the appropriate order of things, and any disruption of this was disliked. A bad harvest also meant that people did not have the resources to take time off and travel to Jagdalpur for Dussehra. Conversely, although 1965 was a year of official scarcity, attendance was about 100,000,[111] possibly because people had become desperate and looked to Pravir to rectify the situation by mediating with the Gods through the celebration of Dussehra. In other words, Dussehra became another way of strengthening Pravir's legitimacy and emphasizing his importance to Bastar, as against that of the government.

---

106 Ibid.
107 *DS*, 11 September 1960.
108 *DS*, 1 October 1961; 15 October 1961; 29 October 1961; 26 August 1962.
109 *DS*, 3 November 1963; 30 September 1962.
110 *DS*, 11 October 1964.
111 *DS*, 17 October 1965.

Rice Situation

In 1965–6, there were severe food shortages all over India due to low stocks and successive bad monsoons, similar in magnitude only to the famine of 1899–1900.[112] The situation was exacerbated by the war with Pakistan (1965). Although massive imports of foodgrain averted disaster, and a policy of zoning was implemented, with the aim of transferring grains from surplus to deficit areas within the country, the situation was grim.[113] The price of rice in Bastar started rising as early as 1961,[114] and scarcity of foodgrains was reported from various parts.[115] The situation continued to be bad in 1963 and 1964, with poor rains and rising market prices, inadequate food allotment from the Centre and rice smuggling to Orissa.[116] In South Bastar, people were said to be subsisting on tamarind seeds.[117] Despite a temporary improvement in late 1964, by early 1965 the situation worsened again, with consumers and retailers complaining of wholesale and millowner blackmarketing. The traders got higher prices at centres of the Bailadilla railway and mining corporation projects, making it even more difficult for adivasis to buy rice.[118] The rains failed again in July. By October, scarcity was officially declared and relief measures started in Kanker and Bhanupratapur.[119]

In 1965, the state government issued the M.P. Paddy Procurement (levy) Order, under which paddy was levied on a compulsory basis according to the number of acres owned. The official intent was to make the district self-sufficient, reducing dependence on outside supplies.[120] Rice was to be purchased through government apex and marketing societies and distributed through fair price shops. But in Bastar, this was not the most rational policy. Although the number of fair price shops in the district had increased to sixty-one, compared to

[112] Dreze (1995:101).
[113] Ibid.:105
[114] *DS*, 29 June 1961.
[115] *DS*, 18 September 1961.
[116] *DS*, 23 June 1963; 28 September 1963. *DS*, 17 June 1964; 11 July 1964.
[117] *DS*, 17 June 1964.
[118] *DS*, 9 August 1964; 23 May 1965.
[119] *DS*, 22 August 1965; 17 October 1965; *MP Chronicle*, 7 January 1966; Samyukta Socialist Party (1966).
[120] Pandey (1967:para 60).

"BIG FOLLOWING"

Sources *The Blitz*, October and November, 1966 Reproduced in Chandidas, et. al, *A Sourcebook on Indian Elections* (New York: Humanities Press : 1968)

India's Food Crises in the 1960s: Glimpses of Public Opinion

forty in 1964, they were negligible for an area of 39,114 sq km.[121] Moreover, a rigorous enforcement of this policy by food and revenue officials and police constables had resulted in rice ceasing to come into local markets altogether. Black market rates for rice varied from Rs 1.25 to Rs 1.30 per kg, as against the official procurement rate of 54 paise per kg.[122] Therefore if people had rice to sell, they would rather have sold it elsewhere than to the government at levy rates. Finally, the standard paddy procurement rates were too high for Bastar, where agriculture is less intensive than in other parts of Madhya Pradesh. The procurement also did not take into account the number of dependents on each land holding. As joint land holdings were and are still common, sometimes going back several generations in a lineage, the number of acres on the land records had no relation to actual family size. Patwaris could not be expected to provide reliable estimates of actual holdings, particularly in a situation where the government was pressing for paddy procurement.

According to Justice Pandey's estimates, the net average out-turn (after including cultivation expenses) in Bastar in 1965–6 was two hundred pounds of paddy per acre. A cultivator with five to eight acres had to give thirty-two pounds per acre while someone with over fifteen acres had to give up hundred and ten out of two hundred pounds per acre, belying the government's claim that the amount levied was small.[123] Moreover, the levy came into practical effect only in January 1966, when most people had already disposed of any surplus, retaining only their precious monsoon stocks. Eventually, the government was able to collect only 1,700 metric tons of paddy as against an initial target of 8,700 metric tons.[124]

Popular Mobilization Against the Levy

The government asked Pravir to help with paddy procurement. Initially he complied, making a few half-hearted village visits.[125]

[121] *DS*, 17 June 1964; 27 February 1966.
[122] *DS*, 7 November 1965.
[123] Pandey (1967: para 58).
[124] Ibid.: para 59.
[125] *DS*, 23 January 1966.

But he also proffered his own solutions, including yagnas to propitiate the rain gods.[126] In February 1966, he began a forty eight day fast demanding that the procurement scheme be revoked or at least suspended till a fresh assessment of the crop output had been made.[127] It was in the villages, however, that the real opposition to the levy took place. The rice issue was mixed up with that of restoring the king to his throne (or to his legal position as ex-ruler to be precise), since it was a common perception among the people that the government could not be trusted and that if the grain was collected and given to the raja instead, he would redistribute it among the poor. They also felt that the king's presence was necessary to overcome the drought, an idea encouraged, not accidentally, by Pravir's speeches and ritual activities. Baldeo of village Karanji reported:

Shri Pravir Chandra Bhanj Deo said that for the restoration of his 'Raj', we would have to stand and do fight and that if we did not do so, there would be no rain and the crops would not ripen and that he would take away the Danteswari Mai with him to some other place. When Shri Pravir Chandra Bhanj Deo said so, we told him that if Danteshwari Mai left this place, what would we do, and how would our children survive?[128]

Women apparently took the lead once the rice situation worsened, and meetings were held in several villages which only women attended. In many villages, a more or less total boycott of the levy was organized and there was an active movement to mobilize women. Kejuram of Village Gopni stated that:

In the beginning of Chaitra last, there was a meeting in my village. Women of 22 villages assembled there. There were about 600 women present on that occasion. Three of them went to my house and enquired from me why I did not send my wife to that meeting. They

---

[126] Pandey (1967:para 56).

[127] *DS*, 13 February 1966.

[128] Deposition by Baldeo, s/o Mahadeo, Cultivator, village Karanji, tahsil Jagdalpur, age 45, 8 August 1966, Bajpai Papers. (R.S. Bajpai is a lawyer in Jagdalpur and as a member of the Praja Socialist Party in the 1960s, he was actively involved in the events of the day, trying to walk a middle path between the king and the Congress. He acted as defence lawyer for many of the villagers implicated in the 1966 confrontation and gave me his copies of the depositions).

threatened me with dire consequences and therefore, I sent my wife to that meeting.[129]

Simultaneously, men came under attack for being spineless and not resisting the levy sufficiently, sometimes leading to domestic conflict. Several accounts describe the women as telling the men to keep away from the fight as they were weak and useless.[130] Village leaders and rich men (landlords, larger tenants, liquor contractors) who were associated with the status quo became special objects of the women's wrath, as they were even more willing to give the grain, or more afraid of the government. Budhu, the patel of village Chaparbhanpuri remembered an incident in Chait (March–April):

The Patwari had come to the village for preparing a voters list. Mst. Parwati who was the memberine of our village had collected women of 16 villages in my village. About 500 women were there. They surrounded the Patwari and snatched away his papers. When I asked the women why they snatched away the papers when no harm was being done to them, they said they would beat me by use of stones and would make water on my head.[131]

The patel then went and reported the incident to the Lohandiguda police station, and a head constable came and threatened all the women with arrest if they did not return the papers. Whereupon they did so. The patel went on:

The women held meetings frequently. The women asked for one pailee (approx. 1.75–2 kg) of rice and one rupee per plough from the residents of my village. They had demanded from me 8 pailees of rice and eight rupees. Then they put me in fear saying that they would set my house on fire and would expel me from the village because I was a man of the Congress Raj.[132]

When the patel was preparing to deliver to the government the twenty bags of paddy required from him under the grain

[129] Deposition of Kejuram, s/o Milsuram, Cultivator, Village Gopni, Jagdalpur Tahsil, age 60, 8 August 1966, Bajpai Papers.
[130] Deposition by Bhadu, s/o Lakhma, Cultivator, Village Chitapur, Jagdalpur Tahsil, 8 August 1966; deposition by Lingraj, s/o Jagbandhu, Cultivator, aged 64 years, Village Mohpal Barai, 8 August 1966, Bajpai Papers.
[131] Deposition of Budhu, s/o Bede, Cultivator, Chaparbhanpuri, Jagdalpur Tahsil, Age 45, 8 August 1966, Bajpai Papers.
[132] Ibid.

levy, about 400–500 women gathered to oppose his breaking of the levy boycott. They snatched away the levy papers when the patwari came to collect it, causing the patwari and his helpers to run away in fear.[133]

In 1965 and early 1966, there were lathi-charges and tear gassing incidents at several markets: Kesarpal, Sargipal, Sheonaguda, Nagarnar, where membrins and members resisted the grain levies. At Kesarpal, the people abused the police and tried to unload the carts on which paddy bags had been stocked.[134] In one case, a group of membrins compelled a trader to lower his rice prices to Rs 1 per paili, less than the rate at which he had bought it.[135] The anti-government feeling spread — school teachers were threatened and schools were boycotted. There were forest fires under mysterious circumstances and there was a widespread resistance to payment of taxes or even voter registration.[136] In November and December 1965, there were several processions through Jagdalpur, demanding that the levy and rice export from the district be stopped; that rice be made available to people at 2 paili per rupee; that in view of crop failure, land revenue be remitted, and *taccavi* loans (for agricultural improvement) advanced. Although the government imposed Sec. 144, it could not hold people back for any length of time.[137] The police arrested seventy-eight leaders including nineteen women, alleged to be inciting people to resist the grain levy,[138] and in early 1966, additional police forces were moved into the district.

On market day (Thursday, 24 March) at Bastar village, a large group of people, mostly women, assembled outside Suryapal Tewari's house, headed by Manglibai of Dongriguda and Ratni Bai. They insisted on seeing him, despite his wife's claim that he was away, and were reported to have been waving the Bastar state flag and demanding the return of the official papers merging Bastar with India, saying: 'Suryapal Tewari has taken

---

[133] Ibid.

[134] Pandey (1967:para 61).

[135] Deposition of Abdul Sattar, s/o Sheikh Tansari, Grain-dealer, village Balenga, Jagdalpur tahsil, age 45 yrs, 8 August 1966, Bajpai Papers.

[136] Pandey (1967:para 61).

[137] Ibid., para 56.

[138] *DS*, 27 February 1966.

the Raja's Raj (kingdom), now he will not even give us rice to
eat.' Police reports successively exaggerated the number of those
present and their actions, claiming that about ten thousand
people were standing in row formation on the banks of three
nearby ponds, 'jumping and dancing' with their bows and
arrows, and other weapons (axes, sticks) at the ready.[139] Unfortunately for the officers and the police, their version of events
was not substantiated by the photographs taken by sub-inspector
M.P. Tewari, which when enlarged revealed that 'the Adivasis
on the banks of the two tanks were both men and women, that
they were only a few hundreds in number, that none of them
carried any bow or arrow, that they were not in formation and
that they were either sitting or standing and looking at something like curious spectators.'[140] Thus, Justice Pandey later concluded that a 'simple incident' which took place on market day
was 'greatly exaggerated by the officers'.[141] Relatively minor
incidents acquired immense proportions in the local official
imagination, which in turn was transmitted through telegrams
to their superiors in Bhopal. This construct became a real part
of subsequent encounters.

25 March 1966

A careful sifting of the conflicting accounts of numerous witnesses by Justice Pandey resulted in the following narrative of
what happened in Jagdalpur on the crucial day of March 25.
Sec. 144 was promulgated by the Collector in the morning to
pre-empt a procession by the adivasis. Police guards armed with
rifles, instead of the usual lathis, were posted at the four main
entrances of the palace premises to enforce this. At the main
gate, in addition, there was a large police force accompanied by
the Additional District Magistrate. An incident with a prisoner
who was under trial and being escorted to the police lock-up in
the palace premises accidentally sparked off an encounter between the people assembled in the palace grounds and the police,

[139] Roznamcha Sanha reports no. 302 and 303, 24 March 1966, Outpost
Bastar, Bajpai Papers; different versions also reproduced in Pandey (1967:
para 70).
[140] Pandey (1967: para 70).
[141] Ibid.: para 71.

with the people shooting bows and arrows and the police responding with tear gas and bullets. One policeman died from an arrow wound and another was injured, whereupon, according to Justice Pandey, 'other members (of the police force) seem to have lost all self-control.' The police then chased the adivasis through the gardens and fired at them in front of the two palaces. Pravir Chandra, who had come out to see what was happening, was shot and killed along with other people. By about 12.45 pm, most adivasis had taken shelter inside the two palaces, and from then till late at night, there was sporadic exchange of arrows and bullets from either side.[142] The government however claimed that the adivasis made two further concerted attempts to attack the police, which Justice Pandey dismissed in scathing terms:

The learned counsel for the officers, however, clothed the Adivasis with heroic fervour born of a supreme sense of duty, which impelled them to come out and make an attack against all odds like Lord Tennyson's Light Brigade. . . . The counsel (for the officers) went on to say that, since the first attack at 1 p.m. had ended disastrously for the Adivasis, Pravir Chandra Bhanj Deo himself led the second attack at 4 p.m. to put courage in the dis-spirited Adivasis and that is how he received bullet injuries and died. This picture, so cleverly and artfully painted, is too good to be true for the illiterate and ignorant Adivasis.[143]

People began to emerge gradually from their hiding places in the palace, in response to a loudspeaker appeal by the Commissioner at night. The bulk of them left after the shooting stopped at midnight, slinking away in the dark, scaling the walls, or exiting through small gates at the sides. The next morning, the last two hundred and fifty came out in response to another appeal by the Commissioner.[144] Two hundred and twenty people in total were arrested and held for questioning by the police, before being let off on bail.[145] People say that the police pursued those who ran away that fateful night, and for many days after, there were repeated police enquiries in the villages as to who had taken part.

[142] Ibid.: para 149-57.
[143] Ibid., para 100.
[144] Ibid.: para 156.
[145] *DS*, 27 March 1966, 3 April 1966.

The number of those who died in the confrontation is a controversial issue. According to Justice Pandey, while the police suffered one death and ten injured, the death toll on the other side was twelve people, including Pravir Chandra. The number of wounded was officially estimated as only twenty, although the police fired over sixty-one rounds.[146] However, a very common story among people retelling the event today is that truckloads of dead bodies were carted away at night and dumped into the Indrawati. On the other hand, several people continue to insist that no one died and that the bullets did in fact turn into water as Pravir had told them would happen. Aitu Nag of Bade Kawali, who helped in the palace for a year, told me that blood was a foot high on the ground and many people died. In the very next statement however, he said that no one in the villages died. When I pointed out the discrepancy in his account, he said: 'Our eyes were cheated. We thought those men were dead. But they weren't.' A similar belief persists in many areas with respect to the raja, i.e. that he never died, since he had extraordinary God-given powers.

When people claim that their side died in large numbers, they also claim to have killed off the police in equally large numbers. In one version deposed during the enquiries, Boga, aged 65, cultivator of village Nandi Sagar, alleged that the police came into the new palace, breaking down the door with their boots:

After the policeman entered the room, all the Adivasis in that room lay on the ground on their chests with faces downwards. While we were so lying, the policemen fired at our backs and killed two of us and injured three of us.[147]

But much much later, in 1993, in response to my questions, Suklo Nag of Barupata told me:

Two Chitapur boys hid behind the doors and cupboards in the Danteswari temple, and killed the police paltan as they entered. All the police died — not a single one remained. But no one knew where the bodies were taken.

[146] Pandey (1967: para 157).

[147] Deposition given by Boga, s/o Mangru, 13 August 1966, to Justice Pandey, Bajpai Papers.

Even if the official figure for the dead was accurate, the number of wounded is likely to have been far higher since people would have been too scared to report their wounds.[148] The day after the firing all the shops in Jagdalpur were shut in mourning.[149] There were also rumours in the press that mango boughs and chillis were continuing to circulate in interior villages, and that a 'Bhumkal Dal' (Rebellion party) had been formed.[150] In Jagdalpur itself, Sec. 144 was extended for another month and police and officers of all levels began patrolling markets and visiting villages.[151] Ironically, the government also suspended land revenue for nearly 2000 villages.[152] The incident created a storm in the state assembly and in both houses of parliament in Delhi. In the state assembly at Bhopal, the charges and counter charges soon degenerated into flying shoe battles.[153] Among opposition parties, there was a widespread demand for a judicial enquiry, and for central government intervention, on the grounds that the state government couldn't be trusted.[154] A one-man commission, comprized of Justice K.L. Pandey of the MP High Court, was appointed. Eventually, when the government changed as a result of the 1967 elections, a second one-man commisssion comprising of Mr T.C.A. Ramanujachari was appointed to re-examine the case.[155]

Re-telling the Story

The retrospective interpretations of every event are almost as interesting as the event itself. One can discern three clear views on this: that of the government, the opposition parties and

[148] For instance, in Kukanar, I was told of one man who was wounded in the firing, his hip turning upwards due to a bullet. But he only died several years later.
[149] *DS*, 27 March 1966.
[150] *DS*, 3 April 1966; 10 April 1966.
[151] Copy of government document titled, "Steps Taken to Restore Order," Bajpai Papers.
[152] *DS*, 27 March 1966.
[153] *MP Chronicle*, 7 April 1966.
[154] *DS*, 5 June 1966.
[155] *DS*, 18 February 1968.

finally, the people of the district themselves. There is, on the one hand, congruity between the government view that violence was premeditated and the impression given by some popular accounts that in fact, careful plans to establish an alternative state had been made. There are other people, however, who claim that they were innocent victims of police firing. The epistemological conditions under which both views came to be formed are interesting.

The government view was that expressed by the Congress state government in power (i.e. the Congress Chief Minister, D.P. Mishra, and members of his cabinet) and the local officials. They blamed the shooting on Pravir's incitement of the adivasis, the adivasis' own propensity to violence, and their combined desire in wanting to secede from the rest of India. The picture they painted was one of planned violence, which they, the officers, had done their best to avoid. A telephone message from the Commissioner to the Chief Secretary on the day after the firing mentioned that 'inside the new palace, cartloads of bows and arrows and large quantities of rice had been stored.'[156] The administration also justified their decision to impose Sec. 144 and post armed police at the palace on the basis of an informer's report, allegedly made on the 25th morning, that:

the jail would be attacked, the Indrawati river bridge would be damaged, the means of communication, that is to say, the telegraph and telephone wires, would be tampered with, the bungalows of the officers would be attacked and the Collectorate and the government godowns and the godowns of *sahukars* would also be looted.[157]

However Justice Pandey took pains to point out several factors which contradict this picture. The informer's report, as well as a number of reports from police stations all around Bastar which tried to paint a picture of weapons being readied and plots being hatched, were dismissed as manufactured *post facto*. In the judge's words, these reports 'were brought into existence after 25 March 1966 in order to prepare an answer to the charge of use of excessive force.'[158] Moreover, shortly before the firing, the Commissioner and Collector went to Bijapur in the extreme west of

---

[156] Reproduced in Pandey (1967: para 77).
[157] Ibid.: para 75.
[158] Ibid.: paras 75–80, 164.

the district on a hunting expedition. As Justice Pandey averred, if they wanted to appear responsible officials, they could not simultaneously claim prior awareness of impending violence.[159]

Whereas the government tried to shift all the blame onto Pravir and the adivasis, the opposition parties portrayed the adivasis as victims of the government, particularly the anti-Pravir policies of the Congress. They were quick to point to Congress opportunism in dealing with Pravir in general, and in fact accused the government of cold blooded murder, insinuating that the Congress had engineered Pravir's death to remove an electoral obstacle.[160] Justice Pandey's report, which in almost every respect is a model of detached impartiality, also subscribes to the view of adivasis as generally innocent victims of the government's food policies and of inept handling by local authorities such as the Additional District Magistrate, the Superintendent of Police and the Collector.[161]

The government saw it as a law and order situation while the opposition saw it as a failure of the government's economic and political policies. Both nevertheless viewed the problem in purely administrative terms, ignoring the internal political dynamic involved: the loss of state legitimacy and the adivasi vision, however inchoate, of a different and more just polity. While both the government and the opposition criticized Pravir for using the economic demands of the people for his own political ends, they in turn used the event and the demands that had previously been expressed by both people and king, to gain votes. The adivasis were simply empty slates on which parties contended to inscribe their own perfections as rulers and administrators. While the Chief Minister justified the actions of his government on the grounds that Bastar was following the secessionist tactics of Nagaland and Mizoram, the opposition claimed that Bastar adivasis were 'as patriotic as any', but that

[159] Ibid.: para 69.
[160] *Statesman Weekly*, 2 April 1966.
[161] Justice Pandey's conclusions were that the posting of police pickets around the palace had been unnecessary in the first place, the claims of conspiracy to rebel having been shown to be post-firing fabrications. While the first round of firing may have been justified in self-defence, the police having been attacked by the adivasis, the subsequent firing, in which most people died, was not. Pandey (1967: paras 158–69).

they couldn't continue to be suppressed. Instead they needed to be 'uplifted'.[162]

The Reincarnation of Gunda Dhur?

At the enquiry itself, there were several witnesses who claimed that plans to stage a major rebellion had been made, though of course, it goes without saying that they personally had had no hand in it, and had, on occasion, valiantly tried to go against the crowd. Jai Deo, a cultivator of village Bhadisgaon, aged approximately 30, said that on that fateful Friday, he was invited by a group of four or five hundred men to accompany them to the palace to fight. But before they could set off, they got news of the firing, and soon dispersed.[163] Sukru, blacksmith of village Bastar, deposed that a month or two before the firing took place, a group of people came to ask him to make arrows. When he refused (or so he claimed), they said that they would beat him, drive him out of the village and raze his house to the ground. Faced with such a threat, he made two hundred and ten arrow heads out of a cart rim they gave him. He was told to go to the palace for his payment, and given twenty five rupees by the head membrin there.[164] If true, this would have indicated an organized attempt at arms collection, emanating from the palace itself. Budhu, the patel of village Chaparbhanpuri remembered an incident in Chait (March-April):

In the month of Chait last, on one Wednesday, Mst. Parvati with about 40 or 50 women was moving about in the village with a mango tree in hand. She was saying that the men of the village had to arm themselves with bows and arrows and axes and had to go to the palace on Thursday night lest they would be seen if they went there during the day time. Since I belonged to the Congress party, they did not ask me to go there with bows and arrows. The women had said there would be a meeting on Friday at Jagdalpur and thereafter when they would return on the following day, they would behead me, the manjhi and the kotwar. The women had said that if after the meeting there

---

[162] Debates in Vidhan Sabha on March 26, reported in *MP Chronicle*, 27 March 1966.

[163] Deposition of Jai Deo, 6 August 1966, Bajpai Papers.

[164] Sukru, s/o Sonadhar, Age 30, Village Bastar, Jagdalpur Tahsil, Deposition, 6 August 1966, Bajpai Papers.

was any disturbance, the raja would lead them and if there was firing, water would come out of the guns.[165]

It is noteworthy that all such depositions were given by men, and quite often, influential men like headmen, who might have had an interest in keeping good relations with the administration. It is also possible that these accounts were given under police compulsion. But whether they were true or not, they subsequently entered the popular imagination. In 1992–3, I often heard from villagers that had the incident with the undertrial prisoner which sparked off the firing not messed up matters, the raja and his people would have been able to successfully push their plan. If the government officers were keen on exaggerating the popular intent to rebel in order to exonerate themselves, some people were also keen, in retrospect, on exaggerating their own organization and resistance. Both sides promote the same image of a secret plan to repeat the rebellion of 1910 in all its details — the burning of schools, police stations and government offices, the driving away of outsiders and government servants etc. On the one hand, the government exaggerated the situation as a way of legitimising its actions, while on the other hand, in the villagers versions, it becomes a means of delegitimation. The stories of hundreds of bodies being loaded into trucks is part of this construction.

Thirty Years Later: Membrins Revisited

In Dussehra 1992 on one rare evening in Vedwati's house, a group of former membrins opened up, described what it was like, mimicked the police and sang songs. Their conversation was somewhat rambling, and did not fit a neat chronology of events as I knew them. However, they provide a vivid sense of the times as they experienced them. Encounters with the police were repeatedly described, indicating what a major source of oppression the police were, as well as giving a touching and inspiring sense of what it must have been like to face up to this and not be scared. The membrins came from all sorts of backgrounds, with and without land, married and with children,

---

[165] Deposition of Budhu, s/o Bede, Cultivator, Chaparbhanpuri, Jagdalpur Tahsil, Age 45, 8 August 1966, Bajpai Papers.

and unmarried women and widows. Many of the membrins were strong, independent women, but several were shy, and came alive only in remembering those times.

Lachni Bai, a thin grey-haired woman from Keslur, described how at the police station she was repeatedly asked by a big officer, a policeman and finally the peon, why she came to the raja's house. Finally, she replied that she and the others came because they and their children were having great difficulty and they wanted the raja to pray for them to Danteswari. She then imitated the police asking her to come back for another hearing:

Policeman: (threatening) Oh, so you won't come?
She: (defiant) No, we won't come.
Policeman: (angry) See here, your date will go by on the 9th. If you go to Raja's house on the 8th, we'll send 100 men from Keslur to jail, *mailotia* (motherfuckers).
She: (coolly) I haven't killed anyone, I haven't done anything. Why do you bother our one village, Keslur, what have we done that you want to send us all to jail?
Policeman: (shouting) *Bhosdi ke sale*, why do you go to fight, leaving your husbands and children at home?
She: (turning to her companions) Come *baile man* (women folk), let's go.

After they had gone some distance, she says the other women had asked her why she talked like that, and she had replied: 'Talk like what?' Then turning to me, she said, 'The policeman thought he could threaten us and put us in jail. Had we been the sort to get scared we would have got cowed. I have never been afraid of anything.' Our conversation shifted to Suryapal Tiwari, the hated Congressman of 1966. Ludri Bai of Bade Marenga remembered that:

The Raja had said: 'Bai Log go, all the bai log go. Burn his grain storage room'. We went, we went a long way looking for it. His younger brother was in our party, the Raja's party. He made us stay in his *kothar* (grain storage room) and gave us rice and lentils. Suryapal hid.
Nandini: Why were you angry with him?
Ludri Bai: Raja had a doubt (using the English word) about him. . .
While returning to Jagdalpur, in all directions the police stopped us. Like the male race, women also carried big sticks, as big as our heads, in a huge crowd. We went to the sirasar to establish the victory post. Police said: 'You

people, don't go in now. Go in the morning.' We insisted but they wouldn't let us in. Then an old membrin, Kosalya and I said: 'Why should we be scared of the police. We'll talk just like them.' We weren't scared at all, and we went straight inside. What could they do to us?

When questioned as to why Dussehra was important, and why Pravir's presence was important,

Rukni Bai said: Its no good if there is no Dussehra. It is being celebrated since raja's parents and their parents. Indira *dokri,* that old woman Indira (Gandhi), mother of Rajiv (Gandhi), had our raja killed, so that is why the government has to listen to us. . . . . Now its no longer the raja's raj. When our raja died, no shops were shut. When Indira dokri died, the shops were shut all year. Our raja has no memorial. . . . But on 25th March, in his name, we light a lamp. The city people don't respect him, but the Muria, Mahara, Bhatra, all believed in him. Raja was our Pujari. . . . If Danteswari isn't worshipped, people will become wounded, mad, ill. So the whole raj contributes. She is the biggest of them all.

Parvati bai added: It was Indira dokri who caused our Raja to die, and for that very reason she herself was killed in a firing. I heard this in Bailadilla.

On the main incident of the 25th itself, they said that when the firing started in the morning, some of them were cooking, and some just starting to cook.

Sukri: How do we know how it happened? The government was armed with rifles and the public was absolutely unarmed, just like we are now. Everyone had come to watch the prayer, to ask for water. Everyone had come with their little bundles and camped here; from every village. It was absolutely dry. All the fish died and the ponds were dry.

Parvati: They (police) put off the lights and threw chilli smoke (tear gas) at us. But even this we survived. Then they jailed the women who helped him. The government said: Somehow or the other we'll get rid of the raja and rule in his place. Raja said: I won't give my Bailadilla, my mines. I won't give my kingdom. The government was angry with him for not leaving. How would you like it if someone told you to leave your house?

Lachmi: Yes, the fight was because of Bailadilla mines.

Sukri: I told you it was because of water. Our fields were dry. The government punished us for rice. We were afflicted for our cattle. . . . Now clothes are so expensive, rice is so expensive. In the rani's time, rice used to be Rs 1 for 8 paili, 1 *dhoti* was 8 annas. God knows where the government took her and made her disappear. She was a Lakshmi, a real Lakshmi (Goddess of prosperity).

Rukni: In this situation, we all went to the raja.

Nandini: What did the raja say?

Parvati: What could he say? Raja made us sit under the bison head in the palace, all the women, and said: 'Bai log, I know. My kingdom has gone, they have punished me. . . . Membrin folk, I will sell the palace.' The membrins replied: 'Maharaj, you have so many children (the peasants), where will you go? If you sell the palace, what will you eat? We will do something, gather the strength, we won't let the palace be sold.' The Raja said it was too late, but the membrins assured him they were there. In every village they collected contributions.

Rukni: There was a big membrin from Lendra, Lachni, like this Manki Bai here. You know what she did? She sold the rice we had collected and bought a buffalo. Then we fought and told the Raja: the big membrin does this and that. The Raja said: Go and call her. But she hid for fear thinking he would beat her. Then she became mad and kept asking for water. The buffalo she bought also died. What else can you expect from someone who steals from the Raja? Bai, I didn't steal anything and here I am alive.

A Matkot membrin said that she had just finished a week's duty in the palace and gone home when the firing took place. The headman of her village told her not to go back because there had been some trouble. 'My heart thumped with fear', she said, and she went into hiding. She went on to recount:

Very late at night I heard of the firing. I sat on a truck and came home. My daughter was there and gave me food. But I cried and cried and couldn't eat. The villagers said: You didn't cry this much even when your parents died as you are crying because the Raja died. My husband said: You will die if you cry like this, don't eat and don't work. I replied: But he was like a father to us.

This idiom of familial closeness and the mutual protectiveness between the raja and the membrins helped to bring forth the women's participation in that instance, but it seems ultimately to have been disempowering. By 1992, the membrins had largely tranferred their attachment to Vedwati, who was ill throughout the period I was there. Their activism now is limited to over-seeing the Dussehra function and waving the lamp in front of the chariots and shouting *'Jai'*. On occasion, they are caustic about the government but within the limited sphere of its handling of Dussehra or the pensions of majhis. This degeneration of spirit on the part of the membrins was partly because of the way the movement dwindled into a power struggle between members of Pravir's family and lost all connection with issues concerning land and forest. Although other groups later continued this struggle, e.g. the communists and naxalites, their support came from a younger constituency. These members and membrins were perhaps too imbued with their relations with the ruling family, and too tired or terrorized by the fall-out of the 1966 events, to become active again in the same way.

In the opportunism and dynastic sycophancy that has come to be characteristic of the major political parties in India, both the Jan Sangh and the Congress began to make contacts with Vedvati.[166] Eventually Vedvati supported Jansangh while Hitendra Kumari, wife of Vijay Chandra, and Kunwar Balmukund Singh, another member of the royal family, supported the Congress.[167] Vedvati also tried to revive the Adivasi Seva Dal, but as an ostensibly non-political organization to protect adivasi rights in land and trees.[168] The post-Pravir period was marked by an unseemly tug of war over Dussehra, with tussles over who would ascend the chariot and who would receive Danteswari during the Mawli parghav. Eventually in 1970, both the maharanis agreed that only the umbrella of Danteswari carried by the priest of the temple would ride the chariot, although both held their own Muria durbars. In that year management of Dussehra arrangements reverted back to the administration. It was reported to be a very poorly attended event.[169] After Pravir's death, invitations to Dussehra were issued in the name of the majhi of Amorapati pargana, and now with the displacment of majhis by MLAs, they go out in the name of one of the MLAs,

[166] *DS*, 4 December 1966.
[167] *DS*, 7 February 1967.
[168] *DS*, 28 April 1968.
[169] *DS*, 4 October 1970.

Conclusion

One can discern two broad positions in existing scholarship on kingship in the post-colonial Indian polity. In one, which I call the culturalist model because it posits the notion of a specific Indian cultural idiom in which politics occurs,[170] there is a long and unbroken tradition of personalized rule. Price argues that the segmentary nature of the state coupled with the focus on monarchical authority resulted in the percolation of kingly values down to the local level, and instilled dependence on superior beings, rather than allowing the notions of rights from a welfare state. This is found in politicians who rule through personal charisma, expect and get unquestioning loyalty from their followers right down to small administrators who run their departments like personal durbars.[171] Personalized politics may be a remnant of an earlier tradition, but it is not some inevitable 'essence' of Indian politics, and requires fresh evaluation in the particular context where it arises. Not only are there historical counter-traditions like that of the Charavaks, who denied the existence of a God beyond themselves, but also enough evidence to show that when subaltern groups get the chance, they prefer autonomy to dependence on a patron, despite the greater security the latter might give them.[172]

In the other model, the changed context of kingship is emphasized. Electoral and other forms of popular support for kings are seen as a manifestation of the 'modernity of tradition'.[173] Richter, while discussing princely participation in post-colonial politics, notes that support for them was not automatic but does not give any detailed understanding of why and how support, where it did or does exist, was mobilized.[174] Bailey argues that rather than politicians modelling themselves on ex-rulers, rulers now model themselves on politicians. In the

[170] Price (1989); Mayer (1991).
[171] Ibid.:572.
[172] Breman (1974).
[173] Rudolph and Rudolph (1967).
[174] Richter (1978).

initial post-colonial period, support for former rulers existed
due to lingering sentiment which produced small vote banks.
Where they continue to have support for a long period, it is
because old ties, which had been reduced to mere sentiment
were now reactivated in the new forms of democratic action.[175]

Neither of these two models is adequate to explain the
popularity of Pravir or of the particular course followed by the
movement. To some extent, Bailey is useful in explaining the
existence of old ties in terms of new forms of democracy, but
his notion of 'democracy' is very much based on a British
parliamentary ideal type. Pravir's success did not represent an
adaptation of 'traditional' kingship to 'modern' electoral politics. Nor was it a continuation of divine kingship, though of
course there was some element of that which he purposely played
upon. While the ritual importance of the king in warding off
drought was common to both 1876 and 1966, the public
expression of this demand was quite different in both cases.
Pravir's popularity and the movement arose at a particular
historical juncture and represented a critique of the post-colonial
state. It was born of the alienation caused by the electoral
opportunism of the mainstream political parties and the loss
of real power that land and forest policies entailed. Pravir
succeeded in mobilizing people because his movement articulated more than his own personal goals, it took up local issues
and latent desires.

In terms of achieving popular democratic goals, it is true
that the movement seems anachronistic on the surface. There
seems little to choose from in a contest between a mad king
and an insensitive government. On the other hand, it is
important to study the movement not for its instrumental
success alone but for its expressive significance. In some sense,
the movement can be read as an expression of subaltern
'consciousness', operating through the common modalities of
resistance outlined by Ranajit Guha: 'negation' or the extension
of opposition to everything and everyone connected with the
government; the reversal of normal forms of deference to the
police and other authorities; the 'ambiguity' regarding 'crime'
as a form of heroism, as witnessed in the land grabbing

[175] Bailey (1963).

incidents; and 'solidarity' expressed by threats against anyone who tried to break the grain levy boycott.[176] However, these were not remnants of a 'pure' pre-colonial subaltern consciousness, but a consciously historical mode of organization, i.e. one that invoked past myth as a guide to present action. The reverbrations of the Bhumkal of 1910 in 1966 bring us alive to the way in which the past and its mythology functions in the service of the future.

Marx's formulations in the *Eighteenth Brumaire* provide the best way of understanding the phenomenon of Pravir's popularity, the manner in which class struggle 'created circumstances and relationships that made it possible for a grotesque mediocrity to play a hero's part.' In his inimitable words:

Hegel remarks somewhere that all facts and personages of great importance in world history occur, as it were, twice. He forgot to add: the first time as tragedy, the second as farce. . . . Men make their own history, but they do not make it just as they please; they do not make it under circumstances chosen by themselves, but under circumstances directly encountered, given, and transmitted from the past. The tradition of all the dead generations weighs like a nighmare on the brain of the living. And just when they seem engaged in revolutionizing themselves and things, in creating something that has never yet existed, precisely in such periods of revolutionary crisis they anxiously conjure up the spirits of the past to their service and borrow from them names, battle cries, and costumes in order to present the new scene of world history in this time-honoured disguise and this borrowed language.[177]

Perhaps even more than what it reveals about subaltern consciousness, studying the movement is useful for what it reveals about the political legitimacy of the state.[178] In this case, it points to the incapacity of the existing post-colonial state to find an echo in everyday aspects of people's lives: their rhythms of production, their rituals and their desires, as well as its longer term destructive effect on these. What also comes through, especially in the accounts of women who participated, is the sense of responsibility and release it gave them, and the way this has been buried in the structures of both the traditional village

---

[176] Guha (1983).
[177] Marx (1972:15).
[178] Fields (1985:22).

polity and the new electoral mechanisms. More than anything else, therefore, it reveals the gendered nature of the polity, the enormous waste of and violence towards women. As comparable accounts of women's participation in popular struggles show, unless there is an explicit attempt to address questions regarding their personal lives, patriarchal structures reassert themselves even in the otherwise most radical movements.[179] It is difficult to say whether participation in the membrin movement made any difference to their personal lives later on in any significant way, but certainly they did not achieve a presence in village panchayats which went back to being male dominated. Nor were they able to keep up the organized struggle as membrins for access to land and forest, though women in Bastar have subsequently organized around similar issues.

In conclusion then, to what extent did the struggle embody a potential for real change? Here, while there was a keen appreciation of government insensitivity and the opportunism and corruption of electoral parties like the Congress, there was no similar understanding of Pravir's role. There was no way he could have provided a state which fulfilled the promises of independence, of land and access to natural resources, which the existing state had failed to provide. The result was a tragic farce where those who lived by honest dreams, ended up defending the bad against the worse.

---

[179] *See* for instance Stree Shakti Sanghatana (1989); Sen (1990); Rowbotham, Segal and Wainwright (1979).

8

The Baba and the Bhagats

While members of the royal family were busy trying to cash in on Pravir's popularity, others were intent on becoming Pravir himself! There were at least sixteen putative re-incarnations of Pravir before the last and most successful of them all — Baba Bihari Das — appeared on the scene. The first attempt was by one Ghumri Kuruk who apparently looked like Pravir, with 'long hair and flowing beard'. By claiming to be Pravir, he and his twenty two companions had been garnering free rations and supplies in several villages. Unfortunately for him and his band, this bonanza ended with arrests.[1]

In 1971, however, there appeared a man who came to be popularly known as Baba Bihari Das. His claim to be a re-incarnation of Pravir was supported by two former activists of the Adivasi Seva Dal, Khosru and Bali, both Bhatras, and thus acquired greater credibility among others.[2] In some versions, it was the raja's men who first noticed the likeness between Bihari Das and Pravir and persuaded him to adopt the role.[3] The fact that the Baba was considerably darker was accounted for by the fact that he had been scorched by bullets and spent several years hiding in the jungle. The Baba added to this aura by making mysterious appearances in the half-light on the banks of a pond near Narayanpal. At the same time, his support also depended on the fact that anyone who opposed him was beaten up.[4] Many people refused to believe that Pravir had actually died in the firing — for that would have been to doubt his supposed tantric powers, and the fact that he could turn bullets into water. According to Dr B.D. Sharma, who was Collector at the time, people thought that Pravir coming

---

[1] *DS*, 12 February 1967.
[2] Bhatt (1983).
[3] Lakshman Jhadi, 17 December 1992.
[4] Information collected and corroborated from several villagers in the course of numerous conversations in 1992-3.

back would mean that the land and forest situation would improve.[5]

In what has become a classic pattern of bhagat (reform and revival) movements in India,[6] the Baba advised his followers to give up drinking liquor and eating meat and to wear *kanthis* — beads made of the wood of the tulsi plant — around their necks. Because of this last injunction, the Baba is commonly called *kanthi-wale* baba. The movement also had millenarian overtones. One had to tie the kanthi to be saved from impending doom. People believed that there would come a 'long dark night, when demons shall eat up all non-kanthi wearing people, when a great havoc shall be caused by an earthquake or deluge in which all except those wearing kanthi shall perish.'[7] In some versions, this long darkness was specified as three days and three nights.[8] The Baba also told people to abandon all their black animals before then, lest they turn into dangerous beasts. In Durras, a hamlet of Kukanar, a substantial number of Dhurwas are Bhagats. The elders who I talked to remembered a particular conversion rate: black goats would turn into cheetahs, black pigs into bears and black bulls into lions; on eating fish, humans would turn into fowl and on eating *chapda* (red ants, with which a very popular chutney is made), they would quiver like chapda. In several places, people told me they had believed that they would die if they ate meat after tying the kanthis. So, rather than simply dispose of their animals, they ate them all up in one huge feast beforehand. A similar phenomenon had occurred before in Bastar, laying the seedbed for future credulity. Grigson recorded that:

In 1932 a rumour went through all the tribes of Jeypore and spread thence into Bastar that a God had descended on one of the mountains of the Eastern Ghats and commanded all men to give up keeping black poultry and goats, wearing clothes or using umbrellas or blankets with any black in them, and using beads or articles made of aluminum alloy. The message was rapidly bruited abroad, and everywhere villages had 'bohorani' ceremonies for purifying themselves from disease, and cast out black goats, cocks, hens, umbrellas, 'waskats', beads, aluminum ornaments and domestic utensils on the village boundary.

[5] Dr B.D. Sharma, 1 May 1993.
[6] Hardiman (1987); Baviskar (1995:97–103).
[7] Bhatt (1983:240), corroborated by Sadashiv Majhi, Hamirgarh, 1993.
[8] Dr B.D. Sharma, 1 May 1993.

Mohammedans began to make a good thing out of slaughtering the goats or exporting them. Strenuous propaganda by the State soon stopped this impoverishing rumour, and some of the villagers in the end recovered much of their property from the police, who had been ordered to take charge of it.[9]

The Baba's Following

The Baba established an ashram at Chapka, a village about 30 km north of Jagdalpur, and thousands of people began flocking there.[10] Vikas Bhatt writes that initially the movement had been popular only among the Bhatras, Halbas and Murias in the area, but it soon spread to other groups and other areas of the district. In Kukanar, when I asked how they had heard of the Baba and why they were attracted to the movement, people said simply that they had heard that a Baba had arrived, and that one just had to go to Chapka and get a kanthi. So a couple of people from every hamlet set off on foot to get kanthis for everyone else.

Baba Bihari Das started celebrating major festivals at Chapka, such as Goncha (in June) and Dussehra, much like Pravir used to celebrate them in the palace. These became major crowd pullers and supplanted the festivals celebrated in Jagdalpur. He also began touring villages, collecting money, performing prayer rituals, dispensing wisdom — all the usual occupations of Indian holy men. In that first year alone, the Baba was said to have collected 1.7 lakh rupees.[11] Apart from the normal subscriptions collected, the Baba made money by selling holy water in bottles[12] and organizing major yagnas where people would come and bring gifts. At one particularly large ceremony held in 1974, 25–30,000 people are said to have attended.[13]

Whole villages became Baba followers in the initial period, walking hundred miles or more to his ashram at Chapka. But soon, the movement created severe dissension within villages

[9] Grigson (1991:76).

[10] Curiously, Chapka had been the site of a previous attempt at starting a Bhagat movement. A Raj-Gond state pensioner had tried to hold a Dhur-Gond sabha there, with the intention of raising tribal status. Microfilm Acc no. 352, CRR, ESA, Fortnightly Reports, March 1939, NAI.

[11] *DS*, 22 August 1971.

[12] *DS*, 26 December 1971.

[13] Bhatt (1983:230).

between followers of the Baba, the Bhagats, and those who continued or fell back into their former ways. The Bhagats would not eat or drink with the non-Bhagats or intermarry with them. They would not even draw water from the same well and if they had to, would wash their pots out with flowers and pray over them.[14] Gradually, however, more and more people fell away as old habits began to reassert themselves, hastened in some cases by retaliation from the drinkers who would pour liquor into their wells for fun.[15] In any case, there were always slippages. There are many stories of people who would take off their kanthis, have a quick swig and put them on again, in the belief that what the kanthi didn't witness couldn't upset the faith! A couple of people said, laughing ruefully, that they just got greedy, while in Chindgarh, one of these relapsed people muttered scornfully: 'Oh, they (Bhagats) live for the next world, but we live for this world.'

Administrative Measures and Political Expediency

If the movement had been restricted to temperance and vegetarianism, the administration might have ignored it, and in fact there are allegations that they actively encouraged it at first, as a form of 'uplift'. However the severe economic loss to the people caused by their disposal of black animals, including cattle – which were sold for throwaway prices, and sometimes just dumped or drowned – needed intervention. Accordingly, Dr B.D. Sharma promulgated Sec. 144 in July 1971, this time to prevent a gathering of more than five animals in any one place and time, as well as their export from the district.[16] In one week that August, the police seized over 900 goats and 400 birds being smuggled out of the district in violation of the order.[17] The administration also suffered a severe loss of excise income as people gave up drinking and liquor shops were forced to shut down. The loss of revenue by some estimates was roughly Rs 20 lakh.[18]

[14] Sahadev Nag, Kukanar, 1993.
[15] Narmada Prasad Shrivastav, Jagdalpur, 1992.
[16] Bhatt (1983:229).
[17] *DS*, 28 August 1971.
[18] *DS*, 4 July 1971.

Although the administration tried to warn people against the Baba, the traders, who were keen on getting animals cheap, twisted this to say that the government was advising people to visit the Baba within seven days. Other traders also inserted their own rumours to increase the sale of their goods, e.g. by saying that eating in leaf cups would cause poison, thus building up sales of steel plates.[19] Finally, B.D. Sharma succeeded in getting the Baba out of the district before Dussehra in 1971.[20] But when an otherwise unknown candidate, Peeluram, won a 1971 by-election because he was supported by the Baba, the Congress discovered the Baba's electoral value and wanted him back.[21] Various police charges against the Baba were dropped, while B.D. Sharma himself was transferred out.[22] The Baba now began to actively campaign for the Congress. As a result, the Congress won nine out of eleven seats in the 1972 state assembly elections, seven of which were with the Baba's help.[23] The fact that Pravir's widow, Vedvati, denied that the Baba was her former husband come alive, and campaigned against him, made little difference, and the Jansangh which she supported won only two seats.[24]

Table VII: *Baba Bihari Das' Influence in Elections (Fate of Congress Candidates in 1967 and 1972 Elections)*

Constituencies toured by Baba Bihari Das	1967	1972
Chitrakot	Defeated	Won
Bakavand	Defeated	Won
Kondagaon	Defeated	Won
Dantewada	Defeated	Won
Keshkal	Defeated	Won
Narayanpur	Defeated	Won
Jagdalpur	Defeated	Defeated

Source: Adapted from Bhatt (1983:235).

[19] Dr B.D. Sharma, 1 May 1993.
[20] *DS*, 10 October 1971.
[21] Bhatt (1983:233).
[22] Dr B.D. Sharma, 1 May 1993.
[23] *DS*, 12 and 19 March 1972.
[24] *DS*, 18 February 1972.

Eventually, when the election was over, and the Baba had outlived his usefulness, the administration was once again allowed to remove him. His property at Chapka was confiscated and he himself was arrested under MISA (Maintenance of Internal Security Act) in 1975, remaining in Raipur jail for eighteen months.[25] He was arrested again in Orissa in 1981 for raping a tribal girl whose family were Bhagats and had been staying in his ashram in Raigarh in Orissa at the time.[26] He eventually came back to Bastar, and still commands a following. But many people have become disillusioned, realising that he is no reincarnation and that he has monetary rather than spiritual interests. Despite certain millenarian aspects, it is difficult to grant Baba Bihari Das's movement the status of what is commonly understood as a millenarian movement, as Anderson and Huber do.[27] Unlike millenarian movements described by Worsley, Fields or Thompson, which help in articulating the tensions in the transition to capitalism, and have their own internal logic,[28] Baba Bihari Das's movement created divisions within Bastar society and went against the deeply ingrained cultural logic of appeasing their Gods with sacrifices of meat and liquor. In short, the Baba represented a move towards personal 'millionarism' rather than millenarianism.

Baba Bihari Das, 1990–93

My first personal encounter with the Baba was through a video screen in Chapka. The Baba himself was away but I sat with his two wives and their several children and watched videos of previous functions in the ashram, made to take from village to village to propagate the faith. The Baba's head floated around in a halo (a photographic technique popular in wedding videos), accompanied by disco prayer music. The Baba's organization is

[25] Bhatt (1983:239).
[26] *DS*, 21 June 1981.
[27] Anderson and Huber (1988:106–11). Huber (1984) argues that externing black animals was coterminous with the indigenous practice of disease riddance. By being cathartic it represented a transition to the promised millenium. But this was rarely mentioned to me as a reason for people taking to the movement.
[28] Thompson (1963:49–50); Worsley (1968); Fields (1985).

called the Bastar Seva Samiti and its members, 'Shanti Sevaks and Sevikas'. They pay five rupees for membership privileges. Like Pravir, the Baba has created his own parallel system of workers and majhis, who handle all the arrangements at any function and are generally distinguished by their bright yellow clothes. The Baba himself wears flowing yellow robes and dark glasses and gives long, loud monologues on subjects ranging from temperance to organic manure and afforestation. He also talks about duty to the nation and has replaced Dussehra with Republic Day as an important festival in his calendar.

According to him, he was born in village Gadhtor in district Kalahandi, Orissa, to a family of mendicants. His grandfather was originally a herbal doctor in Bastar and moved to Kalahandi, where the Baba's parents are still farming. He himself was educated by living in various ashrams and had as his main guru, one Maniram Das, who has an ashram in Ayodhya. The Baba says he came to Bastar as a wandering mendicant and settled in Chapka because it was quiet and beautiful. As for being a re-incarnation of Pravir, he can't say how that rumour came about. He said self-righteously:

Even now people say Maharaj ki Jai, Pravir Chandra Ki Jai. How can I stop them, when it makes them happy? It is not good to put an obstacle in someone's faith and devotion. They treat me like a Guru. It is a great sin to insult anyone (by refusing their adulation).[29]

The Bhagats of Kukanar

The Bhagats in Kukanar village (except for one or two families) are among those who have become disillusioned with the Baba's corruption. Recently, when he wrote to them saying he would be honouring one of their village festivals with his presence, they replied saying that he could attend if he wanted to, but would have to make his own arrangements as they couldn't afford his expenses.

However, they continue to follow rituals shown to them by the Baba. But this too has a twist. Their acknowledged leader is Dayaro Pujari of Bodaras, a Parja priest. Dayaro was one of those who continued to drink even after his initial conversion,

[29] Baba Bihari Das, Jagdalpur, 8 April 1993.

and is said to have been one of the most accomplished drinkers in the village, consuming five bottles of mahua in one afternoon. It was only after he survived a serious illness in which the sirahas pronounced him dead, that he adopted his present puritanism, extending to the rejection of any food other than fruit and roots. Many visionaries commence their careers with such cathartic experiences and Dayaro conformed further to the pattern by 'going mad', according to popular saying, for five years. He was sent to jail for three days with his own family's collaboration and eventually released after his followers petitioned the authorities.

Dayaro says that a stray statement by the Baba telling his followers to search for their roots inspired him to meditate for long periods. He then had visions of the 'original' Parja religion, which involved the offering of fruits, flowers and leaves, rather than the current system of animal sacrifices and libations of liquor. His life's mission now is to convert his people into non-alcoholism and vegetarianism, not in the name of Hinduism, but the original Parja Raj which he uses in the inclusive sense of Praja (people). His following extends to people in distant places, including various missionaries who see him as a prize catch to co-opt. The conversations they have with him inevitably end with both Dayaro Pujari and the visitor feeling they have successfully converted the other.

The Bhagats celebrate their own festivals, always a few days ahead of the rest of the unreformed villagers. Even at weddings and funerals they sit apart from the other villagers and cook their own food. To some extent, this has become a normal feature, and money collected for such communal occasions is divided between meat and liquor for the drinkers, and lentils and sugar water for the Bhagats. But underlying this amity are some deep-rooted tensions, aggravated by the fact that the Bhagats are the richer and more dominant group in the village, being among the first settlers. Dayaro Pujari especially exploits this fact to push his reforms. He has built his house and temple in front of the original village *gudi* and gets annoyed if an animal sacrifice is made there during periods when he is performing his own puja. For a time he had succeeded in preventing them altogether, but some people rebelled. 'What if our Devi gets angry?', they said, resentfully.

The politics of religion play a major role in Kukanar. In 1990, a sect of Kumbhi Buchiyas, whose followers wear ochre clothes and pray to the sun, established itself in the village. Converts were usually created by curing people from various illnesses. The Kumbhi leader in Bodaras took on as his third wife one of the women he had cured and in the ensuing fight with her husband, cursed him. The unfortunate man died within a year. A public meeting was held where other people also claimed intimidation by the Kumbhi faithful, and although the Kumbhi Buchiyas denied any wrong doing, the rest of the villagers beat them up, destroyed their shrine and excommunicated them. The Kumbhi Buchiyas in turn accused Dayaro Pujari of having instigated the attack and took them all to court. And so it goes on, with both parties having to make endless, expensive, time consuming trips to the court in Jagdalpur, seventy kilometres away.

More recently (1996), two sects — Gayatri and Brahmakumari — have made great headway in South Bastar. Five of the Bhagat families in Bodaras have become Brahmakumaris and now do not mingle with the Bhagats, leave alone the drinkers. They have taken over the schoolmaster's old house and every evening they gather to hear the latest broadsheet which comes from Jagdalpur. A single red bulb casts its shadow over the reader, sitting in front of a poster of Shiv Baba. He monotonously intones the text, translating from Hindi to Dhurwa, with a few English words like 'liberate' thrown in. The audience of ten to fifteen people is utterly quiet. However, all these pieties have not helped Aitu, one of the Brahmakumari converts, to get his *marhan* (revenue encroachment) land back from Muda, who usurped it to build his Indira Awas house. While Muda is not a Brahmakumari himself, the rest of his family is, and it came to his support against Aitu. Muda is an active member of the CPI and was elected to the district level panchayat. He is also by no means landless (as one has to be to qualify for an Indira Awas house) — in fact his family is the second richest in the hamlet. Aitu on the other hand has only two fields and is dependent on this encroached land. When he tried to protest, Muda threatened to take him to court.

Finally we come full circle, with history repeating itself — but in new contexts: so-called millennial movements that promise redemption but succeed instead in further entrenching people in the present world of courts and lawyers. 'For races condemned to one hundred years of solitude, there can be no second coming on earth.'[30]

Uncertain Futures

The past leads us
Only when we force it to
Otherwise it shuts us
In its asylum with no gates
We make history
Or it makes us.

Marge Piercy

9

Conclusion

1908: San Andres de Sotavento
The Government Decides That Indians Don't Exist

The governor, General Miguel Marino Torralvo, issues the order
for the oil companies operating on the Colombian coast. The
Indians do not exist, the governor certifies before a notary and
witnesses. Three years ago, Law No. 1905/55, approved in Bogota
by the National Congress, established that Indians did not exist
in San Andres de Sotavento and other Indian communities where
oil had suddenly spurted from the ground. Now the governor
merely confirms the law. If the Indians existed, they would be
illegal. Thus they are confined to the cemetery or exile.

                              Eduardo Galeano, *Century of the Wind*

The history of Bastar as it is written in the pages of this
book is a broadly familiar one — the slow expansion of a
centralized administrative apparatus in colonial and post-
colonial times; restrictions on popular access to land, water and
forests, to facilitate their diversion to commercial uses; and
changes in the locus of political authority. What then makes
this story worth retelling? Perhaps the need to people this
process, to bring to this tale the courage, humour, cunning and
fortitude manifested by those who have lived it. And in doing
so, we might find the paths that lead to the future.

The narrative began by showing how people conceive of their
'past'. The pre-colonial polity, cobbled together partly through
force and partly through ritual, tried to weld together a hetero-
genous, partially stratified and often fractious populace. This was
later ironed out to create the appearance of binary opposition
between people and state that has come to be the hallmark of
'tribal' areas. In both society and polity, there is a sense of ceaseless
movement that was suddenly stilled under colonialism in order
to make other controlled sorts of movements possible and to
give rise to particular administrative and political categories.

The system of indirect rule built upon and simultaneously displaced the indigenous polity. In Bastar, resistance took on different expressions at different times, e.g. the appeal to a 'just king' in 1876, rebellion against the entire colonial apparatus and those associated with it, including the king, in 1910, and finally, rallying around the former king as a protest against the policies of the independent Indian state in 1966. This changing mode of relating to the king calls into question essentialized notions of divine kingship. A king who did not fulfil his duties to his subjects found his divinity quickly fractured; conversely, not all kings played the role of divine monarchs equally well. In the 1876 rebellion, Raja Bhairam Deo's plaintive complaint about being hit with clods of earth indicates a scepticism about the king's divinity that was shared by ruler and ruled alike. The fact that in 1910 the king was seen as part of the administration or at best ignored, indicates the progressive denigration of the indigenous polity even as the facade of indirect rule was zealously maintained.

There are several similarities as well as contrasts between the rebellions of 1876 and 1910. Both were part of a tradition of rebellions across India in defence of land and forest rights.[1] Both were directed against extractions of begar, excessive rents and other forms of everyday oppression practiced by village lessees and officials. In the 1910 case in addition, forest reservation was a major issue. But whereas the 1876 seige was confined to the palace and involved only a few parganas around Jagdalpur, the 1910 rebellion was dispersed and covered most of the state, 'a tract about 85 miles from north to south by 60 miles from east to west.'[2] The former seems to have been more spontaneous, the last straw as it were, being the raja's behaviour towards his coolies at Marenga. The Bhumkal of 1910, by contrast, involved weeks of planning among the villages and consultations with elites in the town. In 1876, the protest was put down in a month, while in 1910 it took the colonial authorities from February to mid-May to capture and punish all the rebels. In both cases, the majority of rebels appear to have been from tribal and scheduled caste groups like Parjas, Marias, Murias and Bhatras,

---

[1] Gadgil and Guha (1992:146–80); Desai (1979).
[2] DeBrett, Confidential no. 4417.

Dhakads, Lohars and Maharas. The collaborators in 1910, however, came from all groups. The loyalty of some of the zamindars
to the British was only to be expected, but there were also tribal
headmen as in Kukanar and the Maria Peddas of Massenar in
Dantewara. Perhaps these included some majhis who had been
given leases by the British after 1876. The extended spread of
the 1910 Bhumkal as well as the existence of both rebels and
collaborators reveals the greater entrenchment of colonial rule
by 1910.

Comparative studies of why and how people rebel in different
places are inadequate to the extent that they do not account
for the role of popular memory in fuelling resistance. This
memory need not always be present as an articulate ideology
or remembrance — consciousness, after all, emerges and is
accessible to the analyst through practice as much as through
overt statements. Thus in each case of 'encroachment' on forest
land in order to satisfy the right to life, villagers were operating
on the strength of ideologies expressed in the rebellion of 1910.
In popular accounts of 1966, we find echoes of 1910 — the
same imagery with respect to bullets turning into water, the
same refusal to acknowledge defeat in the face of death, the
same belief that the leader had not died, the same belief that
if the requisite prayers had been completed, the peasants would
not have lost. In some cases, this was a conscious attempt to
recreate past inspiration, and in others the inspiration came
forth through the fault lines of history. As each new event
drew upon the past, it also re-wrote that past, turning victims
into heroes, celebrating survival with a bottle of liquor and a
leg of meat. But inevitably, there has also been a process of
forgetting, as the state enforces its own version of events. And
different sections of the population remember differently, based
on their interests and closeness to the administration of the
day. Thus Inder Baghel, one time BJP Sarpanch of Kukanar,
one of the most fluent Dhurwa speakers of Hindi in the village
because of his constant dealings with the administration, and
very much a man of the status-quo, explains Gunda Dhur's
name by the fact that he was a goonda (goon).

Moreover, not all those who celebrate the events today would
be deemed its natural heirs. Dusting my way through the files
in the English record room at Jagdalpur, I came across a 1974

letter from the MP government at Bhopal to the Collector at Jagdalpur, requesting details of freedom struggles in the district, including that of 1910. The irony is that any similar movement today would rapidly meet its demise at the hands of the same state. Immigrant Bengali youth enact plays about the glorious Gunda Dhur to which the district administration's presence is earnestly solicited — a history of Bastar's role in the 'national freedom struggle', with the majority of its inhabitants, the adivasis, conveniently erased. And shopkeepers who are out to dominate the adivasis, sigh mournfully in memory of the 1966 events and desire to hold exhibitions of Pravir memorabilia to commemorate his passing.

Despite this convenient toying with interpretations of the past, we might yet discern a somewhat consistent strand in the fundamental assumptions and operation of the state from colonial to post-colonial times. It is true of course, that official documents display a variety of views, drawing on the position or provenance or ideology of the author. But as with popular consciousness, where the hardships of life will people into periodic protest, the constraints of rule structure an underlying attitude. In all three cases, 1876, 1910 or 1966, the colonial authorities and the independent Indian government were reluctant to concede culpability for the discontent, preferring to blame it on the hapless kings, or as in the 1966 case, incitement by a deranged demagogue. Even in 1992, protest against displacement by the proposed steel plants was attributed entirely to the machinations of Dr B.D. Sharma and his environmentalist associates. Yet, in the very stridency of statements about state innocence and public misbehaviour is the acknowledgement of popular right. In each case, the government reconsidered its strategies — by tinkering with the rates of land revenue after 1876, slashing the forest area to be reserved after 1910, abolishing corvée and giving powers to 'customary' councils in the 'twenties and 'thirties, putting an end to the forcible grain levy in 1966, and temporarily halting the Bodhghat Hydroelectric project and the steel plants in the 'eighties and 'nineties respectively.

However, these concessions have inevitably been limited and, in fact, have helped to further entrench and normalize certain administrative categories and institutions. Although the British 'rescue' of the king from his rebellious subjects in 1876 led to the corrupt officials being removed, it also served to enhance colonial notions about indigenous inefficiency and the need for their own judicial and administrative mechanisms to be set in place. Similarly, the Bhumkal was followed by a long period of paternalist rule towards tribals, in which colonial authorities were believed to perform much better than other 'caste' Indians. While ostensibly rolling back the state, this was also a period when the category of the 'tribal' was most firmly consolidated: as simple and needing 'uplift', but simultaneously strong and dangerous and requiring repression. This was carried over into the post-colonial state, where, given the structures of administration already set in place, capitalist pressures on the economy, and opportunistic and divisive party politics, the scope for genuine articulation of popular demands within the existing polity has been significantly reduced.

Discourses of Development

Following Foucault in attending to discursive practices, a few scholars have tried to bring out the way in which the whole model and apparatus of 'development' constitutes its object.[3] In the process of making up what is seen as a deficiency or absence of material wealth, 'scientific' knowledge and a 'modern' lifestyle among the majority of the world's population, the development discourse provides jobs, contracts, markets, raw material and labour to a minority. Although the history of 'development' as a specific idea dates only to the post World War II period,[4] there are basic similarities between the 'development regime' and the colonial state. While both couch their policies in terms of public progress, their major contribution is to the development and extension of state power and capitalist market systems.[5] In a place like Bastar, there are further continuities between the colonial and post-colonial regimes in that the individuals who are doing the 'developing' continue to see themselves as more 'advanced' than the 'natives' being 'developed', and have retained the language of a civilizing mission.

[3] Ferguson (1990); Escobar (1995).
[4] Escobar (1995:21–54)
[5] Ludden (1992:251–2).

In his study of development in Lesotho, James Ferguson argues that development projects are, ipso facto, anti-politics machines. They are powerful precisely because of their unintended or 'instrument' effects: 'alongside the institutional effect of expanding bureaucratic state power is the conceptual or ideological effect of depoliticizing both poverty and the state.'[6] Depoliticization occurs as political questions regarding the distribution of land, wages etc. get transformed into issues of technocratic or administrative expertise. By its supposedly neutral thrust, development 'may also very effectively squash political challenges to the system.'[7] While much of this is true, his own comparative account of the impact of development projects also suggests plenty of resistance on the part of those being affected.[8] Moreover, in a post-liberalized world, the connections of 'development' to naked capitalism are becoming ever more apparent, with or without the mediation of restructured states.

Like the colonialism which preceded it, India's 'development regime' (in both its *dirigiste* and *laissez-faire* avatars) has set in place an ongoing struggle over the terrain of popular consciousness. On the one hand, there has been a change in needs and desires among some sections of adivasis, as marked, for instance, by the supplementing of communal singing by all-night community video shows as modes of marking major life-cycle ceremonies like weddings and funerals. On the other hand, 'development' has resulted in an even further dispossession of certain groups in favour of others. According to the CSE Report of 1984–5, Bastar generated an annual revenue of Rs 470 million, yet only Rs 50 million was spent on the region itself.[9] Everyday life in Kukanar illustrates the first face. While it is not necessarily a representative village, its level of 'development' and mix of population provides an indication of the way the rest of the district is headed. Here confrontation and collaboration takes place on a daily basis, not just between different sets of people, but within the private selves of individuals. The second aspect is visible taking Bastar as a whole. The contradictions are

[6] Ferguson (1990:256).
[7] Ibid.:270.
[8] Ibid.:262–7.
[9] CSE (1985:93).

primarily between those who would lose or gain from the further expansion of capitalism, though it is often misleadingly expressed as an encounter between adivasis and the state, or between the ways of 'indigenous knowledge' and 'modernity'.

Thakurs and Tribals in Kukanar

Although the number of Thakur families in Kukanar is small compared to the number of adivasis, the village is often called a Thakur stronghold, testimony to the kind of dominance they exercise. At the beginning of the century there were about three households of UP traders, all claiming to be Rajputs, but there are now approximately forty, as brothers, uncles, relatives came to visit and settled down to do business. Most came only in the last two decades, attracted by the illegal tin smelting in the area and the trade in NTFPs, and pushed by the land fragmentation in their own villages in UP. A couple of them have set up shops where they buy grain and forest produce, and sell oil, salt, rice and other groceries. Sitting in the wide verandahs of one of the Thakur houses, which stretch along the main road on either side, the older men — pot bellied in their vests and white pyjamas — play cards and keep a watch on everyone and everything. The younger Thakur men, whose primary business is to purchase mahua and tamarind, cover a circle of weekly markets in the area, each of which takes place on a different day. Some of them own trucks in which they transport the weekly collection to the central market at Jagdalpur. Others sell in turn to Marwaris from nearby Tongpal (a slightly bigger centre than Kukanar) who take it to Jagdalpur, from where it is sent to larger centres like Calcutta. The Thakur women generally stay at home, some of them helping out in the family shop. While the expansion of households signifies that NTFPs are good business, the Thakurs themselves complain that 'there are too many scales', and their profit margin has gone down. They also, quite unashamedly, complain that the adivasis have got street smart and can no longer be cheated as easily as before.

The Thakurs are friendly with all the lower government staff posted to the area. Since Kukanar is a big village, it has several primary schools, an ayurvedic dispensary, a fair price shop and a rural bank. Many school teachers who work in other hamlets of Kukanar or even in neighbouring villages prefer to commute from the Thakur hamlet, regarding it as an oasis of north Indian 'civilized' culture in the midst of adivasi life. This works to the mutual advantage of the Thakurs and the government functionaries in a variety of ways. Given its status as a backward tribal area, there are a number of development programmes which have been introduced in Bastar – the nationwide Integrated Rural Development Programme (IRDP); Jawahar Rozgar Yojana (JRY), an employment programme; as well as purely Bastar-specific projects – e.g. the Bastar Development Authority, and the Abujhmar Development Programme. These generate their own sort of 'welfare colonialism'.[10] Loans given out under government schemes to increase rural assets often end up decreasing them, as the 'beneficiaries' are unable to pay off the loans and lose their lands in the process. In the early 1980s, in the circle of the Kukanar rural bank, IRDP loans to landless families to purchase bullocks ended up in disaster, as most of the bullocks died within a few months, being weak and sickly. They had evidently not been worth the price that had been entered for them in the loan books; yet the loan had to be paid off in full. In the meantime, the banker, cattle trader, and the president of the local Twenty Point Programme Committee (a Kukanar Thakur), made a handsome profit. The Thakur subsequently built himself a big house and provisions store in the main market square of Kukanar, which is popularly known as the *thotha bailla* (landless bullocks) house.

Much of the time, the adivasis participate in their own exploitation. Many of them prefer to take their tamarind or mahua to the Thakurs, even when adivasi boys from their own hamlet have tried to enter the trade and do the purchasing. Partly of course, this is due to a need to maintain networks of patronage for difficult times. But there is also a sense of being honoured by having Thakurs hob-nob with you. It is not uncommon to see someone laughing, a shade over-enthusiastically, when a Thakur or some other outsider makes a derogatory comment about adivasis. Thakur men occasionally roar up to the adivasi hamlets on their motorbikes, looking upon them as sources of alcohol, which they cannot legitimately drink in their

---

[10] The term is taken from Beckett (1987).

own houses. A few of them are known to have adivasi mistresses. One unfortunate woman hanged herself after she got pregnant and the man refused to provide upkeep. Thakur women are pitied by the adivasis because they are kept confined at home and often treated badly by their in-laws, which is in sharp contrast to the freedom of adivasi women. But at the same time, the more 'civilized' they get in their own eyes, the more they copy Thakur lifestyles.

The local sirahas and waddes, or medicine men are still the first option in a situation where there is no doctor and the nearest proper hospital is in Jagdalpur, seventy kilometres and a substantial sum of money away. But Ramji, the Chattisgarhi peon at the Ayurvedic dispensary, also does good business going around the village on his cycle injecting people. And in one scene at examination time in the local primary school, I was witness to a sad and paradoxical conversion. Sonu Guruji, acting here as external examiner, asked the children their names. He is one of a few Dhurwa schoolteachers, and is keen to revive the use of Dhurwa. Yet as they called out each distinctive adivasi name — like Gagru or Aitu or Devli, he ironed it out to Gagru Ram, Aitu Ram, Devli Kumari etc. Dayaro Pujari, chief guest at his hamlet's primary school function for Republic Day, admonished the children to come to school regularly so that they too could wear full pants, or salwar kurtas and spectacles like the live-in anthropologist. But in other contexts, Dayaro is a custodian of Parja history, refusing to have it subsumed by other narratives. Everyday life is thus conducted through a mixture of active collusion, compromise or call it innovative fusion, resignation or call it avoidance — while at the same time the framework of Thakur dominance gets more entrenched.

Things have changed a bit in recent years, however, especially since the CPI came to power in the village. The process started in the late seventies, when the Thakurs beat up some Gonds from Katulmiri, a sub-hamlet of Bodaras. They went home and held a panchayat, came back with a large number of other villagers and stoned the Thakur houses. The police thana was re-established in Kukanar after this. Since 1910, when the original thana was burnt down, the nearest station had been in Tongpal, thirteen kilometres away. When Dayaro Pujari started on his Bhagat beliefs, he gave over the task of helping officials like the patwari, to his middle son, Sonadhar. The patwari who was posted to Kukanar in 1987–8 was apparently extremely corrupt. He would demand Rs 100 for every entry in the land records, on the pretext that it was due to the government, a pretence that Sonadhar who was helping him, soon dismantled. But complaints to the Collector and the local Congress MLA, Parshuram Nag, were fruitless. Finally, in desperation, Sonadhar contacted Lakshman Jhadi at the CPI office in Jagdalpur, having heard that they helped in cases of this sort. Luckily, at that time, the CPI happened to be demonstrating for other demands. Three or four truckloads of people from Kukanar joined the *gherao* of the Collector's office, adding their demands to the list. The patwari was removed the very next day (but subsequently promoted to Circle Inspector, which makes them all bitter). Around the same time, the CPI-led youth also managed to get an abusive policeman named Pande transferred. The villagers were so impressed by all this that they voted for the CPI in a big way in the panchayat elections of 1989. The Congress and BJP, whose stronghold it had been for the past fifteen years primarily due to the Thakurs, had to forfeit their deposits.[11]

The assertion of 'adivasi' identity under the CPI, or even under some nativist Dhurwa banner, does not automatically translate into increased respect for 'traditional' knowledge or traditional lifestyles. Although the CPI youth affect to despise the Thakurs, they continue to associate with them. Most of them are educated, at least upto the 8th standard. Some are alienated from ploughing and aspire to more urbanized lifestyles. So far, within the village, because of the heavy emphasis on the kin idiom, accumulation at the expense of others or a refusal to share was difficult, and the overt economic differentiation was never very sharp.[12] However, as the last chapter showed, this is increasingly difficult to maintain. While the dominance of the founding lineages is mitigated by the fact that they have to sacrifice more days in ritual activity, attending to village affairs or dealing with the government, there is also increased competition for new benefits. In 1995, Buda, son

[11] Narrated to me by Lakshman Kashyap, block head of the CPI, and Sonadhar Nag.

[12] Though as Gell (1986) points out, the collective ethos among Murias which militates against ostentatious private consumption, paradoxically leads to the rich getting richer.

of the former patel of Kukanar won with Thakur support on a BJP ticket, defeating Sonadhar of the CPI. The choice of candidates was a logical one due to long standing dissensions between the two families, both of whom claim to be original founders. One's family, moreover, is leader of the Bhagats, while the other's leads the drinkers in Kukanar as a whole. Thus new divisions enhance or bring into existence old ones, as history gets entangled in the quarrels of the present.

This focus on party politics is not typical of Bastar as a whole, or even of everyday life in Kukanar. People's routine lives revolve around cultivation, waiting for the rains, making sure the right sacrifices are performed, looking after children, collecting and selling tendu and tamarind, drinking, making love, births, deaths and weddings. It is sometimes a desperate, hungry life; a life of great sadness, as children, laughing and playing, are quick to sicken and die. Women, particularly, age rapidly, wracked by the pressures of stretching meagre resources. Of course, there are small pleasures to be enjoyed — sweets eaten at the mandai, a visit to one's natal home, gossip at the bathing ghat, the everyday joy of conviviality. Nevertheless, there is a subterranean change that integration into more than a century of capitalism has introduced. People are called upon to define themselves more sharply, to justify their human presence in a world of profit.

Insiders vs Outsiders

In an interview I had with him apropos the steel plants proposed to be set up in Bastar (see introduction), the then Collector, Mr J.P. Vyas, argued that there had never been any precedent for informing the people beforehand about impending displacement: 'If the people were consulted beforehand and asked for permission, inherent in this is the possibility that they might refuse. And then where would the government be?'[13] Where, indeed? In any case, he argued, the people were ignorant and once the experts had decided where a project was going to be located, there was nothing more to be said. He went on to offer several other astonishing insights, such as the fact that the

[13] Interviewed in the Collector's Bungalow, Jagdalpur, 15 December 1992.

government was doing the adivasis a favour by uprooting them because long occupation created stagnation and stagnation was a form of death. 'Mobility is a sign of progress,' he said, 'Look at me'.[14] As to the demand for shares in the factory to be given to those displaced by it: 'This is a very wrong demand and totally alien to their culture. It will create possessiveness as tribals are very selfless people.'[15] During the agitation about the steel plant, the walls of Jagdalpur were plastered with slogans asking tribal activists and other 'outsiders' protesting against the project to go 'home'. On the other hand, the businessmen who were responsible for this, and who are all recent migrants, are at pains to justify their own presence in Bastar, saying: 'it is all one country, we're free to settle anywhere.' They commonly invoke the myth of their own hard work and adivasi profligacy in explaining how they got the riches they currently own.

In the past year, 1995-6, the question of the indigenous, or of insiders versus outsiders came to a head with a proposal by the Congress government in MP to apply the Sixth Schedule of the Constitution to Bastar, thereby creating an autonomous district council. There were rallies and counter rallies in Jagdalpur in support of and against the proposal. The pro-schedule lobby under the banner of the Bastar Swashasiya Raj Samiti consisted of the CPI, a faction of the Congress, including Mankuram Sodi and Arvind Netam, former MPs from Bastar, the Bharat Jan Andolan, and their respective supporters. Throughout the first half of 1995, the CPI held several block and village level meetings to apprise people of the provisions of the Sixth Schedule and its possible benefits. The anti-Schedule group was organized under the name of the Bastar Zilla Sangharsh Samiti, and was a predominantly BJP outfit, supported by another faction of the Congress under Mahendra Karma, MP from Bastar.[16] A committee under the chairmanship of Dr B.K. Roy Burman was set up by the Madhya Pradesh government in 1995, to look into the applicability of the Sixth Schedule to

---

[14] Ibid.
[15] Ibid.
[16] Conversation with Lakshman Jhadi and M.A. Iqbal of the pro-6th Schedule group, Pandripani, 11 February 1996.; Ravi Shankar Bajpai, of the anti-6th Schedule group, Jagdalpur, 14 February 1996. For the CPI's stand on the Sixth Schedule, *see* Bakshi (1994).

M.P. In the meantime, another committee was set up by the
Central Government under the chairmanship of Dilip Singh
Bhuria. On 24 December 1996, its recommendations were
enacted as 'The Provisions of the Panchayats (Extension to the
Scheduled Areas) Act, No. 40 of 1996'. As one of the architects
of the Act, Dr B.D. Sharma argues that it represents a long
awaited recognition of the tribal community as a functioning
collectivity and that it will restore power to the villagers at the
level at which they live their everyday life – the hamlet or a
group of hamlets, depending on how 'community' is locally
defined. There are many things to recommend the Act, including
the proposal to put development activities and the management
of local natural resources under the control of the *gram sabha*,
to sanctify the local settlement of disputes, and to amend the
Land Acquisition Act to seek villagers' permission before acquir-
ing their land for development projects or the exploitation of
minor minerals. But based as it is on an idyllic notion of a
tribal village community as an arena of participative democracy,
and a paternalist plan of implementation from above, this Act
too, may go the way of the 1940s attempts at giving power to
customary bodies.[17]

Whatever the outcome, the very thought of the Sixth Schedule
or the Bhuria Committee proposals appears to have terrified
the immigrants – the traders, lawyers, journalists and the lower
rungs of the bureaucracy. If created, an autonomous district
council could revoke licenses for illegal practices in the past.
Lawyer's practices too, could be significantly reduced. All cases
would go first to the gram sabha and very few would come to
court. At the moment there are more than two hundred (almost
all non-tribal) lawyers in the Jagdalpur court, organized into
forty chambers. At a meeting called by the Kanker Chamber of
Commerce on 23 April 1995, the participants – again, all non-
tribals – unanimously decided that enough money had been
pumped into development for the Bastar adivasis. Why, they
asked sanctimoniously, when they had lived harmoniously with
the adivasis all this time, was the government introducing
dissension? A campaign was launched to convince non-tribal

[17] For details of the Bhuria Committee Proposals, *see* Sharma (1995).

groups like Sundis, Kallars and Maharas, that they would suffer under an autonomous council, with the Gonds being in power.[18]

While the traders and others have been the worst offenders in terms of denying adivasi autonomy and insinuating themselves into dominant positions in Bastar, the government is no less culpable. It too has overturned the concept of insider versus outsider to suit itself. The term 'outsider' is used for instance against the Naxalites. Over the years, several battalions of police, including a special Bastar battalion, have been inducted to counter them, and draconian laws like TADA have been applied. The District Magistrate interviewed by the PUCL in 1989 referred to the Naxalites as 'a gang of dacoits moved into Bastar from the border beyond'. In fact, the Bastar activists of the PWG hail mostly from the region and as the PUCL report noted, 'to the adivasis of South Bastar, Kursum Rajakka, the 24 year old Naxalite woman who was killed in an encounter at Mukabelli . . . is just a fellow Dorla tribal woman.'[19]

Leave alone Naxalites, even the Bhatra, Halba and Mahara women of Asna village near Jagdalpur who in 1987 organized to prevent the encirclement of their local forests by barbed wire and subsequently formed a forest protection committee to safeguard it, have on occasion been regarded as 'outsiders'. A group of the women formed a collective under one of the government's schemes and contracted for the purchase of sal seeds and tendu leaves as agents for the forest department, for fishing rights in the village ponds and the raising of a nursery under the forest department's social forestry schemes.[20] There have been repeated political pressures to remove them and give the contracts to unemployed Brahman youths on the grounds that they were more deserving than uneducated tribal women. Under corrupt contractors expert at underweighing, making wrong entries and sheer blustering, tendu and sal seed purchasing contracts can be very lucrative indeed. Although the collective has been able to fight back due to the efforts of a local activist, in every other center in that block, the party in power has

---

[18] Undated press clipping from NavBharat Times, April 1995, Ravi Shankar Bajpai Collection.

[19] PUCL (1989:4).

[20] Sundar (1993).

managed to get its own people – mostly non-tribals – appointed as contractors for minor forest produce.[21]

Thus, the government's use of the term 'outsider' has lost all connections with its official dictionary meaning. The term 'outsider' is used to refer to anyone who disagrees with the state's concept of development, or anyone who voices dissent over its undemocratic acts. It is used by newly arrived business interests to refer to those who stand against the logic of capital accumulation, and by landlords who have grown old in the ways of exploitation and resent any breath of new thinking among the lower castes or classes.

There is always a danger, of course, that 'subaltern' groups too, could yield to chauvinist or nativist sentiments. To demand priority treatment on the basis of a distinction between some 'original inhabitants' and recent migrants is not a happy direction to take in a situation where all have needs. And given the extent to which capitalism has involved the large-scale movement of populations – as plantation workers, industrial wage workers, agricultural labourers, sugarcane cutters, makers and vendors of recycled goods in degraded urban surroundings – there can be no complacency about the ease with which one can identify 'local' rights or customary usages. With what sounds like indubitable logic, Dayaro Pujari once said in the context of the struggle over the steel plants:

Did our village come first or did the government come first? Our ancestors cut the forests and levelled the fields in the days when there were no government loans for this work or even a government at all. It is we, who through our labour, built the roads that let the government officials into our villages. Then how did the government, simply by means of a little *'likha-padhi'* (reading-writing) acquire the right to our land, to order us around and move us about? Since they were not the ones to establish us in our village, they have no right to take it away from us.

But rather than simply take such accounts literally in every case, we need to pay attention to the way in which they also articulate a particular stance on history, and a particular type of claim. We know from several sources, including the history of Bastar itself, that villages were often depopulated and resettled by successive

[21] M.A. Iqbal, pers. com.

governments; and the government often entered into the very constitution of the village and was not merely an external imposition.[22]

In India today land is considered merely a form of property which can be given or taken away by the state. For example, it can be given through the regularization of 'encroachment' on forest land, or taken away through the Land Acquisition Act, in the name of public purpose, albeit with 'due compensation'. But a democratic perspective needs to go beyond a merely legalistic definition to view access to land or to a job as an integral part of the right to life and livelihood. In the context of growing population, it is true that access to land can no longer be mediated in the old way and a resort to some notion of 'customary law' is impossible and often undesirable, especially in that it denies equal land rights to women. But these are questions that can only be properly addressed through a democratic process, through consultation between all the parties involved. In movements fighting for local rights, there is often a common use of language which suggests nostalgia for 'original rights' in some pre-colonial order or which implies an innate environmental conservationism among tribal or peasant groups.[23] No doubt there are also contradictions within the movements between intellectuals and the actual workers or peasants, between people's needs and desires and what is deemed sustainable. Nevertheless, a common thread linking these struggles to others is the need to defend democratic rights within an economic and political order that is continually eroding them.

Towards the Future

How did the world change so suddenly and insiders become outsiders? Clearly, the situation is not unique to Bastar. In his essay on 'Custom, Law and Common Right,' E.P. Thompson concludes by noting that local right was not a form of primitive communism but that 'enclosure, in taking the commons away from the poor, made them strangers in their own land'.[24] In this

[22] *See for instance* Breman (1988).

[23] *See for instance*, pamphlets circulated by the Bharat Jan Andolan or the National Alliance of People's Movements.

[24] Thompson (1993:184).

book I have tried to understand the process whereby other people's definitions of Bastar have come to be inscribed as authoritative, whereby the people of Bastar have become strangers in their own land. But I have also tried to show that they have not been silent victims and have resisted at different times. I would like this to be not merely a straightforward chronological history with a closure but a history whose rationale is provided by the future. 'The past leads us only when we force it to . . . we make history or it makes us'.

Dayaro Pujari invokes an old Parja story according to which the Parja (praja) was the elder brother and the Raja the younger. They were walking along with one horse between them. The younger brother then climbed the horse and made the elder brother bear his burden. Having fallen behind under force, the elder brother – the one who came first – was dispossessed. 'The raja's time is over now,' says Dayaro, 'we need to establish the praja raj again.'

Glossary of Terms

adhkari	tax collector
adivasi	tribal ('original inhabitant')
aikul	*Setaria italica*
andil	elder sister-in-law (Dhurwa)
anna	unit of currency (16 annas = 1 rupee)
anya	maternal uncle's wife or father's sister
aonla	*Emblica officinalis*
ashram	place of holy man
atpaharia	person appointed by village to do various chores
baba	old man/holy man
bahidar	record-keeper
bai/bai log/ *baile man*	woman/women folk
bairagi	mendicant
bamboos	*Dendrocalmus sirictus, Bambusa tilda*
bat penda	shifting cultivation on flat ground
beedi	local cigarettes
begar	corvée
bethia	mutual help system
bhandarin	person in charge of stores (Dhurwa)
bhum	earth
bhumiswami	legal term for rights over trees in one's own land
bhumkal	rebellion/political council
bija/bijasal	*Pterocarpus marsupium*
bisaha	free or subsidised supplies that peasants were obliged to give touring officials
bodka	Dhurwa functionary who cooks and cleans in earth shrine
chalki/chalan	the majhi's deputy
chapda	red ants
char	*Buchanania lanzan*
chind	*Phoenix sylvestris*

chirmul	gaur/ wild buffalo (Dhurwa)
chupras	badges
chuprassi	peon
cowrie	shell used as currency
dangdi/dangda	ancestral spirits; young girls and boys (Halbi)
dant	teeth
darogah	head constable
devi	goddess
devi-shakti	power given by the devi
dewan/diwan	chief administrator; manager of the state
dhan	paddy
dhaora	*Anogeissus latifolia*
dhoti	sarong
dhup	sal resin used as incense
dhya/dahya/ dahi	shifting cultivation on old fallows; also generic term for shifting cultivation (Halbi)
dogani	unit of currency (10 doganis = 1 rupee)
dokra/dokri	old man/woman (Halbi)
dorel	original lineages (Dhurwa)
duffadar	court peon
dugga	story (Dhurwa)
dukkil	old fallows cultivation (Dhurwa)
durbar	assembly/court
gaita	village headman
garhs/gurhs	an administrative division centred around a fort
ghat	promenade on river bank, usually for bathing
gharpatti	dues paid for the right to collect small timber and NTFPs
gherao	seige
gudi	shrine
haat	weekly market
haldu	*Adina cordifolia*
hikmi	assistant to headman
hurra	*Terminalia chebula*
jaga	earth (Dhurwa)
jai	cry hailing victory
jatra	sacrifices to mother Goddesses to avoid sickness

jhipa	grass seeds (Halbi)
joharni	greeting (Halbi)
kabadi	bonded labourer
kalas-sthapan	ceremony involving installment of sacred water pots
kamdar	literate managers/revenue collectors for khalsa
kanthi	tulsi beads worn around neck
kapurdar	valet
katav	history (Dhurwa)
kavad	porters
kayasth	scribal upper-caste
khalsa	lands whose revenue was directly collected by the state
khandi	a weight (1 khandi = 20 paili)
kicek	person who lights fire (Dhurwa)
kirich	*Elaeodendron glaucum*
kisan	farmer
kodon	*Paspalum scrobiculatum*
koi/koitor	human/person (Gondi)
kont penda	hillside shifting cultivation (Dhurwa)
kothar	grain storage shed
kotwar	village watchman
kuraal	a multigenre ritual performance in Dhurwa villages
kutcheri	court
kutki	*Panicum miliaceum*
lakh	hundred thousand
lal	member of the younger lineage (e.g. the Raja's younger brother)
landa	rice beer
lathi	bamboo stave used by police
magar-muhi	base of Dussehra chariot
mahua	*Bassia latifolia*
majhi	the headman of a pargana (or in some cases, a large village)
malguzar	holder of rights to revenue
malguzari	revenue paid to an intermediate rights-holder
mama	maternal uncle
mandai	pargana level festival
mandia	*Eleusine coracana*

marhan	shifting cultivation on level ground/encroachment (Halbi)
mata	mother goddess
mati	earth
mati-pujari	priest of the earth god
matidar	original lineage
maund	measure of grain
mazdoor	worker
membrin	woman members of Raja Pravir Chandra's organisation
muafis	khalsa lands which were granted revenue-free status
munshi	accountant/clerk in traditional judicial system
muqaddam	Mughal (Persian) term for village headman
murtak	old man (Dhurwa)
murtal	old woman (Dhurwa)
nad	a micro-region (Tamil)
nagar	plough (one of the bases for assessing land revenue)
nakedar	guard in charge of customs checkpost
naik	head of a caste/settles disputes
nayakhani	new-eating ceremony
negi	administrative assistant
nistar	forest produce allowed to villagers free or on concessional rates
paili	measure (1 paili = 1.5–2 kg)
paltan	platoon
panchs	members of a panchayat
panchayat	village decision-making body
pardesi	foreigner/outsider
parishad	council
parads	hunting expeditions
pargana	an administrative division comprising several villages
pata	wheels of Dussehra chariot
patel	village headman
patrani	junior rani
patwari	official responsible for keeping land records
pedda	village headman
penda	shifting cultivation on hill slopes

perma/pelas	earth priest
praja	people/ public
puja	prayer ceremony
pujari	priest
rajguru	king's chief advisor
rath	chariot
rathel	particular millet
raut	cowherd; cook for officials
ryots	peasants
saga	affines/guests
sahukars	traders/moneylenders
saja	*Terminalia tomentosa*
sal	*Shorea robusta*
samiti/sangh	committee/collective
sangharsh	struggle
sarkar/sirkar	government
sarpanch	elected village headman
sakta-pithas:	cult centres of sakti or female power
sein	ancestral spirits; friends (Halbi)
semur:	*Salmalia malabaricum*
ser	a measure (1 ser = approx. 2 lbs.)
seva	service
sevak/sevika	one who does service (male/female)
shanti	peace
shisham	*Dalbergia sissoo*
siadi	*Bauhinia Vahilii*
siraha	shaman
sirasar	durbar hall
sulphi	*Caryota urens*, whose fermented juice is very popular
swadeshi/ swashasiya	self-rule
taccavi	a loan for agricultural improvement
tahsil	sub-division of a district
tahsildar	administrative head of tahsil
tallur muttay	earth mother (Muria Gondi)
tar	*Borassus flabellifer.*
tendu	*Diospyros melanoxylon* whose leaf is used for local cigarettes

thana	police station
thanagudi	village hut for visiting officials to stay
thanedar	police head
thekedar	a revenue collector/landlord for khalsa lands
Toler Vaub	fraternal lineages (Dhurwa)
ur	village/place (Tamil)
vilaitee	foreigner
wadde	medicine man (Gondi)
wajib-ul-arz	village record of rights
yagna	fire sacrifice
yayal mutte	name for Danteswari (Muria Gondi)
zamindar/	
zamindari	tributary chiefships
zilla	district

Bibliography

Archival Sources

Files pertaining to Bastar were consulted in the following archives:

National Archives of India, New Delhi (NAI)

Foreign Department: 1850–1913.
Foreign & Political Department: 1914–1936.
Political Department: 1937–1947.
Political Department and Ministry of States: 1947.
Ministry of States: 1948–1954.
Crown Representative Records, Eastern States Agency (Microfilm).

Madhya Pradesh Record Room, Nagpur (MPRR)

Nagpur Residency and Secretariat records, Revenue and Miscellaneous, 1821–1874.
Compilations, Political Department, 1854–1892.
C.P. Civil Secretariat Records, Political & Military Department, 1906–1916.
Printed Selections.
Chattisgarh Divisional Records.

Jagdalpur Record Room, District Collectorate, Bastar (JRR)

Compilations Nos.:
I. Affairs
II. Annual Administration Reports (1886–90, 1896–7, 1898–1947)
    Assorted Annual Reports on the Zamindaris.
III. Census
IX. Sukma Zamindari
X. Darbar and Darbaries
XII. Disturbances & Rebellion

XV. Excise
XVII. Famine
XXII. Forced Labour
XXIII. Forest
XXIV. Human sacrifice
XXVII. Judicial
XXIX. Landed Property
XXX. Landed Property held by the Officials of the Feudatory states
XXXIII. Medical
XXXVI. Minor Monopoly, Sale of
XXXVIII. Office HQ & Tahsils
XLVI. Raj Family
LI. Settlement

India Office Library, London (IOL)

Elwin Papers (1902–1964).
A.N. Mitchell Memoirs.

Other Manuscript Sources

Institutions/Libraries

Hyde Papers, Cambridge South Asia Centre, Cambridge.
Methodist Reports Collection, United Methodist Church, Madison, New Jersey.

Individual Collections in Bastar

R.S. Bajpai (Depositions pertaining to the events of 1966).
Kirit Doshi (Miscellaneous Newspaper Clippings).
M.A. Iqbal (Miscellaneous newspaper clippings; Leaflets and Circulars of the Bastar Prakriti Bachao Samiti/BASCON).
Lallu Pujari (Speeches, letters, etc. of Pravir Chandra Bhanj Deo).
Pyare Lal Vishwakarma (Letters on Bodhghat).

Newspapers

Dandakaranya Samachar, Jagda!pur: 1959-71
M.P. Chronicle, Raipur: 1962-6

Statesman Weekly (Press Cuttings, Hyde Papers)

NB: Dandakaranya Samachar is used extensively for chapter 8 because it is the only detailed and generally neutral source of information for that period.

Government Documents

A. *Major Reports Referred to:*

Agnew, Major P. Vans. 1915. Report on the Subah or Province of Chattisgarh. Nagpur, Printed Selections (rpt. from 1820). MPRR.

Craddock, R.H. 1889. Note on the Status of the Zamindars of the C.P. Nagpur, Printed Selections. MPRR.

Elliott, Lt. Col C. 1856. Report on the Bustar Dependency of Raepore District. JRR (Typed Mss.).

Glasfurd, Capt. C.L.R. 1862. Report on the Dependency of Bastar. JRR (Typed Mss.)

Jenkins, Richard. 1901. Report on the Territories of the Raja of Nagpur submitted to the Supreme Government of India. Nagpur, Printed Selections (rpt. from 1827). MPRR.

Temple, Richard. 1863. Report on the Zamindaries and other Petty Chieftaincies in the Central Provinces in 1863. Nagpur, Printed Selections. MPRR.

Ward, Lt. Col H.C.E. 1884. Report on the Administration of Bastar State, in For Pol A, Jan 1884, Pro. nos. 117–125 (Pro. 123), NAI.

B. *Government of India Documents*

Census of India, 1871–1991.

Constituent Assembly Debates, (Official Report), vol. 9, 30th July–18th September 1949. New Delhi: Lok Sabha Secretariat.

Government of India. 1984. *Task Force Report on Encroachment in Forest Areas in India.* Ministry of Agriculture. New Delhi: Government of India Press.

—— 1960. *Report of the Committee on Special Multipurpose Tribal Blocks* (Chairman Verrier Elwin), Ministry of Home Affairs. New Delhi: Government of India Press.

Pandey, Justice K.L. 1967. *Report on the Disturbances which took place at Jagdalpur on the 25th and 26th March, 1966.* Madhya Pradesh, Home Department. Bhopal: Government of Madhya Pradesh.

Sharma, B.D. 1990. *Report of the Commissioner for Scheduled Castes and*

Scheduled Tribes: 29th Report, 1987-89. Delhi: Government Publication.

Sharma, B.D. 1988. *Report of the Commissioner for Scheduled Castes and Scheduled Tribes: 28th Report, 1986-87*. Delhi: Government Publication.

C. Government of Central Provinces/Madhya Pradesh Documents

Census of India. *Central Province Census Reports*, 1881-1941.

— *MP District Census Handbooks*, Bastar District, 1951-1981.

DeBrett, E.A. 1988. *Central Provinces Gazetteers: Chattisgarh Feudatory States*. (rpt. from 1909) Bhopal: Vanya Prakashan.

Central Provinces Government. 1929. CP Feudatory States Manual.

— 1937. CP & Berar Constitutional Manual Nagpur, vol. I. Nagpur: Govt. Press.

Government of M.P. 1995. *Madhya Pradesh Human Development Report*. Bhopal.

— 1991. *Madhya Pradesh Environmental Status Report*, vol. II. Bhopal.

— 1984. *Bastar Development Report*. Madhya Pradesh State Planning Board, Bhopal.

— 1950. *History of Services of Gazetted Officers in the Civil Departments in the C.P. & Berar*. Nagpur: Govt. Press.

Grant, Sir Charles. 1984. *The Gazetteer of the Central Provinces*. New Delhi: Usha Publications (rpt. from the 2nd Edition, Nagpur: 1870).

Kamath, H.S. 1941. *Grazing and Nistar in the Central Provinces Estates: The Report of an Enquiry*. Nagpur: Government Printing Press.

Ramadhyani, R.K. 1942. *Report on Land Tenures and the Revenue System of the Orissa and Chattisgarh States*, vol. I. Berhampur: Government Printing Press.

D. Bastar State/District Documents

Conservator's Office, Jagdalpur. *Working Plan Report for the Reserved Forests of Jagdalpur, North Kanger and South Kanger Ranges of North Bastar Forest Division and the Chintalnar, Tongpal . . . Reserves of South Bastar Forest Division, 1957-58 - 1972-73*. Gwalior, 1963.

— *Working Plan for Central Bastar Forest Division and Tongpal Range of South Bastar Forest Division, Jagdalpur Circle, 1988-89 to 1997-98*, vols. I & III, Text by A.K. Dubey, Dy. Conservator of Forests, 1988.

— *Working Plan for the Gollapalli Reserve, Konta Range, ESA, 1934-54*, by S.R. Daver, Jagdalpur, 1935.

Conservator's Office, Jagdalpur. *Working Plan for South Bastar Forest Division and Pamed Range of West Bastar, 1982-83 - 1996-97*, vol. I Text by R.P. Singh, June 1981.

Jagdalpur Tahsil Office. Documents pertaining to Dussehra Arrangements, 1992.

Bastar District Collectorate Library, Bastar State Judicial circulars 1907.

— Bastar State Revenue Circulars 1907.

— Bastar State Forest Manual 1908.

— Bastar State Police Manual 1908 (Hindi).

— Bastar State Revenue Manual 1931.

— Bastar State General Manual 1932.

— Land Alienation Act (170 A or 170 kh).

Bastar District Collectorate (Hindi Record Room). Kukanar Misal Bandobast (Settlement Record), 1934-35, 1952.

Secondary Sources: Books, Articles, Theses

Adas, Michael. 1995. 'The Reconstruction of "Tradition" and the Defence of the Colonial Order: British West Africa in the Early Twentieth Century', in Jane Schneider and Rayna Rapp (eds), *Articulating Hidden Histories*. Berkeley: University of California Press.

— 1993. *Islamic and European Expansion*. Philadelphia: Temple University Press.

— 1983. 'Colonisation, Commercial Agriculture, and the Destruction of the Deltaic Rainforests of British Burma in the Late Nineteenth Century', in Tucker and Richards (eds), *Global Deforestation and the Nineteenth-Century World Economy*. Durham: Duke University Press.

Agarwal, Bina. 1994. *A Field of one's own: Gender and land rights in South Asia*. Cambridge: Cambridge University Press.

Agarwal, Prem Chandra. 1979. *Human Geography of Bastar District*. Allahabad: Garga Bros.

Amanullah, Mohammad. 1988. *Dashera of Bastar: A Pictorial Representation*. Bhopal: Vanya Prakashan.

Anderson, Michael. 1990. 'Classifications and Coercions: Themes in South Asian Legal Studies in the 1980s', in *South Asia Research* 10 (2).

Anderson, Perry. 1968. 'Components of the National Culture', in *New Left Review* 62.

Anderson, R.S. and Huber, W. 1988. *The Hour of the Fox*. Seattle: University of Washington Press.

Appadurai, Arjun et al. 1991. *Gender, Genre and Power in South Asian Expressive Traditions*. Philadelphia: University of Philadelphia Press.

Archer, William G. 1984. *Tribal Law and Justice: A Report on the Santhal*. New Delhi: Concept Publishing Co.

Arnold, David. 1989. 'Famine in Peasant Consciousness and Peasant Action, Madras 1876-8', in Guha (ed.), *Subaltern Studies III*. Delhi: Oxford University Press.

Arthurs, H.W. 1985. *Without the Law*. Toronto: University of Toronto Press.

Asad, Talal. 1973a. 'Two Images of European Rule', in Asad (ed.), Anthropology and the Colonial Encounter. London: Ithaca Press.

— (ed.) 1973b. *Anthropology and the Colonial Encounter*. London: Ithaca Press.

Bailey, F.G. 1963. *Politics and Social Change*. Berkeley: University of California Press.

Bailey, F.G. 1961. 'Tribe and Caste in India', in *Contributions to Indian Sociology* 5 (1).

Baker, D.E.U. 1993. *Colonialism in an Indian Hinterland: The Central Provinces, 1820-1920*. Delhi: Oxford University Press.

— 1979. *Changing Political Leadership in an Indian Province: The Central Provinces and Berar, 1919-1939*. Delhi: Oxford University Press.

Bakshi, Chittaranjan. 1994. *Madhya Pradesh ke adivasi anchal aur chhatti anusuchi ka saval*. Bhopal.

Ball, V. 1985. *Tribal and Peasant Life in India*. Delhi: Manohar (rpt. from London, 1880).

Banaji, Jairus. 1970. 'The Crises of British Anthropology', in *New Left Review* 64.

Bates, Crispin. 1995. 'Race, Caste and Tribe in Central India: Early Origins of Indian Anthropometry', in Peter Robb (ed.), *The Concept of Race in India*. Delhi: Oxford University Press.

Bates, Crispin and Carter, Marina. 1992. 'Tribal Migration in India and Beyond', in Gyan Prakash (ed.), *The World of the Rural Labourer in Colonial India*. Delhi: Oxford University Press.

Baviskar, Amita. 1995. *In the Belly of the River: Tribal Conflicts over Development in the Narmada Valley*. Delhi: Oxford University Press.

Bayly, C.A. 1988. *Indian Society and the Making of the British Empire*. The New Cambridge History of India II.1. Cambridge: Cambridge University Press.

— 1983. *Rulers, Townsmen and Bazaars*. Cambridge: Cambridge University Press.

Beckett, Jeremy. 1987. *Torres Strait Islanders: Custom and Colonialism.* Cambridge: Cambridge University Press.

Benedict, Burton. 1983. *The Anthropology of World's Fairs.* London: Scolar Press.

Benjamin, Walter. 1969. *Illuminations.* New York: Schocken Books.

Beteille, Andre. 1974. *Six Essays in Comparative Sociology.* New Delhi: Oxford University Press.

Bhanj Deo, Pravir Chandra. 1965. *I Pravir the Adivasi God.* Raipur.

—— 1963. *Lohandiguda Tarangini.* Raipur: Lakshmi Press.

Bhatt, Vikas. 1983. 'A Baba in Bastar', in K.S. Singh (ed.), *Tribal Movements in India,* vol. II. New Delhi: Manohar Publishing House.

Bilaspuri, Ganpat Lal Sau. n.d. *Bastar Ka Khuni Itihas.* Allahabad: Shakti Prakashan.

Blackburn, Stuart and A.K. Ramanujan (eds) 1986. *Another Harmony.* Berkeley: University of California Press.

Blackburn, Stuart et al. 1989. *Oral Epics in India.* Berkeley: University of California Press.

Blum, Jerome. 1961. *Lord and Peasant in Russia.* Princeton: Princeton University Press.

Blunt, Capt. J.T. 1924. 'Narration of a Route from Chunargarh to Yertnagoodum in the Ellore Circar', in Wills, *European Travellers in the Nagpur Territories,* (rpt. from 1795).

Brecht, Bertolt (ed. by John Willett and Ralph Manheim). 1976. *Poems, 1913-1956.* New York: Methuen.

Breman, Jan. 1988. *The Shattered Image: Construction and Deconstruction of the Village in Colonial Asia.* Dordrecht: Foris Publications. Comparative Asian Studies 2.

—— 1974. *Patronage and Exploitation: Changing Social Relations in South Gujarat, India.* Berkeley: University of California Press.

Burger, Julian. 1987. *Report From the Frontier.* London: Zed Books.

Burman, Sandra and Barbara Harell-Bond (eds) 1979. *The Imposition of Law.* New York: Academic Press.

Burrow, T. and S. Bhattacharya. 1953. *The Parji Language.*

Carter, Paul. 1987. *The Road to Botany Bay.* Chicago: University of Chicago Press.

Centre for Science and Environment. 1985. *The State of India's Environment, 1984-1985: the Second Citizen's Report.* New Delhi: CSE.

—— 1982. *The State of India's Environment, 1981-1982.* New Delhi: CSE

Chandidas, R. et al. 1968. *India Votes: A Source Book on Indian Elections.* Bombay: Popular Prakashan.

Chanock, Martin. 1991. 'Paradigms, Policies and Property: A Review of the Customary Law of Land Tenure', in Richard Roberts and Kirsten Mann (eds), *Law in Colonial Africa*. London: James Currey.

Chanock, Martin. 1985. *Law, Custom and Social Order. The Colonial Experience in Malawi and Zambia*. Cambridge: Cambridge University Press.

Cinemart Foundation. 1984. *Scenario of the Seven Percent*, vol. 1. New Delhi.

Clementi-Smith, E. 1945. 'The Bastar Rebellion, 1910', in *Man in India*, (Rebellion Number) vol. xxv.

Clifford, James. 1988. *The Predicament of Culture*. Cambridge: Cambridge University Press.

Clifford, James and George Marcus. 1986. *Writing Culture*. Berkeley: The University of California Press.

Cohn, Bernard. 1989. 'Law and the Colonial State in India', in Starr and Collier (eds), *History and Power in the Study of Law*. Ithaca: Cornell University Press.

— 1990. *An Anthropologist Among the Historians and Other Essays*. Delhi: Oxford University Press.

Comaroff, John and Jean. 1992. 'Images of Empire, Contests of Conscience', in *Ethnography and the Historical Imagination*. Boulder: Westview Press.

Coomaraswamy, Ananda. 1978. *Spiritual Authority and Temporal Power in the Indian Theory of Government*. New Delhi: Munshiram Manoharlal.

Cooper, Frederick. 1992. 'Colonizing Time: Work Rhythms and Labor Conflict in Colonial Mombasa', in Dirks (ed.), *Colonialism and Culture*. Ann Arbor: University of Michigan Press.

— 1993. 'Africa and the World Economy', in Cooper et al, *Confronting Historical Paradigms: Peasants, Labor and the Capitalist World System in Africa and Latin America*. Madison: The University of Wisconsin Press.

Corbridge, Stuart. 1988. 'The Ideology of Tribal Economy and Society: Politics in the Jharkhand, 1950–1980', in *Modern Asian Studies* 22 (1) pp. 1–42.

Corrigan, Phillip and Derek Sayer. 1985. *The Great Arch: English State Formation as Cultural Revolution*. Oxford: Basil Blackwell.

Crosby, Alfred. 1986. *Ecological Imperialism*. Cambridge: Cambridge University Press.

Daji, Homi. 1978. *Massacre at Bailadilla*. New Delhi: Communist Party of India.

Daniel, Valentine. 1989. 'Three Dispositions Towards the Past', in

H.L. Seneviratne (ed.), *Identity, Consciousness and the Past: The South Asian Scene. Social Analysis* 25.

Das, N.K. 1982. 'Tribal Unrest in Bastar', in Buddhadeb Chaudhuri (ed.), *Tribal Development in India*. Delhi: Inter India Publications.

Davis, Sheldon. 1977. *Victims of the Miracle: Development and the Indians of Brazil*. Cambridge: Cambridge University Press.

Desai, A.R. 1979. *Peasant Struggles in India*. Delhi: Oxford University Press.

Dirks, Nicholas. 1993. *The Hollow Crown*. Ann Arbor: University of Michigan Press.

— 1992a. 'From Little King to Landlord: Colonial Discourse and Colonial Rule', in *Colonialism and Culture*. Ann Arbor: The University of Michigan Press.

— (ed.) 1992b. *Colonialism and Culture*. Ann Arbor: University of Michigan Press.

— 1989. 'The Original Caste: Power, History and Hierarchy in South Asia', in *Contributions to Indian Sociology* 23, 1.

Dove, Michael. 1993. *A Revisionist View of Tropical Deforestation and Development*, East West Center Reprints, Environment Series no. 19.

Dreze, Jean. 1995. 'Famine Prevention in India', in Dreze, Sen and Hussain (eds), *The Political Economy of Hunger*. Oxford: Clarendon Press.

Dubey, K.C. and M.G. Mohril. 1961. *Fairs and Festivals of Madhya Pradesh*. Census of India.

Dumont, Louis. 1962. 'Reply to F.G. Bailey's Caste and Tribe in India', in *Contributions to Indian Sociology* 6.

Dwivedi, H.N. 1986. Commentary on the MP Land Revenue Code (20 of 1959). Gwalior: Law Journal Publications.

Elwin, Verrier. 1991. *The Muria and their Ghotul*. Delhi: Oxford University Press. (Vanya Prakashan).

— 1988. *The Tribal World of Verrier Elwin*. Delhi: Oxford University Press.

— 1977. *Maria Murder and Suicide*. Bombay: Oxford University Press.

— 1954. 'A Policy for India's Tribesmen', in *The Sunday Statesman*, October 3.

— 1943. *The Aboriginals*. Oxford Pamphlets on Indian Affairs, no. 14. Bombay: Oxford University Press.

— 1942. 'The Sago Palm in Bastar State', in *Journal of the Bombay Branch of the Royal Asiatic Society*, N.S. vol. 18.

Eschmann, Anncharlott. 1986. 'Hinduisation of Tribal Deities in Orissa', in Eschmann, Kulke and Tripathi (eds), *The Cult of*

Jagannath and the Regional Tradition of Orissa. Delhi: Manohar Publications.

Escobar, Arturo. 1995. *Encountering Development: The Making and Unmaking of the Third World*. Princeton: Princeton University Press.

Fallers, Lloyd. 1969. *Law Without Precedent*. Chicago: Aldine.

Feely-Harnuk, Gillian. 1985. 'Issues in Divine Kingship', in *Annual Review of Anthropology*, vol. 14, Palo Alto: Annual Review Inc.

Ferguson, James. 1990. *The Anti-Politics Machine: 'Development', Depoliticisation and Bureaucratic Power in Lesotho*. Cambridge: Cambridge University Press.

Feuchtwang, Stephen. 1973. 'The Colonial Formation of British Social Anthropology', in Asad (ed.), *Anthropology and the Colonial Encounter*. London: Ithaca Press.

Field, Daniel. 1989. *Rebels in the Name of the Tsar*. Boston: Unwin Hyman.

Fields, Karen. 1985. *Revival and Rebellion in Colonial Central Africa*. Princeton, NJ: Princeton University Press.

Fisher, Michael H. 1991. *Indirect Rule in India*. Delhi: Oxford University Press.

Fox, Richard. 1969. *Kin, Clan, Raja and Rule*. Berkeley: University of California Press

Fukazawa, Hiroshi. 1991. *The Medieval Deccan*. Delhi: Oxford University Press.

Fuller, C.J. 1992. *The Camphor Flame: Popular Hinduism and Society in India*. Princeton: Princeton University Press.

Furedi, Frank. 1989. *The Mau Mau War in Perspective*. London: James Currey.

Furer-Haimendorf, Christoph von. 1982. *Tribes of India: The Struggle for Survival*. Berkeley: University of California Press.

Gadgil, Madhav and Ramachandra Guha. 1992. *This Fissured Land: An Ecological History of India*. Delhi: Oxford University Press.

Gailey, Christine Ward. 1985. 'The State of the State in Anthropology', in *Dialectical Anthropology* 9 (1–2).

Galeano, Eduardo. 1988. *Century of the Wind*. New York: Pantheon.

Gell, Alfred. 1986. 'Newcomers to the World of Goods: Consumption among the Maria Gonds', in Arjun Appadurai (ed.), *The Social Life of Things*. Cambridge: Cambridge University Press.

—— 1983. 'The Market Wheel: Symbolic Aspects of an Indian Tribal Market', in *Man* (N.S.) 17.

Gell, Simeran. 1992. *The Ghotul in Muria Society*. Berkshire: Academic Publishers.

Ghurye, G.S. 1963. *The Scheduled Tribes*. Bombay: Popular Press.

Giddens, Anthony and David Held (eds) 1983. *Classes, Power and Conflict.* London: MacMillan.

Gluckman, Max. 1966. *Custom and Conflict in Africa.* Oxford: Oxford University Press.

—— 1963. *Order and Rebellion in Tribal Africa.* Oxford: Oxford University Press.

Gough, K. 1968. 'New Proposals for Anthropologists', in Social Responsibilities Symposium, *Current Anthropology* 9.

Grigson, W.V. 1993. *The Aboriginal Problem in the Central Provinces and Berar.* Bhopal: Vanya Prakashan, (rpt. from Nagpur, 1944).

—— 1991. *The Maria Gonds of Bastar.* (Delhi: Oxford University Press for Vanya Prakashan, rpt. from London, 1949).

Grove, Richard. 1995. *Green Imperialism: Colonial Expansionism, Tropical Edens and the Origins of Environmentalism.* Delhi: Oxford University Press.

—— 1993. 'Conserving Eden: The (European) East India Companies and their Environmental Policies on St. Helena, Mauritius and in Western India, 1660-1854', in *Comparative Studies in Society and History* 35 (2).

Guha, Ramachandra. 1989. *The Unquiet Woods.* Delhi: Oxford University Press.

Guha, Ranajit. 1983. *Elementary Aspects of Peasant Insurgency in Colonial India.* Delhi: Oxford University Press.

—— (ed.) 1982-1987. *Subaltern Studies, Volumes I- VI* Delhi: Oxford University Press.

Guha, Sumit. (Forthcoming).'Kings, Commoners and the Commons: People and Environments in Western India, 1600-1900', in *Modern Asian Studies.*

—— 1996. 'Forest Polities and Agrarian Empires: The Khandesh Bhils *c.* 1700-1850', in *Indian Economic and Social History Review,* no. 2.

Gupta, S.K. 1965. *Maharaja As I Saw Him.* Delhi: Ganpat Lal Sao Bilaspuri.

Habib, Irfan and Hiroshi Fukazawa. 1982. 'Agrarian Relations and Land Revenue', in Tapan Raychaudhuri and Irfan Habib (eds), *The Cambridge Economic History of India, vol. I, c.1200-1750.* Cambridge: Cambridge University Press.

Hajra, Durgadas. 1970. *The Dorla of Bastar.* Delhi: Manager of Publications, GOI.

Hardiman, David. 1987. *The Coming of the Devi: Adivasi Assertion in Western India.* Delhi: Oxford University Press.

Haynes, Edward. 1990. 'Rajput Ceremonial Interactions as a Mirror of a Dying Indian State System, 1820–1947', in *Modern Asian Studies* 24 (3).

Hecht, Susanna and Alexander Cockburn. 1990. *The Fate of the Forest (Developers, Destroyers and Defenders of the Amazon)*. New York: Harper.

Hettne, Bjorn. 1978. *The Political Economy of Indirect Rule*. London: Curzon Press.

Hira Lal, Rai Bahadur. 1916. *Madhya Pradesh ka Itihas*. Kashi.

—— 1909–1910 'Inscriptions of Bastar State', in Sten Konow and Rai Bahadur V. Venkaiyya (eds), *Epigraphica Indica, Vol. X*. Calcutta: Government Press.

—— 1907–1908. 'Inscriptions of Bastar State', in E. Hultzch and Sten Konow (eds), *Epigraphica Indica*, vol. IX. Calcutta: Government Press.

Homans, G.C. 1942. *English Villagers of the Thirteenth Century*. Cambridge: Cambridge University Press.

Hookey, John. 1984. 'Settlement and Sovereignty', in Peter Hanks and Bryan Keon-Cohen (eds), *Aborigines and the Law*. Sydney: George Allen and Unwin.

Huber, Walter. 1984. *From Millennia to the Millennium: An Anthropological History of Bastar State*. M.A. Thesis. Vancouver: University of British Columbia.

Huizer, G. and Mannheim (eds) 1979. *The Politics of Anthropology: From Colonialism and Sexism Towards a View from Below*. The Hague: Mouton.

Hunt, Roland and John Harrison. 1980. *The District Officer in India, 1930–1947*. London: Scolar Press.

Hutton, J.H. 1991. 'Introduction' 11 October 1936, in Grigson, *The Maria Gonds of Bastar*. Delhi: Vanya Prakashan (rpt. from London, 1949).

—— 1941. 'Primitive Tribes', in L.S.S. O'Malley (ed.), *Modern India and the West*. London: Oxford University Press.

Iyer, Raghavan. 1960. *Utilitarianism and All That*, in Iyer (ed.), St. Anthony's papers #8 South Asian Affairs, no. 1. London.

Jagdalpuri, Lala. 1994. *Bastar: Itihas Aivam Sanskriti*. Bhopal: Adarsh Publishers.

Jeffrey, Robin (ed.) 1978. *People, Princes and Paramount Power: Society and Politics in Indian Princely States*. Delhi: Oxford University Press.

Jha, J.C. 1987. *The Tribal Revolt of Chota Nagpur (1831–1832)*. Patna: KP Jayaswal Research Institute.

Jones, S. 1978. 'Tribal Underdevelopment in India', in *Development and Change* 9.

Joshi, G.M. 1990. *Tribal Bastar and the British Administration.* New Delhi: Indus Publishing Co.

Joshi, M.M. 1967. *Bastar - India's Sleeping Giant.* Delhi: People's Publishing House.

Kahn, Joel. 1985. 'Peasant Ideologies in the Third World', in *Annual Review of Anthropology.* vol. 14. Palo Alto: Annual Reviews Inc.

Kelkar, Govind and Dev Nathan. 1991. *Gender and Tribe.* New Delhi: Kali for Women.

Kosambi D.D. 1983. 'At the Cross–Roads: A Study of Mother-Goddess Cult-Sites', in *Myth and Reality.* Bombay: Popular Prakashan.

Kulke, Hermann. 1986. 'Royal Temple Policy and the Structure of Medieval Indian Kingdoms', in Eschmann, Kulke and Tripathi (eds), *The Cult of Jagannath and the Regional Tradition of Orissa.* New Delhi: Manohar Publishing House.

Lan, David. 1985. *Guns and Rain: Guerrillas and Spirit Mediums in Zimbabwe.* Berkeley and LA: University of California Press.

Lazarus-Black M. and S. Hirsch. 1994. *Contested States: Law, Hegemony and Resistance.* New York: Routledge.

Lelyveld, David. 1993. 'The Fate of Hindustani: Colonial Knowledge and the Project of a National Language', in Carol Breckenridge and Peter Van der Veer (eds), *Orientalism and the Post-Colonial Predicament.* Philadelphia: University of Pennsylvania Press.

—— 1985 'Of Kings and Kings of Kings: Ideologies of Ruling Power in Indian History'. Paper presented to the China-India Seminar, Fairbanks Center, Harvard University, 1985.

Low, D.A. 1973. *Lion Rampant: Essays in the Study of British Imperialism.* London: Frank Cass.

Ludden, David. 1992. 'India's Development Regime', in Dirks (ed.), *Colonialism and Culture.* Ann Arbor: University of Michigan Press.

Madhya Pradesh Adivasi Lok-kala Parishad. 1988. *Suraj.* Bhopal.

Mahapatra, L.K. 1987. 'Ex-Princely States of Orissa: Mayurbhanj, Keonjhar and Bonai', in Surajit Sinha (ed.), *Tribal Polities and State Systems in Pre-Colonial Eastern and North Eastern India.* Calcutta: Centre for Studies in Social Science.

Majumdar, D.N. 1939. 'Tribal Culture and Acculturation'. Presidential Address, Anthropology Section, Proceedings of the 26th Indian Science Congress, Lahore.

Mandlebaum, David. 1984. *Society in India.* Bombay: Popular Prakashan.

Mann, Kirsten and Richard Roberts (eds) 1991. *Law in Colonial Africa.* London: Heinemann Educational Books.

Marcus, George and Fischer. 1986. *Anthropology as Cultural Critique.* Chicago: University of Chicago Press.

Marquez, Gabriel Garcia. 1971. *One Hundred Years of Solitude.* New York: Avon Books.

Marx, Karl. 1972. *The Eighteenth Brumaire of Karl Marx.* New York: International Publishers.

Mayer, Adrian. 1991. 'Rulership and Divinity: The Case of the Modern Hindu Prince and Beyond', in *Modern Asian Studies* 25 (4).

Menon, J.C.K. 1938. *The Dashera Festival in Bastar.* Box 8, File C, Hyde Papers, Cambridge South Asia Centre.

Menon, V.P. 1985. *Integration of the Indian States.* Hyderabad: Orient Longman.

Mitchell, Timothy. 1988. *Colonising Egypt.* Cambridge: Cambridge University Press.

Mohanty, Gopinath. 1987. *Paraja* (translated from the Oriya by Bikram K. Das). Delhi: Oxford University Press.

Moore, Sally Falk. 1993. 'Changing Perspectives on a Changing Africa: The Work of Anthropology', in Robert Bates, V.Y. Mudimbe and Jean O'Barr (eds), *Africa and the Disciplines.* Chicago: University of Chicago Press

— 1989. 'History and the Redefinition of Custom on Kilimanjaro', in Starr and Collier (eds), *History and Power in the Study of Law.* Cornell, Ithaca: Cornell University Press

Nandi, R.N. 1973. *Religious Institutions and Cults in the Deccan.* Delhi: Motilal Banarsidas.

Nash, June. 1981. 'Ethnographic Aspects of the World Capitalist System', in *Annual Review of Anthropology* 10.

Nehru, Jawaharlal. 1977. 'An Approach to Tribal Problems', in H.M. Mathur (ed.), *Anthropology in the Development Process.* New Delhi: Vikas Publishing House.

— 1959. 'Foreword', in Elwin, *A Philosophy for NEFA.* Shillong: Sachin Roy on behalf of NEFA.

Neruda, Pablo. 1991. *Canto General.* Berkeley: University of California Press.

Padel, Felix. 1995. *The Sacrifice of Human Being.* Delhi: Oxford University Press.

Pande, Arjun Prasad and Harshnath Joshi. n.d. *360 Aranyak Brahmin Samaj ka Udbhav Avam Goncha Parva.* Jagdalpur (pamphlet).

Pati, Biswamoy. 1993. *Resisting Domination: Peasants, Tribals and the National Movement in Orissa, 1920-1950.* Delhi: Manohar Publications.

Perlin, Frank. 1985. 'State Formation Reconsidered', in *Modern Asian Studies* 19 (3).

Popoff, Terrel. 1980. *The Muriya and Tallur Mutte: A Study of the Concept of the Earth Among the Muria Gonds of Bastar District, India.* University of Sussex, D.Phil Thesis.

Prakash, Gyan. 1990a. *Bonded Histories: Genealogies of Labour Servitude in Colonial India.* Cambridge: Cambridge University Press.

—— 1990b. 'Writing Post-Orientalist Histories of the Third World: Perspectives from Indian Historiography', in *Comparative Studies in Society and History.* 32 (2).

Prasad, Archana. 1994. 'Forests and Subsistence in Colonial India: A Study of the Central Provinces, 1830–1945'. Ph.D. Thesis, Jawaharlal Nehru University.

Pratt, Mary Louise. 1992. *Imperial Eyes: Travel Writing and Transculturation.* New York: Routledge.

Price, Pamela G. 1989. 'Kingly Models in Indian Political Behaviour', in *Asian Survey*, vol. XXIX, no. 6, June 1989.

Price, Richard. 1990. *Alabi's World.* Baltimore: Johns Hopkins University Press.

PUCL (People's Union for Civil Liberties). 1989. *Bastar: Development and Democracy.* Hoshangabad: Kishore Bharati.

Rangarajan, Mahesh. 1996. *Fencing the Forest: Conservation and Ecological Change in India's Central Provinces, 1860–1914.* Delhi: Oxford University Press.

—— 1994. 'Imperial Agendas and India's Forests: The early History of Indian Forestry, 1800–1878', in *Indian Economic and Social History Review*, vol. 31.

Rao, B. Shiva. 1968. *The Framing of India's Constitution: A Study.* Bombay: N.M. Tripathi Pvt. Ltd.

Rebel, Hermann. 1989. 'Cultural Hegemony and Class Experience: A Critical Reading of Recent Ethno-Historical Approaches (Parts 1 and 2)', in *American Ethnologist* 16 (1 and 2).

Rennell, James. 1976. *Memoir of a Map of Hindoostan.* Calcutta: Editions Indian (rpt. from London, 1793).

Richter, William. 1978. 'Traditional Rulers in Post-Traditional Societies: The Princes of India and Pakistan', in Jeffrey (ed.), *Peoples, Princes and Paramount Power.* Delhi: Oxford University Press.

Roberts, Andrew (ed.) 1990. *The Colonial Moment in Africa.* Cambridge: Cambridge University Press.

Roberts, Richard and Kirsten Mann (eds) 1991. *Law in Colonial Africa.* London: James Currey.

Roseberry, William. 1989. *Anthropologies and Histories*. New Brunswick: Rutgers University Press.

—— 1988 'Political Economy – A Review Article', in *Annual Review of Anthropology* 17.

Rowbotham, Sheila, Lynne Segal and Hilary Wainwright. 1979. *Beyond the Fragments*. London: Merlin Press.

Rudolph and Rudolph. 1967. *The Modernity of Tradition – Political Development in India*. Chicago: University of Chicago Press.

Russell and Hiralal. 1969. *Tribes and Castes of the Central Provinces, Volume 1-4*. Oosterhout: Anthropological Publications. (rpt. from London, 1916)

Sabean, David Warren. 1984. *Power in the Blood: Popular Culture and Village Discourse in Early Modern Germany*. Cambridge: Cambridge University Press.

Saha, S. 1988. 'The Territorial Dimension of India's Tribal Problem', in Shepperdson and Simmons (eds), *The Indian National Congress and the Political Economy of India*. Brookefield: Avebury.

—— 1986. 'Historical Premises of India's Tribal Problem', in *Journal of Contemporary Asia*, vol. 16 (3).

Samyukta Socialist Party. 1966. *Bastara: Itihasa Tatha Janasruti Aur Dastavez*. Allahabad: Rajranjana Publishers.

Savyasachi. 1993. 'An Alternative System of Knowledge: Fields and Forest in Abujhmarh', in Tariq Banuri and F.A. Marglin (eds), *Who Will Save the Forests? Knowledge, Power and Environmental Destruction*. London: Zed Books.

—— 1992. 'A Sociology of Agriculture'. University of Delhi, D.Phil thesis.

Scott, James. 1990. *Domination and the Arts of Resistance*. New Haven: Yale University Press.

Sen, Ilina (ed.) 1990. *A Space within the Struggle, Women's Participation in People's Movements*. New Delhi: Kali for Women.

Sengupta, Nirmal. 1988. 'Reappraising Tribal Movements – I, II, III, IV', in *Economic and Political Weekly*, May 1988.

—— 1986. *The March of an Idea: Evolution and Impact of the Dichotomy Tribe-Mainstream*. Madras: MIDS Offprint.

Sharma, B.D. 1995. *Whither Tribal Areas? Constitutional Amendments and After*. New Delhi: Sahyog Pustak Kutir.

—— 1984. *Planning for Tribal Development*. New Delhi: Prachi Prakashan.

—— 1979. *Bezubaan*. New Delhi: Prachi Prakashan.

Sharma, Suresh. 1994. *Tribal Identity and the Modern World*. New Delhi: Sage Publications.

Sherwani, H.K. 1973. *History of Medieval Deccan (1295-1724), Volume I.* Hyderabad: Government of Andhra Pradesh, Printing and Publication Bureau.

Shiva, Vandana. 1988. *Staying Alive: Women, Ecology and Survival in India.* New Delhi: Kali for Women.

Shivaramakrishnan, K. 1995. 'Colonialism and Forestry in India: Imagining the Past in Present Politics', in *Comparative Studies in Society and History.*

Shukla, Hira Lal. 1992. *History of the People of Bastar.* Delhi: Sharada Publishing House.

—— 1988. *Tribal History: A New Interpretation.* Delhi: B.R. Publishers.

Singh, Chhatrapati. 1986. *Common Property and Common Poverty.* Delhi: Oxford University Press.

Singh, K.S. (ed.) 1989. *Jawaharlal Nehru, Tribes, and Tribal Policy.* Calcutta: Anthropological Survey of India.

Sinha, Surajit. 1962. 'State Formation and Rajput Myth in Tribal Central India', in *Man in India* vol. 42 (1), January–March.

Sinha, Surajit (ed.) 1987. *Tribal Polities and State Systems in Pre-Colonial Eastern and North Eastern India.* Calcutta: Centre for Studies in Social Science.

Skillen, Anthony. 1978. *Ruling Illusions.* New Jersey: The Humanities Press.

Sontheimer, Gunther-Dietz. 1989. *Pastoral Deities in Western India.* New York: Oxford University Press.

Southall, Aidan. 1988. 'The Segmentary State in Africa and Asia', in *Comparative Studies in Society and History*, vol. 30 (1).

—— 1956. *Alur Society.* Cambridge: Cambridge University Press.

Spear T.G.P. 1978. 'Stern Daughter of the Voice of God: Ideas of Duty among the British in India', in O'Flaherty, Wendy and J.D.M. Derrett (eds), *The Concept of Duty in South Asia.* New Delhi: Vikas Publishing House.

Spurr, David. 1993. *The Rhetoric of Empire.* Durham: Duke University Press.

Starr, June and Collier, Jane F. (eds) 1989. *History and Power in the Study of Law.* Cornell: Cornell University Press

Stein, Burton. 1980. *Peasant State and Society in Medieval South India.* Delhi: Oxford University Press.

Stocking, George (ed.) 1991. *Colonial Situations: Essays on the Contextualisation of Ethnographic Knowledge.* Madison: University of Wisconsin Press.

—— 1984. *Functionalism Historicized: Essays on British Social Anthropology.* Madison: University of Wisconsin Press.

Stocking, George (ed.) 1983. *Observers Observed: Essays on Ethnographic Fieldwork.* Madison: University of Wisconsin Press.

Stoler, Ann. 1989. 'Making Empire Respectable', in *American Ethnologist* 16 (4).

Stree Shakti Sanghatna. 1989. *We were Making History: Women in the Telengana Struggle.* London: Zed Press.

Subrahmanyam, Sanjay. 1990. *Merchants, Markets and the State in early Modern India.* Delhi: Oxford University Press.

Suleri, Sara. 1992. *The Rhetoric of English India.* Chicago: The University of Chicago Press.

Sumner, Colin (ed.) 1982. *Crime, Justice and Underdevelopment.* London: Heineman.

Sundar, Nandini. 1995. 'The Dreaded Danteswari: Annals of Alleged Sacrifice', in *Indian Economic and Social History Review,* 32 (3).

—— 1993 'Direct Action for Forest Protection', in *Economic Times,* August 1, 1993.

Taussig, Michael. 1987. *Shamanism, Colonialism and the Wild Man.* Chicago: University of Chicago Press.

Thakkar, A.V. 1941. *The Problem of Aborigines in India.* Gokhale Institute of Politics and Economics, R.R. Kale Memorial Lecture 1941.

Thakur, Pandit Kedarnath. 1982. *Bastar Bhushan.* Ratanpur: Itihas Deepan. (rpt. from Benares: Bharat Jiwan Press, 1908).

Thapar, Romila. 1978. 'The Image of the Barbarian in Early India', in *Ancient Indian Social History.* New Delhi: Orient Longman Ltd.

Thomas, Nicholas. 1994. *Colonialism's Culture.* Cambridge: Polity Press

—— 1990. 'Sanitation and Seeing: The Creation of State Power in Early Colonial Fiji', in *Comparative Studies in Society and History* 32 (1).

Thompson, E.P. 1993. *Customs in Common.* New York: The New Press.

—— 1975. *Whigs and Hunters.* New York: Pantheon Books.

—— 1963. *The Making of the English Working Class.* New York: Vintage Books.

Thusu, Kedar Nath. 1977. *The Pengo Porajas of Koraput.* Calcutta: Anthropological Survey of India.

—— 1965. *The Dhurwa of Bastar.* Memoir no. 16. Calcutta: Anthropological Survey of India.

Tiruvalluvar. 1990. *Tirrukural* (Trans. from the Tamil by P.S. Sundaram). Delhi: Penguin Books.

Tyler, Stephen. 1978. 'Fields are for Planting: Swidden Agriculture among the Koyas of South India', in Surajit Sinha (ed.), *Field Studies on the People of India.* Calcutta: Indian Anthropological Society.

Vansina, Jan. 1990. *Paths in the Rainforest*. Madison: University of Wisconsin Press.

— 1985. *Oral Tradition as History*. Madison: University of Wisconsin Press.

Venkataramanayya, N. and M. Somasekhara Sarma. 1982. 'The Kakatiyas of Warangal', in G. Yazdani (ed.), *The Early History of the Deccan, Volumes I and II*. New Delhi: Oriental Books Reprint Corporation

Verma, V.P. 1974. *Studies in Hindu Political Thought and its Metaphysical Foundations*. Banaras: Motilal Banarsidas.

Verma, V.S. 1958. 'Dussehrah in Bastar (The Changing form of a Festival)', in *Bulletin of the Tribal Research Institute*, II (3).

Vidyarthi, L.P. 1978. *Rise of Anthropology in India, Vol I (The Tribal Dimension)*. Delhi: Concept Publishing Company.

Vincent, Joan. 1990. *Anthropology and Politics: Visions, Traditions and Trends*. Tucson: University of Arizona Press.

— 1989. 'Contours of Change: Agrarian Law in Colonial Uganda, 1895–1962', in Starr and Collier (eds), *History and Power in the Study of Law*. Cornell: Cornell University Press.

— 1988. 'Sovereignty, Legitimacy and Power: Prolegomena to the Study of the Colonial State', in Ronald Cohen and Judith D. Toland (eds), 'State Formation and Political Legitimacy', *Political Anthropology*, vol. 6. New Brunswick, NJ: Transaction Books.

— 1982. *Teso in Transformation: The Political Economy of Peasant and Class in Eastern Africa*. Berkeley: University of California Press.

Vitebsky, Piers. 1993. *Dialogues with the Dead*. Cambridge: Cambridge University Press.

Washbrook, David. 1981. 'Law, State and Agrarian Society in Colonial India', in *Modern Asian Studies* 15:3.

White, Hayden. 1978. *Tropics of Discourse*. Baltimore: John Hopkins University Press.

Wills, C.U. 1919. 'The Territorial Systems of the Rajput Kingdoms of Medieval Chattisgarh', in *Journal of the Asiatic Society of Bengal*, New Series, vol. xv, pp. 197–262.

Wilson, H.H. 1940. *A Glossary of Judicial and Revenue Terms*. Calcutta: Eastern Law House.

Wolf, Eric. 1982. *Europe and the People Without History*. Berkeley: University of California Press.

Worsley, Peter. 1968. *The Trumpet Shall Sound*. New York: Schocken Books.

Yazdani, G. (ed.) 1982. *The Early History of the Deccan, Volumes I and II*. New Delhi: Oriental Books Reprint Corporation.

Index